DAILY LIFE IN

VICTORIAN ENGLAND

Recent Titles in
The Greenwood Press "Daily Life Through History" Series

Immigrant America, 1820–1870
James M. Bergquist

Pre-Columbian Native America
Clarissa W. Confer

Post-Cold War
Stephen A. Bourque

The New Testament
James W. Ermatinger

The Hellenistic Age: From Alexander to Cleopatra
James Allan Evans

Imperial Russia
Greta Bucher

The Greenwood Encyclopedia of Daily Life in America, Four Volumes
Randall M. Miller, general editor

Civilians in Wartime Twentieth-Century Europe
Nicholas Atkin, editor

Ancient Egyptians, Second Edition
Bob Brier and Hoyt Hobbs

Civilians in Wartime Latin America: From the Wars of Independence to the
Central American Civil Wars
Pedro Santoni, editor

Science and Technology in Modern European Life
Guillaume de Syon

Cooking in Europe, 1650–1850
Ivan P. Day

DAILY LIFE IN

VICTORIAN ENGLAND

Second Edition

SALLY MITCHELL

The Greenwood Press "Daily Life Through History" Series

GREENWOOD PRESS
Westport, Connecticut • London

Library of Congress Cataloging-in-Publication Data

Mitchell, Sally, 1937–
    Daily life in Victorian England / Sally Mitchell. — 2nd ed.
        p. cm. — (Greenwood Press "Daily life through history" series,
    ISSN 1080–4749)
    Includes bibliographical references and index.
    ISBN 978–0–313–35034–4 (alk. paper)
    1. England—Social life and customs—19th century.   2. Great Britain—
History—Victoria, 1837–1901.   I. Title.   II. Series.
    DA533.M675 2009
    941.081—dc22   2008031363

British Library Cataloguing in Publication Data is available.

Library of Congress Catalog Card Number: 2008031363
ISBN: 978–0–313–35034–4
ISSN: 1080–4749

First published in 2009

Greenwood Press, 88 Post Road West, Westport, CT 06881
An imprint of Greenwood Publishing Group, Inc.
www.greenwood.com

Printed in the United States of America

The paper used in this book complies with the
Permanent Paper Standard issued by the National
Information Standards Organization (Z39.48–1984).

10 9 8 7 6 5 4 3 2 1

CONTENTS

PREFACE

For this second edition of *Daily Life in Victorian England*, I have made corrections and improvements to the text of the first edition. I have not, however, added more information about all the things people have asked for—ranging from how one found a rental house in London to books used at Oxford to details about cathedral clergymen's duties and titles to (the most frequent question of all) how much something would cost at a particular date. Instead I have created an appendix on research that will help to track down information about almost anything from the books and other resources that literate Victorians could have used. As recently as 2006 it would have required a trip to England to see most of these sources; now it is possible—with persistence and a little ingenuity—for anyone using a computer and fast internet connection to see vast quantities of information published in the nineteenth century. The research resources I explain in the appendix do not require access to academic libraries or paid database subscriptions; they range from Web sites created to support the British elementary school history curriculum to the thousand-page volumes that would have been used by Victorian physicians and barristers.

Once again, as for the first edition, my own primary debt is to the worldwide members of the VICTORIA discussion list, and to Patrick Leary for founding it in 1993, when internet resources were in their infancy. Permission to reproduce photographs and illustrations was granted by the sources named in credits to individual pictures. The illustrations not credited to any library, museum, or agency are from materials in my own collection and were scanned by Shawn Ta of the Instructional Support Center at Temple University.

CHRONOLOGY: CHIEF EVENTS OF THE VICTORIAN AGE IN ENGLAND

1837 King William IV dies on June 20, leaving no legitimate offspring. His 18-year-old niece Victoria (granddaughter of George III) becomes queen of the United Kingdom of Great Britain and Ireland.

1839 Government begins to provide money for elementary schools.

1840 Queen Victoria marries her cousin Prince Albert of Saxe-Coburg-Gotha. Penny post (fast, inexpensive mail service) established.

1842 Railway between Manchester and London opens. London police establish detective department.

1843 First telegraph line is in service.

1844 Factory Act limits working day to 12 hours for people under 18.

1845 Irish potato famine; starvation and emigration cause population of Ireland to drop from 8.2 million in 1841 to 6.5 million in 1851.

1848 Cholera epidemic reveals need for public health measures.

1851 Great Exhibition at the Crystal Palace celebrates progress and industry.

1853 Queen Victoria uses chloroform at the birth of her eighth child, thus ensuring its place as an anesthetic.

1854 Crimean War (1854–1856); Earl of Cardigan leads charge of light brigade at Balaclava (October 25).

1855   Florence Nightingale introduces hygienic standards into military hospitals.

1857   Indian Mutiny, a rising by subject peoples in India. Matrimonial Causes Act makes divorce available without special act of Parliament. Sentence of criminal transportation is abolished, although some long-term convicts are still sent to Australia.

1858   Medical Act establishes register of qualified physicians. Lionel de Rothschild is first Jew seated in Parliament.

1859   Charles Darwin publishes *On the Origin of Species through Natural Selection.*

1860   Nightingale Training School for Nurses is established.

1861   Prince Albert dies of typhoid. Louis Pasteur proposes germ theory of disease.

1863   The London Underground (subway) begins regular passenger service.

1866   Women form committee to seek voting rights; they present a petition signed by 4,999 women to Parliament. Transatlantic telegraph cable begins operation.

1867   Second Reform Bill reduces property qualification for male voters; John Stuart Mill's amendment to substitute *person* for *man* and thus enfranchise women is defeated.

1869   Suez Canal opens. Imprisonment for debt is abolished.

1870   W. E. Forster's Education Act makes elementary education available to all children in England and Wales and establishes local School Boards. Everyone who pays property taxes is eligible to vote for school-board members, and women may be elected to the boards.

1871   Trade unions are legalized.

1872   First women are admitted unofficially to Cambridge University examinations (women awarded Cambridge degrees: 1947).

1876   Women win right to become licensed physicians.

1878   Electric lights are installed on some London streets. University of London opens all degrees (including medicine) to women.

1879   London's first telephone exchange opens.

1880   Elementary education becomes compulsory (from age 7–10). Stores begin to sell canned fruits and meats.

1882 Final version of Married Women's Property Act protects women's right to all property they earn or inherit before or after marriage.

1884 Third Reform Bill extends vote to all male householders.

1885 Football League is formed to control professional soccer matches.

1886 Safety bicycles go on sale.

1888 County councils are established; women are granted right to vote in county council elections. Jack the Ripper murders five women in London.

1889 London dock strike is a success; trade unionism spreads. Employment of children under age 10 is prohibited.

1890 First moving-picture shows appear.

1891 Elementary education in state schools becomes free.

1897 Queen Victoria's Diamond Jubilee.

1899 War with Boers in South Africa (1899–1902). School attendance becomes compulsory up to age 12. First motor bus is in service.

1901 Queen Victoria dies, January 22; Edward VII becomes king.

INTRODUCTION: THE VICTORIANS AND THEIR WORLD

Many of us have vivid mental pictures of Victorian England: a Charles Dickens Christmas with a large happy family surrounding a table crammed with food; the dark and terrifying slums in other Dickens novels; Sherlock Holmes in London by gaslight; timeless country estates where laborers nodded in deference to the squire while ladies paid social calls and talked about marriage. In addition, *Victorianism* remains a living concept in social and political debates, although its meaning is ambiguous: it is used to describe exploitation and class division, sexual repression, hypocrisy, values of hard work and self-help, moral certainties about family life, and a wide variety of arrangements intended to solve public problems.

The first thing to understand about the Victorian age in England is that it was enormously long and that there were significant changes in almost every aspect of politics, law, economics, and society. Furthermore, the texture of daily life—the physical and technological surroundings in which people lived, the patterns of their education and work and recreation and belief—were utterly transformed. In 1837, when 18-year-old Victoria became queen, the majority of England's people lived in the countryside and relatively few of them ever traveled more than 10 miles from the place where they were born. Goods and messages moved no faster the horses that carried them. Most food was cooked over an open fireplace. Little more than half of the population could read and write; children as young as five years of age worked long days underground in coal mines or tending dangerous machinery in factories. Political and legal power was entirely in the hands of a small minority: men who held property.

By the time Queen Victoria died in 1901, the modern world had taken shape. Most of England's people were town or city dwellers. The British Empire covered one-fourth of the globe, and London was the capital of that empire. London had subway trains and electric streetlights; telegraph messages sped around the world in minutes; luxurious steamships plied a busy transatlantic trade. Education was compulsory; public hanging of criminals had been abolished; a man's religion (or lack of it) no longer barred him from attending a university or serving in Parliament; and the legal and political status of women in all classes was significantly improved.

The Victorian age was first and foremost an age of transition. The England that had once been a feudal and agricultural society was transformed into an industrial democracy. Between 1837 and 1901, social and technological change affected almost every feature of daily existence. Many aspects of life—from schooling to competitive sports to the floor-plan of middle-class houses to widely held ideals about family life—took the shape that remained familiar for most of the twentieth century.

Much of the current popular interest in things Victorian emphasizes the extremes, concentrating either on criminals and the very poor or on the elite classes with their country estates, town houses, and elaborate social life. In this book I make a determined effort to balance information about slums and high society with descriptions of the vast majority of English Victorians: ordinary working-class people and the growing white-collar class of teachers, clerical workers, nurses, shop assistants, managers, and engineers. Information about women's lives (and women's issues) is integrated into every section of the book.

I have deliberately restricted my discussion to the Victorian period and to England. That is, the book covers the years between 1837 and 1901, when Victoria was queen, rather than the entire nineteenth century, and it does not consider life in Scotland, Wales, and Ireland, although they were united politically to England under a single government. Because of the way statistics were gathered during the period, however, some numbers will necessarily include the population of Wales in the figure for England.

Students in the United States may wonder why I have paid almost no attention to race. Some Africans and other people of color (especially from India) lived in England during the Victorian period, but their number was small—and also unknown; the form used by census takers reported each person's name, age, marital condition, occupation, and place of birth, but no data about race were included. The government's very lack of interest is evidence of a kind: not only were there very few people of color, there was apparently no community of interest or (in the strict sense) of racial identity. Personal prejudices existed, but segregation and institutional discrimination did not; race is simply not visible in descriptions of Victorian daily life.

In addition to conveying the concrete and physical texture of daily life, I have tried to answer many of the questions that high school and college students generally ask and to clear up some common misapprehensions about the class system, money, marriage, the laws of inheritance, and the social importance of religion. My sources include standard histories of the period as well as specialized histories (of technology, for example, or of criminal law), but I've also drawn on many years of reading not only the Victorian books that are generally taught in college classrooms but also dozens and dozens of forgotten popular novels, nineteenth-century magazines, household guides, etiquette manuals, autobiographies, schoolbooks, children's stories, and other contemporary materials. Many of the illustrations and quotations are drawn from these sources; through them, the book attempts to convey the flavor as well as the facts of daily life in Victorian England.

1

A BRIEF HISTORY OF VICTORIAN ENGLAND

The primary subject of this book is social history: how people lived and acted and spent their time, what they ate and wore and cared about. Conventional history—politics, economics, legislation, wars—is important, however, when it helps to explain the forces that shape daily life. This chapter provides an overview of nineteenth-century historical circumstances that framed ordinary people's thoughts and experiences.

BEFORE THE VICTORIANS

Three events before 1837 had a crucial impact on Victorian life. (1) The Duke of Wellington's victory over Napoleon at Waterloo in 1815 created an atmosphere of national pride. (2) The Industrial Revolution transformed England from an agricultural nation to one based on industry and made it for most of the century the world's greatest economic power. (3) The Reform Bill of 1832, which doubled the number of men eligible to vote, began a gradual progress towards democratic rule and governmental responsibility for the safety and well-being of all citizens.

England and France were at war for much of the time between 1793 and 1815, but none of the battles took place in England; the war did not concern most people. During the period known as the

Regency, from 1811 to 1820, the Prince of Wales (later George IV) acted as Regent, or ruler, because his father George III had become incurably insane. The Regency, in popular imagination, was a period of aristocratic gaiety, license, and extravagance, when elegant men in tight breeches and women in filmy white dresses floated through a round of balls and social events. For most of the population, however, times were not easy. The government raised taxes to fight the war; food could no longer be imported from those parts of Europe that had been conquered by Napoleon; and the common land on which rural workers had traditionally grazed animals and gathered wood was enclosed for farming, which made it even harder for ordinary people to obtain an adequate diet.

In 1814, the French emperor Napoleon Bonaparte was defeated and exiled to the island of Elba. In 1815, however, Napoleon escaped. He returned to France on March 1, quickly recovered the loyalty of the French army, and by March 20 had entered Paris and regained power. The drama of Napoleon's return aroused all of Europe. England was swept by fear of an invasion. The army was mobilized; even the guards regiments, normally quartered in London to defend the monarch and the seat of government, were fitted out for combat and sent across the channel.

The climactic battle took place at Waterloo, in Belgium, on June 18, 1815. The British forces commanded by the Duke of Wellington, together with their Dutch and Prussian allies, won a decisive victory over Napoleon and the French. The battle remains a classic drama of confrontation and tactics: tightly formed squares of red-coat infantry held firm by discipline, courage, and honor; stirring cavalry charges; peaks of individual heroism. For the rest of the century Waterloo Day was celebrated with memorials and schoolroom ceremonies. Waterloo was the first battle in English history for which every single soldier who took part was awarded a medal. The victory created a new sense of patriotism, a national mythos of discipline, self-confidence, pride, security, and entitlement.

In conducting the war against Napoleon, English naval blockades did serious damage to the French economy. At the same time, English industrial production was growing by leaps and bounds. Thus England's control of the seas at the end of the Napoleonic wars put the country in an unrivaled position to sell its manufactured goods on the world market.

Furthermore, England was the first country to move from an agricultural economy to one based on manufacturing. The industrial revolution began about 1780, initially in the cotton industry.

Machines were invented to do the spinning and weaving, which had traditionally been done by hand. First water power and then steam engines were used to drive the machines. Because it took little muscular strength to tend the power-driven machinery, women and children—whose labor was inexpensive—became the principal workers in textile factories. The vast quantity of cloth produced by fast machines, combined with the low cost of labor, made British textiles far cheaper than those in other countries. When, in addition, the British had control of the seas after 1815, new wealth flowed into England. The profits, in turn, stimulated the development of new technology, growing trade, and yet more new wealth. England's economic and industrial dominance lasted until almost the end of the nineteenth century and had a dramatic impact on daily life.

In the political realm, historians often date the beginning of the Victorian age from the Reform Bill of 1832 rather than Queen Victoria's accession in 1837. Great Britain was governed by a Parliament made up of an elected House of Commons and a House of Lords in which, until 1999, most members inherited their right to sit. In the early nineteenth century, only men who held property had the right to vote for representatives in the House of Commons. (The amount of property needed was determined by complicated rules.) Furthermore, the districts entitled to a seat in the Commons were based on old patterns of landholding. Some big manufacturing towns had no representative at all; in other places there were "rotten boroughs" with so few voters that one landowner could be sure his candidate would be seated in Parliament.

The Reform Bill of 1832 did not bring democratic government, but it began the process. Parliamentary seats were redistricted and the number of eligible voters doubled to about 1 million. Most electors before 1832 were landowners or men of the upper classes; after 1832 large numbers of middle-class men also had the vote. In addition, for the first time, the word *male* was specifically added to the description of eligible voters. Women had not voted for hundreds of years, and even then only a few really important and rich women did so. Nevertheless, the addition of male suggests that lawmakers were beginning to realize that some women might want to claim the privilege.

Another significant influence in the early part of the nineteenth century was the Evangelical Revival, which will be more fully discussed in chapter 11. People turned away from the excesses of the Regency and developed a new concern for social problems. Charities were founded; voluntary associations began to educate poor children. The new moral and social concern led to new laws that would affect many people's daily lives during the remainder of the century. In 1833, for the first time, government factory inspectors enforced restrictions on working conditions. Textile mills could no longer employ children under the age of nine. Parliament abolished slavery in all parts of the British Empire from the first of August, 1834. The Poor Law Amendment Act of 1834 drastically changed the conditions under which aid was given to people who could not support themselves. Its provisions, which will be discussed in chapter 5, had a major impact on the Victorian poor.

THE EARLY VICTORIANS (1837–1851)

Victoria became queen on June 20, 1837. She was daughter of Edward, Duke of Kent, the fourth son of George III. Her father had died while she was an infant, and Victoria had been raised quietly by her mother in Kensington Palace. Because none of George III's

---

QUEEN AT 18: AN EXTRACT FROM VICTORIA'S JOURNAL

Tuesday, 20th June [1837].—I was awoke at 6 o'clock by Mamma, who told me that the Archbishop of Canterbury and Lord Conyngham were here, and wished to see me. I got out of bed and went into my sitting-room (only in my dressing-gown), and *alone*, and saw them. Lord Conyngham (the Lord Chamberlain) then acquainted me that my poor Uncle, the King, was no more, and had expired at 12 minutes p. 2 this morning, and consequently that I am *Queen*. Lord Conyngham knelt down and kissed my hand, at the same time delivering me the official announcement of the poor King's demise. The Archbishop then told me that the Queen was desirous that he should come and tell me the details of the last moments of my poor, good Uncle; he said that he had directed his mind to religion, and had died in a perfectly happy, quiet state of mind, and was quite prepared for his death. He added that the King's sufferings at the last were not very great but that there was a good deal of uneasiness. Lord Conyngham, whom I charged to express my feelings of condolence and sorrow to the poor Queen, returned directly to Windsor. I then went to my room and dressed.

Since it has pleased Providence to place me in this station, I shall do my utmost to fulfil my duty towards my country; I am very young and perhaps in many, though not in all things, inexperienced, but I am sure, that very few have more real good will and more real desire to do what is fit and right than I have.

first three sons was survived by a legitimate child, Victoria inherited the throne after the death of her uncle, William IV. Although the monarch's actual powers were severely limited by the nineteenth century, the young queen took a keen and intelligent interest in the affairs of state, conferred regularly with government ministers, carefully considered the papers that were sent to her, and used her public role to exercise personal and moral influence.

The first years of the reign were marked by social and political turmoil, largely in response to the rapid changes that came with industrialization. In 1801 most people lived in villages or on farms; by 1851 more than half of the population was urban. Only one-fourth of the people who lived in a city such as Manchester had been born there. Teenagers and young adults flooded in from the country to factories where the jobs were. Industrial cities were overcrowded, insanitary, and unplanned. Friedrich Engels, who in 1848 was co-author with Karl Marx of the *Communist Manifesto,* learned about the economic misery of working people from his experience in England's industrial cities. Often several families lived in one room of a rickety house with no indoor plumbing and little heat or light.

Social problems dominated the economic and political scene in the 1840s. The term *hungry forties* is sometimes applied to the first part of the decade. Food prices were high. A depression threw many people out of work. In 1842, more than 15 percent of the population received public assistance; many more people were helped by private charities; and the crime rate was higher than any other time during the century. The London police force established its first detective division in 1842, and Pentonville Prison was built.

When potato blight destroyed the chief Irish food crop, vast numbers of hungry laborers fled to England (as well as across the Atlantic to Boston and New York and Philadelphia). The price of bread—the staple food of England's working people—was kept high by the Corn Laws, which put a heavy tax on imported grain. (In England, the word *corn* includes all grains—wheat, rye, barley, and oats as well as the Indian corn or maize that came from the Americas.) Intended to promote domestic agriculture, the Corn Laws protected landowners' income as well as providing revenue for the government. If there had been no import duty, English bread would have been made from cheaper grain produced in European countries with longer growing seasons. The upper classes, who owned land, supported the policy that kept their income high, but workers hated the Corn Laws for making food expensive. So did manufacturers—they had to pay higher wages so their employees could eat, and therefore they lost some of their competitive advantage in foreign markets.

During the 1830s and 1840s, the Chartist movement brought about the first large-scale political activism by English working-class people. Although inspired by hard times, the Chartists did not simply have economic goals. Instead, they wanted what we now understand as democracy. They produced a People's Charter (hence, the name Chartists) with six demands: annual parliaments, voting rights for all adult men, the end of property qualifications for members of the House of Commons, voting by secret ballot, equal electoral districts, and salaries for members of Parliament so that men without private wealth could afford to run and be elected. After several months of speeches, meetings, and demonstrations the Charter was presented to the House of Commons in July 1839 with 1,280,000 signatures—and was overwhelmingly rejected. Additional petitions, with even more names, were drawn up. Large mass meetings were held in 1842 and 1848. Although some people at the time were afraid there would be armed revolution—as there was in a number of European countries in 1848—the Chartist movement in England faded away as prosperity began to grow.

The new prosperity arose in part from a crucial early-Victorian technological revolution—the coming of railways. Primitive steam locomotives were used in industry to pull freight cars along rails during the 1820s, but the boom in rail construction coincided almost exactly with the beginning of Victoria's reign. By the mid-1840s, vast building projects transformed the landscape and provided work for thousands of laborers. Rail construction dramatically increased the production of coal and iron. New skills and new techniques were developed in engineering and machine technology; bridges and tunnels and locomotives came into being.

By 1850 the new transportation system reached most parts of the country. Later Victorians saw the railroads as marking a great divide: before rail travel was the past, after it was the present. Aside from the economic and technological changes, rapid rail transportation built a national culture. London's daily papers could be read at breakfast almost anywhere in England. Local dialects and regional customs began to fade. Quick and inexpensive shipping of perishable goods made it possible for many more people enrich their diet with fish and fruit and milk. In 1849 the Corn Laws were repealed. By that time steamships were crossing the Atlantic in under 20 days, bringing the American continents into England's economic orbit.

Some other significant innovations in the early Victorian period also influenced daily life. In 1839 the government began for the first time to provide money for elementary education, although schooling would not become compulsory until 40 years later. Communications were vastly improved by an inexpensive and efficient postal service, by the invention of the telegraph, and by the development of electrotyping and high-speed presses for mass printing. Gaslights came to major streets, making it much safer to be out-of-doors at night.

In the late 1840s, the first organized movements for women's rights began to form. Middle-class women sought serious education, rather than the painting, piano playing, social graces, and general knowledge that were usual in girls' schools. They also began trying to extend the range of women's employment. Working-class girls and women supported themselves as domestic servants, factory workers, agricultural laborers, and garment workers, but virtually the only middle-class career open to women was that of governess. Women reformers at midcentury began looking for ways that women could be trained and employed in clerical work, bookkeeping, typesetting, social welfare, and other reasonably well-paid occupations.

THE MID-VICTORIANS (1851–1875)

Most people's mental image of the Victorian period is based on the years between 1850 and the mid-1870s. England enjoyed domestic stability, progress, and growing prosperity. The leading novelists were Charles Dickens and George Eliot; Alfred, Lord Tennyson, was poet laureate; Matthew Arnold, John Ruskin, and John Stuart Mill were influential critics and philosophers; Charles Darwin published his significant scientific work. Both agriculture and industry prospered. Not only profits but also wages rose, so that large numbers of people had a more adequate standard of living.

The period began with the Exhibition of 1851, which celebrated progress, invention, and British supremacy in world markets. Essentially the first world's fair, its official name was "The Great Exhibition of the Works of Industry of All Nations," and it was open from May until October. The central building, soon nicknamed the "Crystal Palace," was a triumph of engineering and design. The first large structure to be built of metal and glass, its components were prefabricated and interchangeable, with identical girders, columns, and panes of glass throughout the building. (When the

Exhibition was over, the Crystal Palace was taken apart and reassembled to a different pattern in South London, where it was in public use until destroyed by a fire in 1936.) Three times the length of St. Paul's Cathedral, the building displayed over 100,000 exhibits: exotic art from China and India; furs from Canada and Russia; furniture and housewares; sculpture and stained glass; the Koh-i-noor diamond; working examples of industrial triumphs such as power printing presses, agricultural machines, locomotives, and an electric telegraph; and newly invented domestic appliances including a gas cooking stove.

During the Exhibition's five-month run it was seen by some six million visitors; in some periods the daily attendance was well over 100,000. The new railway network made it possible for people to come from all over England on cheap one-day and two-day excursions; 10 years earlier it would have been a long slow trip from most parts of the country, requiring several days away from home and far greater expense. The money earned from admission fees for the Exhibition was used to buy the land in South Kensington where the Victoria and Albert Museum, the Science Museum, and the Imperial College of Science and Technology were built. All three institutions still contain some of the materials that were on display at the Crystal Palace, and they remain the inheritors of its spirit.

In the years after the Exhibition, London became the world's central metropolis, and many of its distinctive features appeared. The new Houses of Parliament (with the Big Ben clock tower) replaced the structure that had burned in 1834. Work on the subway system began in 1854. Sewers and water pipes were laid. New "departmental stores" came to line Oxford Street, Regent Street, and Piccadilly Circus. Ring after ring of newly built brick housing pushed the city's borders outwards. Other cities, especially the thriving manufacturing centers such as Manchester and Birmingham, invested in public buildings (city halls, law courts, concert halls, museums) built in the substantial and dignified Gothic Revival style. America grew far closer; steamships regularly crossed the Atlantic in nine days, and in 1866 the telegraph cable allowed almost instant transmission of news and business messages. The Suez Canal, which opened in 1869, dramatically shortened the sea routes to India and the Far East.

Two overseas military events marred the peace of the 1850s. From 1854 to 1856, England and France were allies in a war against Russia in the Crimea, which lies between the Black Sea and the Sea of Azof and was then a part of the disintegrating Turkish Empire.

The causes of the Crimean War have never been entirely clear, but it was part of a struggle between England and Russia to maintain influence in the Middle East and thereby protect trade routes into Asia. The war in the Crimea was noteworthy for the heroic (or suicidal) charge of the Light Brigade, for Florence Nightingale, and—most significantly—for being the first war fought in the glare of daily publicity.

Military news in earlier wars had come from official sources or from officers' letters, which traveled slowly home by mail and were printed weeks after the event in newspapers so expensive that only the well-to-do could afford to read them. By 1854 telegraph lines stretched across Europe. High-speed presses, cheaper paper, and railroads for distribution had made the London *Times* a national presence. William Howard Russell, sent out to the Crimea as the first "war correspondent," virtually perfected the trade at the same moment that he invented it. Refusing to depend on statements from headquarters or reports made by officers, he witnessed the battles of Alma, Inkerman, and Balaklava; talked to ordinary soldiers; and sent home dispatches highly critical of official conduct. Unable to land essential supplies, the army faced winter without enough food, clothing, ammunition, medicine, or fodder for the horses. Public outcry over Russell's descriptions of chaos in the army hospital at Scutari moved the government to accept Florence Nightingale's offer to supply trained nurses for military service. Money poured into a *Times* fund that was used to give Nightingale an independent budget for medical needs. With money at her command, she was able to exert far more power than would otherwise have been possible for a woman with no official rank in the army. Thus the primary consequences of the Crimean War were government inquiries into military training and equipment, reform of the army medical service, the growth of nursing as a respectable profession for women, heightened patriotism, and a demonstration of the press's power to shape public opinion.

The Indian Mutiny of 1857 was also the subject of dramatic newspaper reporting. A rebellion by the people of northern India against being governed by the British, the rising was labeled a "mutiny" because it began when a group of Indian soldiers killed the English officers who commanded them and the women and children who were with the English garrison. This brought savage reprisals against Indian civilians and soldiers. As a consequence of the rebellion, which was suppressed by troops brought from England and China, the East India Company was disbanded and the British

government took over direct rule of India. Newspaper and magazine stories about these events created the first stirrings of popular
imperialism. Most people in England had known very little about
India. The spate of publicity, the improved transportation, and the
growth of opportunities for commercial and government service in
India began to excite public pride in the possession of a rich overseas empire.

Political events at home led to a second Reform Bill in 1867.
Once again the size of the electorate doubled. Most middle-class
men and the more prosperous among the working class gained
the vote, although John Stuart Mill's motion to substitute the word
person for *man* was ridiculed and defeated. Political parties had
grown increasingly well organized during the nineteenth century. Beginning in 1868 there was a period of almost 20 years during which the government was headed alternately by two prime
ministers, Benjamin Disraeli and W. E. Gladstone. Disraeli led the
Conservative ("Tory") Party, presumed to represent landowners,
the Church of England, patriotism, and the preservation of established rights. Gladstone was head of the Liberal Party, which had
been formed in 1859 and held the allegiance of many newer voters among the middle class, organized labor, and people in other
religious denominations. Yet both Conservative and Liberal governments in the 1860s and 1870s carried out measures for social
reform. New laws prevented the adulteration of food, protected
children from abuse, and enforced standards of safety and sanitation in housing. Trade unions were legalized, the universities were
modernized, and the purchase of army commissions abolished.
The Factory Act of 1874 established a maximum working week of
56 hours.

The standard of living for urban workers improved significantly.
Real wages (i.e., the amount of goods that can be bought with a day's
earnings) may have doubled, since better transportation lowered
the cost of food and factory production made clothing, shoes, and
household goods much less expensive. Working-class families had
some money available to spend on things beyond the bare necessities. Union contracts, factory laws, and the newly passed Bank
Holiday Act began to provide some leisure time. Mass newspapers,
cheap magazines, professional sports, and other entertainments
developed and flourished. Effective police forces were established;
cities grew safer as the crime rate diminished.

Although John Stuart Mill's proposed amendment to the 1867
Reform Bill had failed to secure votes for women, their status

improved in a number of ways. Single women who owned property could vote for Poor Law officials and school board members. The Married Women's Property Act of 1870 gave wives some control over their own earnings. Nursing schools were formed, paid positions in social work developed, and improved secondary schooling led to formal qualifications for teaching. Women's colleges were built in Oxford and Cambridge, although the two universities did not award degrees to women until after World War I.

A final and most significant legislative accomplishment of the mid-Victorian period was the Education Act of 1870, which created government-supported schools and required that elementary education be available to every child in England. The improved opportunities for literacy were soon visible in the increasing number of laborers' children who moved into clerical work, teaching, surveying, nursing, engineering, and other employments on the path of upward mobility.

The young queen who came to the throne in 1837 had married her cousin, Prince Albert of Saxe-Coburg-Gotha, in 1840. Over the next 17 years she gave birth to nine children and became increasingly popular as a moral leader and model of family values. In December 1861, Prince Albert died unexpectedly of typhoid fever. The queen, overwhelmed by grief, made very few public appearances during the next 15 years, although she continued faithfully to read and respond to the official papers sent to her by government ministers. When she emerged once more in the late 1870s, it was to an altered role as national and imperial symbol and ultimately, with the marriages of her children and grandchildren, as "grandmother of Europe."

THE LATE VICTORIANS (1875–1901)

The later part of the nineteenth century had a somewhat more difficult and diverse tone than the high Victorian years of mid-century, although not necessarily because times were harder. The balance of domestic political and economic power was shifting, and new groups could make demands of their own. In addition, there seemed to be a cultural transition. George Eliot died in 1880, Thomas Carlyle and Benjamin Disraeli in 1881, Charles Darwin and Anthony Trollope in 1882. The artists and writers who came to prominence in the fin de siècle (Thomas Hardy, Oscar Wilde, George Bernard Shaw, Joseph Conrad, Aubrey Beardsley) produced work of a less comforting—more "modern"—tone.

THE ROYAL FAMILY

Her Majesty Queen Victoria, born May 24, 1819; died January 22, 1901. Succeeded her uncle, William IV, June 20, 1837; crowned June 28, 1838; proclaimed Empress of India January 1, 1877. Married February 10, 1840 to His Royal Highness Albert, Prince of Saxe-Coburg and Gotha, born August 26, 1819, died December 14, 1861.

Children:

1. Victoria Adelaide Maria Louisa, Princess Royal, born November 21, 1840; died 1901. Married Frederick III, Emperor of Germany. Children: William II, Emperor of Germany (Kaiser Wilhelm II), Charlotte, Henry, Sigismund, Victoria, Waldemar, Sophia, and Margaret. Sophia (1870–1932) married Constantine, King of Greece (1868–1923).
2. Albert Edward, Prince of Wales (1841–1910), became King Edward VII. Married Alexandra, daughter of King of Denmark. Children: Albert Victor, Duke of Clarence (1864–1892); George Frederick Ernest Albert, Duke of York, who became King George V (1865–1936). Also Louise, Victoria, Maud (who married the King of Norway).
3. Alice (1843–1878). Married Louis IV, Grand Duke of Hesse-Darmstadt (1837–1892). Children: Victoria (m. Prince Louis of Battenberg), Elizabeth (m. Serge, Grand-Duke of Russia), Irene (m. Henry of Prussia), Ernest, Grand Duke of Hesse, and Victoria Alice (1872–1918), known as Alix (married Nicholas II, Czar of Russia). Also Mary and Frederick (both died in childhood).
4. Alfred, Duke of Edinburgh (1844–1900). Married Grand Duchess Marie Alexandrovna of Russia. Children: Alfred, Marie (married Ferdinand King of Roumania), Victoria, Alexandra, Beatrice.
5. Helena (1846–1923). Married Prince Christian of Schleswig-Holstein. Children: Christian, Albert, Helena Victoria, Louise, Harold.
6. Louise (1848–1939). Married Duke of Argyll. No children.
7. Arthur, Duke of Connaught (1850–1942). Married Louise of Prussia. Children: Margaret (married Gustav VI, later King of Sweden), Arthur, Victoria.
8. Leopold, Duke of Albany (1853–1884). Married Helen of Waldeck. Children: Alice, Countess of Athlone; Charles Edward, Duke of Saxe-Coburg-Gotha.
9. Princess Beatrice (1857–1944). Married Prince Henry of Battenberg. Children: Alexander, Victoria (married Alfonso III, King of Spain), Leopold, Maurice.

An agricultural depression in the 1870s was caused by a series of bad harvests, which coincided with the rapid settlement of prairie land in Canada and the United States. North American railroads and fast steamships brought plentiful wheat that was far cheaper than English grain. Mutton and beef came in cold storage from the grazing lands of Argentina and Australia. English agriculture could no longer compete. As a consequence, aristocrats and landed gentry whose income depended on rent from their land grew less prosperous unless they found other sources of investment. Politically, the dominance of landed interests in national affairs began slowly to wane. An interdependent world economy was in the making; England no longer produced enough food to sustain its own population, but relied on imports instead. New waves of rural laborers came to the cities and manufacturing towns for jobs. Some counties lost one-fourth of their residents, and rapidly growing towns threw out yet more rings of brick suburbs. By 1901, 80 percent of England's people lived in urban areas.

The population also continued to grow much more quickly than it had before the Industrial Revolution. Despite the impression that labor in mines and factories was more brutal than the former rural life, industrialization goes hand in hand with rapid increases in population. There has been some debate about why this is so, but generally it appears that plentiful jobs with good wages allow industrial workers to marry younger, and that the range and variety of foods available to city dwellers have a positive effect on nutrition. These two factors together mean that more children are born and survive to grow up. In the later Victorian years, public health

POPULATION OF ENGLAND AND WALES

Year	Males	Females	Total
1841	7,777,586	8,136,562	15,914,148
1851	8,781,225	9,146,384	17,927,609
1861	9,776,259	10,289,965	20,066,224
1871	11,058,934	11,653,332	22,712,266
1881	12,639,002	13,334,537	25,973,539
1891	14,052,001	14,949,624	29,001,625
1901	15,728,613	16,799,230	32,527,843

British Historical Facts 1830–1900.

measures began to control the epidemic and contagious diseases that had made city life dangerous earlier in the century.

The table also shows that there were significantly more women than men and that the imbalance grew steadily larger. There are also more women than men in the contemporary United States, but the reason now is that women tend to live longer; the "surplus" is made up of women aged 60 and upwards. In the Victorian years, however, there was not much difference between the sexes in average age at death. The imbalance between women and men appeared early, between age 15 and 25. Far more men than women were leaving England for economic opportunities in the colonies or as immigrants to Australia, New Zealand, or North America. The number of young women who could not expect to marry was one reason for the rapid development of new movements for women's economic and political rights.

Large numbers of women took up clerical jobs after the invention of the typewriter and telephone in the 1870s changed the nature of office work. After 1876, women physicians could be licensed to practice. There were many new openings for teachers when elementary education became compulsory in 1880. Unionization spread rapidly among women in skilled and unskilled trades; the first major success by unskilled workers (of either gender) was the victory of the Bryant and May "matchgirls" in their strike of 1888.

Strikes, union advances, and labor organization were powerful forces for change in the last years of the century. A third Reform Bill, in 1884, gave the vote to most urban working men. In 1886 there were 10 times as many voters as there had been in 1831, before the first Reform Bill. In addition, the property qualification for service in the House of Commons had been removed. Working men could now be elected. By 1900 the British Labour Party was founded.

Women made their political presence felt through local government, charitable organizations, settlement houses, pressure groups, and (at the end of the century) renewed agitation for full suffrage and legal equality. The major issue in domestic politics during the last part of the century, however, was whether Ireland should have its own Parliament. Alliances and conversions over this question—which was known as "home rule"—split and realigned the political parties. Anxious and dramatic votes were held, but the issue was not resolved.

The domestic concerns of the last quarter of the century—home rule, women's rights, labor agitation, altered political and economic power, agricultural decline, continued rapid technological change—were muted by dramatic overseas expansion and the patriotic fervor created around imperialism. In 1876, Prime Minister Benjamin Disraeli sent to Parliament a bill that gave Queen Victoria the title "Empress of India," thereby focusing attention on the idea of empire. New territories were acquired: Burma and Malaysia to safeguard the borders of India; islands and ports and coaling stations to secure continued English dominance over the seas; pieces of China and the Middle East to protect trade routes or gain economic advantages. During the final decades of the century, England competed with other European nations in the "scramble for Africa" that made most of the continent into colonial territory.

Queen Victoria's Golden Jubilee in 1887 was an outpouring of national affection and a celebration of 50 years of domestic progress. The Diamond Jubilee of 1897, by contrast, marked the high tide of Empire. It was a massive exhibition of pageantry and power. Subject peoples from around the world sent jewel-bedecked rulers and armies in ethnic dress to pay tribute to the almost mythic empress in London who governed them. The South African war of 1899–1902, in which British and Boer peoples struggled over African territory both wanted, was a rude anticlimax; but by the time peace was negotiated the twentieth century had arrived, Queen Victoria was dead, and the Prince of Wales had taken the throne as King Edward VII.

2

THE FOUNDATIONS OF DAILY LIFE: CLASS, TRADITION, AND MONEY

The basic quality of daily life for people in Victorian England rested on an underlying structure determined by social class and shaped by traditional ways of life in country, town, and city. English society in the nineteenth century was still highly stratified, although some of the old class distinctions were beginning to blur by the end of the period.

SOCIAL CLASS

The concept of class is sometimes difficult to understand. It did not depend on the amount of money people had—although it did rest partly on the source of their income, as well as on birth and family connections. Most people understood and accepted their place in the class hierarchy. When the railroads designated different cars for first class, second class, and third class, passengers knew where they were expected to ride. Even if a working man had just won a lot of money on the races and could afford an expensive ticket, he would not dream of riding home in the first-class car. Class was revealed in manners, speech, clothing, education, and values. The classes lived in separate areas and observed different social customs in everything from religion to courtship to the names and hours of their meals. In addition, Victorians believed that each class had its own standards, and people were expected to conform to the rules for their class. It was wrong, people thought, to behave like someone from a class above—or below—your own.

In the strictest legal sense, England had only two classes: aristocrats (who had inherited titles and land) and commoners (everyone else). Nevertheless, most Victorians understood that their society was three-tiered. In broad terms, the working classes (both men and women) did visible work. Their labor was physical and often dirty; it showed in their clothes and their hands. They were paid a daily or weekly wage. Men of the middle classes did clean work that usually involved mental rather than physical effort. They earned a monthly or yearly salary. The elite or upper classes did not work for money. They included the aristocracy and the landed gentry. Their income came from inherited land or investments.

The Working Classes

Although members of the working class are not much seen in Victorian fiction or in popular conceptions of Victorian life, about three people out of every four did manual work. The largest number were agricultural laborers, domestic servants, and factory hands. In addition there were a great variety of unskilled, semiskilled, and skilled jobs in mining, fishing, transportation, building, the garment industry, and other manual trades.

Most working people earned just enough to stay alive, and could be thrown into poverty by illness, layoffs, or a sudden misfortune such as a factory fire that caused even short-term unemployment. People in unskilled and semiskilled jobs generally needed additional income from several members of the family. Because manual labor was physically demanding, working men were often most highly paid in their twenties, when they were in peak physical condition. They married then; and for a year or two, while both husband and wife continued to work, there was extra money to buy a few things. Once children came, a woman could not usually continue working a 12- or 14-hour day. She might earn something at home by doing piecework or taking in a lodger, but the family would be quite poor while the children were small. In addition, the man earned less as he grew older. Girls and boys had to start work very young. They had little schooling. Even before they were old enough for regular jobs, they often helped in the work done by older members of the family.

Once the children were all at work, the family's income would again rise above the poverty level. The parents might even accumulate some savings—which they would need after the children married and set up their own households. By that time, hard labor and poor food would have weakened the parents' health. They could not earn nearly as much as when they were younger. If they lived to be old, they would probably be very poor. They might end their days in the workhouse unless some of their children earned enough to take care of them.

Skilled workers, who made up perhaps 15 percent of the working class, were in a more fortunate position. Printers, masons, carpenters, bookbinders, expert dressmakers, shoemakers, and the growing number of highly skilled workers in new trades such as toolmaking had a higher and more dependable income. Because these trades were generally learned through apprenticeship, skilled workers came from families that could afford to do without their children's income while the apprenticeship was served. Many of the girls who trained as teachers and nurses in the later part of the century were the daughters of skilled workers. In effect, the skilled formed a separate subclass within the working class, with differences in education, training, interests, and way of life. Artisans such as saddlers, shoemakers, bakers, and builders sometimes became employers and set up their own shops, thus occupying a borderline territory between working and middle classes.

The Middle Classes

The middle class grew in size and importance during the Victorian period. It made up about 15 percent of the population in 1837 and perhaps 25 percent in 1901. This was a diverse group, including everyone between the working classes (who earned their living by physical labor) and the elite (who inherited landed estates). It's important to remember that money was not the defining factor in determining class. The middle class included successful industrialists and extremely wealthy bankers such as the Rothschilds; it also included poor clerks like Bob Cratchit (of Charles Dickens's *The Christmas Carol*). Cratchit earned only half as much as a skilled worker such as a printer or a railway engine driver, but he would nevertheless be considered middle class.

Within the middle class, those with the highest social standing were the professionals (sometimes referred to as the *old middle class* or *upper middle class*). They included Church of England clergymen, military and naval officers, men in the higher-status branches of law and medicine, those at the upper levels of governmental service, university professors, and the headmasters of prestigious schools. Later in the period some additional occupations such as architecture and civil engineering might be added. The professional middle classes were largely urban. They educated their sons at boarding school and university; later in the period they often demanded quality education for their daughters as well.

The newer portion of the upper middle class was made up of large-scale merchants, manufacturers, and bankers—men whose success was a direct consequence of the Industrial Revolution. The wealthiest among them achieved some class mobility in the next generation by sending their sons to prestigious schools and preparing them for a profession; their daughters might hope to marry landowners.

Farmers (who employed farm laborers to do the actual physical work on the land) were also part of the middle class. So were men in a number of newer occupations that required a reasonably good education: accountants, local government workers, journalists, surveyors, insurance agents, police inspectors, and so forth.

Small shopkeepers and most clerical workers are generally considered lower middle class. Such work required literacy but not further education. Children of the lower middle class were probably kept at school until age 12 or 14, after which daughters as well as sons might begin working in the family shop or in some suitable commercial post. As London became a world center of business and finance, the number of people doing what was then called *black coated* work (we now call it *white collar*) grew enormously. The group included clerks, middle managers, bookkeepers, and lower-level government workers. Women increasingly found clean and respectable work in shops, offices, and telephone exchanges and as schoolteachers.

Despite the range in status and income, the middle class was presumed to share a set of standards and ideals. The concept of a distinctly middle-class way of life developed early in the Victorian period. In addition to maintaining a certain kind of house, the middle class despised aristocratic idleness; the majority valued hard work, sexual morality, and individual responsibility. Education was important; sons who were not sent to the elite boarding schools went to local grammar schools or to private schools with a practical curriculum. The middle classes were churchgoers: generally the professional middle class attended the Church of England, while manufacturers and tradesmen were more likely to be Nonconformists. (These terms are explained in chapter 11.)

Family togetherness and the idealization of family life were typically middle class: many among the working class had to send children out to work when they were very young, and upper-class children were raised by servants and saw little of their parents. Other middle-class virtues included sobriety, thrift, ambition, punctuality, constructive use of leisure, and prudent marriage—indeed, the wish to be financially secure before starting a family meant that middle-class men often did not marry until they were past age 30.

A man's status depended primarily on his occupation and on the family into which he was born; a married woman's status derived from her husband. Church of England clergymen in minor parishes could have very small incomes, but they were indisputably gentlemen because of their education, values, and position in the community. It would be inconceivable for such a man's wife or daughters to do paid work. His sons, of course, would support themselves, but extraordinary sacrifices were made to pay for their education so they could enter professions or government service. There were men in skilled trades who earned enough to live in a comfortable house in a decent neighborhood, keep servants, and send their children to good local schools, but they were nevertheless not considered middle class.

The Aristocracy and Landed Gentry

Aristocrats and the gentry made up a hereditary landowning class, whose income came from the rental of their property. A landowner's estate—some of them owned thousands of acres—was divided into farms that were rented out on very long-term leases. The manor or hall in which the landowner lived was a comfortable country house with a staff of servants. The title (in the case of aristocrats) and the land usually passed intact to the eldest son. With the coming of nineteenth-century moral reforms, an upper-class life of pure leisure and dissipation lost favor. When the eldest son inherited the estate, he was expected to do something useful—to sit in Parliament, take part in local affairs, use his influence in a charitable cause—although he did not do any paid work. Younger sons might have some inherited income, but many were prepared to enter a profession, especially as military officers, clergymen, or colonial administrators.

In 1842 there were 562 titled families in England. The peerage has five grades: from highest to lowest they are duke (his wife is a duchess), marquess (marchioness), earl (countess), viscount (viscountess), and baron (baroness). An aristocrat is not promoted up the ranks from lower to higher; he continues to hold the title he inherits. Sometimes, however, a new title is created to reward someone for extraordinary public accomplishments. In late-Victorian times, the banker and philanthropist Angela Burdett-Coutts became the first woman to be made a baroness in recognition of her service to the nation. It may also sometimes appear, in reading novels, that a man has been "promoted," because of the custom of using a courtesy title for an eldest son. A duke or viscount or earl generally holds several additional titles that have passed into his family, over the centuries, through marriage and inheritance. The second-most-important family title is given to the eldest son, by courtesy, while his father is still alive. Thus the Duke of August's son may be known as the Earl of January. When the old duke dies, his son will no longer be called the Earl of January but will become the Duke of August.

The head of a titled family had certain responsibilities and privileges. He was automatically a member of the House of Lords. He could not be arrested for debt. And if he were charged with a criminal offense, he would be tried by a *jury of his peers*—a jury made up of other noblemen, in a special court held in Westminster Hall rather than in an ordinary criminal court.

Knights and baronets are technically commoners; they do not have an aristocrat's privileges, although they are addressed as *Sir*. The baronet's title is inherited. A knighthood must be earned; the title is awarded by the monarch for some important public, military, or artistic accomplishment, and it does not pass down to the knight's sons.

In some European countries, the aristocracy as a whole formed a separate class under law; the children of a titled man were also aristocrats with special rights. In England, the sons and daughters of peers were commoners. If he wanted to be active in government, a peer's son could run for election to the House of Commons. If he broke the law, he would be tried in ordinary criminal courts. Only after his father died would the eldest son become an aristocrat, inherit the title, and take a seat in the House of Lords.

Peers generally had a London residence as well as one or more estates in the country. When Parliament was in session (during spring and early summer), the family lived in their town house and engaged in a round of balls, dinners, and receptions. It held parties

Worsley New Hall, a country house surrounded by its park and gardens, was built in the 1840s for Francis Egerton, a poet, member of Parliament, and art patron who became first Earl of Ellesmere in 1846. Courtesy of The Art Archive/Private Collection.

to attend the regatta at Henley, horse racing at Ascot, and cricket at Lord's. Men and younger women rode in Hyde Park; older women took drives in the afternoon, made calls, and shopped. During the autumn and winter they returned to their estates for foxhunting and houseparties. Sons were generally educated at the great public schools (which are actually expensive boarding schools, as explained in chapter 8). Daughters were taught at home by a governess.

Baronets occupied an anomalous space between aristocrats and commoners. There were about 850 of them in Victorian times. Although their title is inherited, baronets did not sit in the House of Lords. If they were interested in Parliament, they could be elected to the House of Commons. Even in the middle 1860s, about one-third of the men in the House of Commons were either baronets or the sons or grandsons of peers, which helped maintain the political influence of the upper class.

Although aristocrats, who spent half the year in London attending to Parliamentary business, were nationally important, the major local influence in the English countryside rested with the landed gentry. *Burke's Landed Gentry,* which lists their names and lineage, was first published in the year that Victoria became queen (1837). A landed estate typically included a hall or manor house, a home farm that was managed by a bailiff, several farms occupied by tenants, and a village or two in which farm laborers lived.

The landed gentleman usually did not have a house in town. He spent most of the year on his estate and took an active part in local affairs. He was generally called *Squire,* which is not a legal title but rather a customary term for the most influential local landowner. In Victorian times there were about two thousand squires with estates of between one thousand and three thousand acres. Some were knights or baronets, but most had no title. The squire was expected to be a justice of the peace, to take an interest in the countryside, and to promote local charities. His wife and daughters would visit poor people, provide layettes for new babies or soup for the elderly, and probably teach a class in the Sunday school. Theirs was the idealized Victorian life that many people yearn for; there was plenty of time for sports, visiting, hunting, balls, and country festivals.

ALL THINGS BRIGHT AND BEAUTIFUL

Written in 1849 by Cecil Frances Alexander, this hymn from the Church of England's *Hymns Ancient and Modern* was a favorite for use with young children.

> All things bright and beautiful,
> All creatures great and small,
> All things wise and wonderful,
> The Lord God made them all.
>
> Each little flower that opens,
> Each little bird that sings,
> He made their glowing colours,
> He made their tiny wings.
>
> The rich man in his castle,
> The poor man at his gate
> God made them, high and lowly,
> And ordered their estate.

There were vast differences of degree between the upper levels of the nobility and the smaller squires, yet social contact and inter-marriage between the two groups were not impossible. Further-more, the younger sons of both groups might earn their living in a profession. Education at the great public schools created standards of behavior that were shared by boys from the upper middle class, the landed gentry, and the aristocracy. In the latter part of the cen-tury, leading merchants and industrialists also began to send their sons to Eton, Rugby, and other elite boarding schools, where they acquired the values and manners of the landed classes. Class dis-tinctions became more flexible. Society continued to be hierarchical: people saw themselves as occupying a "place," and offered defer-ence to those "above," but some movement was possible. Bankers and businessmen bought country estates and were accepted by the rural gentry. In 1881 the daughter of a manufacturer was, for the first time, presented at court. In the 1890s some industrialists were granted titles.

TRADITIONAL WAYS OF LIFE

Class standing interacted with place of residence to create tradi-tional ways of life. Although actual circumstances were more com-plex than the idealized picture, these traditions had an effect on the way people lived and thought of themselves. It is often suggested that the golden age of traditional society was between 1850 and 1880, with a fading nostalgic afterlife trailing in memory up to the last happy summer before World War I.

Country Life

In its idealized (and simplified) form, rural life was centered on the squire and his family, who lived in a manor house with sta-bles, gardens, and extensive grounds that he had inherited. Nearby stood a village with a church and village green, two or three pubs, a few shops (grocer, chemist, baker, butcher), and some craftspeople such as a blacksmith, a shoemaker, a dressmaker, and a miller. More than half of the village population would be farm laborers; others worked on the squire's estate as carpenters or gardeners. Some women had traditional skills in midwifery, nursing, and laying out the dead. The village well supplied water to all of the dwellings and served as meeting place for women and children (who had to haul the water home). The pub was the men's social center and their source of news and gossip. Women did not drink at the village pub, though they might knock at the back door for beer to take home.

Although the church did not actually belong to the squire, he often had the power to appoint its clergyman. The squire and clergyman might well be the only educated residents; their families generally socialized with one another as well as with neighboring squires. However, the neighborhood might have a few other substantial families—people who were retired or had independent incomes, and had rented large houses in the vicinity. If the squire's property bordered on an aristocratic estate, the nobleman and his family exerted a certain presence when they were in residence. They might hand out the prizes at a village agricultural show or enlist support for candidates during an election campaign. Because aristocrats were in the country for only a small part of the year, however, the squire and his family were far more important to village life. Once a year they opened their gardens, put up a tent, and provided a school treat or church festival or some other entertainment for the tenants and villagers.

The tenant farmers had comfortable houses and a relatively prosperous style of life, although social distinctions were made. For example, gentry and farmers both enjoyed foxhunting during the autumn. The men sat down as equals for all-male dinners, but it was an unstated custom that farmers and their wives did not attend the hunt ball. The squire was expected to maintain good relations with his tenants, to make sure the buildings were repaired, the land drained, and appropriate improvements made. Relationships between farmers and landlords might last for several generations; the terms of a farm lease were often written to cover three lifetimes.

The village school had one room with separate entrances for boys and girls. It usually stood next to the church and was supported by a voluntary society and by the squire's family. Very young children of farm laborers and village tradespeople learned reading, writing, arithmetic, religion, and (if they were girls) sewing. The farmers' children were sent away to boarding school, but not to the same expensive schools that educated the squire's sons.

Most actual work on farms was done without machinery, and therefore required large numbers of agricultural laborers. They lived in one-room and two-room cottages in the village and in tiny settlements of a dozen or so cottages scattered among the farms. Since the squire owned the cottages, a laborer lost his home if he lost his job. Laborers generally had a little plot to grow some food for their own use—a necessity, since their wages were often below subsistence level. Cottage families had a traditional right to gather firewood *by hook or crook*. That is, they could pick up fallen branches or use a hook to bring down dead wood, but they could not cut trees. Married women earned a little money by knitting or braiding straw for hatmaking; they also did field work in busy seasons. Model family budgets in an 1876 schoolbook suggest that the wife's earnings should be used for postponable extras: shoes, clothing, treats such as sugar and currants and meat for Sunday dinner.

Village girls traditionally went into domestic service. At age 12 or 13 the farm laborer's daughter would become underservant for a farmer or helper in a local tradesman's house. After she had some experience and had saved money for her outfit, she would look for a place in town. Thereafter she came home for a week or two every summer, bringing treats for the younger children and some of her employer's cast-off clothing as gifts for her mother and aunts.

Town Society

The rural village was within reach of a market town. In the days before railroads, towns that held a weekly market day were small and close together; later in the century people could travel further to sell produce and make necessary purchases. A market town had more shops than would be found in a village, and it had a range of artisans, including saddlers, glaziers, carpenters, masons, and plumbers. In addition, there were professionals whose services were needed by the surrounding gentry: bankers, medical men, and solicitors who served as business agents and legal advisors. There might be an old grammar school for sons of the smaller-scale professional men and the more prosperous farmers and tradesmen.

In a town that had a cathedral, or a county town with courts and administrative offices, the upper-middle and professional class would be larger. There would also probably be retired military and business men, and some upper-middle-class widows or single women with small private incomes. Cathedral and county towns thus had an active social life of calls, visits, dinners, charitable events, evening parties, and annual balls. In addition, the artisans and tradespeople and small employers had their own social and political life centered around the Baptist or Methodist chapel and the town council's business affairs.

City Life

Urbanization was the most striking phenomenon of the Victorian age. Cities grew chiefly by migration. Entire families left the village for better jobs in factories; rural girls came into domestic service; younger sons of the gentry looked for opportunities in urban professions. Cities developed patterns of living that were segregated by income. In country towns it was still usual for shopkeepers and even bankers to live on the premises where they worked, but in cities the commercial centers were virtually deserted at night.

The rapid growth of industry meant equally rapid growth in manufacturing cities. Workers' living conditions were miserable in the early part of the century. Developers ran up streets of cheap row houses built back-to-back (so that two rows of housing shared the same back wall). Each dwelling had two rooms, one above the other, with only a single window in the front. There was no indoor plumbing; water had to be carried in buckets from a pump; and a small fireplace with a grate served for both cooking and heating.

Bagot Street, Birmingham, is typical of the rows of terraced housing built for factory workers in an industrial city. Courtesy of The Art Archive.

The same conditions were found in the rural cottages from which the first generation of industrial workers migrated—but in cities the sheer mass of people, compounded by the lack of fresh air and sanitation, created public health problems that soon called out for reform.

In the second half of the century, sewers, piped water, gas lighting, and building codes brought massive improvements in city life. There were neighborhoods of substantial homes, "clerks' suburbs" of middle-class row houses, vast areas of rental housing for workers. People lived and shopped and took entertainment in their own neighborhoods. Extensive local social structures were based on church, chapel, trade unions, professional associations, volunteer organizations, sports clubs, amateur musical societies, and so forth. The social relationships of working-class and middle-class urban life became so complicated that they defy any easy description.

MONEY

Although the amount of money people had did not determine their social class, it was evident to Victorians that a certain income was needed in order to maintain a style of living appropriate to the class status one held through birth, education, and occupation. That is, a clergyman's son who was trying to make his living as a novelist would remain middle class even if he earned almost nothing and lived in a single rented room in a working-class neighborhood. But if he wanted to marry and live as a man of his class was expected to live, an income of at least £300 a year was essential. Understanding these target incomes for various standards of living is useful, since it helps in interpreting the sums of money that are often mentioned in novels and biographies.

The Monetary System

In 1971 Britain switched from its old system of currency to a decimal system similar to the one in the United States. The old system used traditional non-decimal English measures such as dozens and scores. The Victorian monetary scheme was based on the penny, the shilling, and the pound. The *penny* was a large copper coin; its written symbol was d. (The plural of *penny* is *pence*.) The *shilling* was a silver coin worth 12 pence; its written symbol was s. The *pound* was equal to 20 shillings or 240 pence; its written symbol was £. The pound coin, made of gold, was referred to as a *sovereign.* In addition, there were coins for the following amounts:

Farthing (one-fourth of a penny)
Halfpenny
Twopence
Threepence
Groat (4 pence)
Sixpence
Florin (2 shillings)
Half crown (2 shillings and sixpence)
Double florin (4 shillings)
Crown (5 shillings)
Half sovereign (10 shillings, or one-half of a pound).

The *guinea* coin, worth 21 shillings, was not minted after 1813. The word remained in use, however, especially for luxury goods. A rich customer would presumably not care if something was priced at 20 guineas rather than 20 pounds, although 20 guineas is another way of saying "20 pounds and 20 shillings" and the customer would therefore actually be paying 21 pounds.

Almost all money circulated in the form of coins. The government did not print paper money. Paper *bank notes* were issued by individual banks. If the bank failed—which was not uncommon— its banknotes became worthless. Five-pound notes were the smallest ones issued. Careful people insisted on using gold coins even for very large amounts. Checks were not commonly accepted. Merchants used other complicated means of transferring large sums of money.

It is not possible to translate the value of Victorian money into modern terms by using a simple system of multiplication. There are too many differences in relative prices, costs, values, standards. House rent, for example, was very low: the middle-class rule of thumb was that 10 percent of one's annual income might be spent on rent. In the contemporary United States, a family generally spends at least one-third of its income on housing costs. On the other hand, even the most modest middle-class Victorian family had at least one servant, although that did not mean that the woman of the house spent her days in idleness. It took much more time and energy to do housework without washing machines, refrigeration, piped water, or central heating. Servants did a great deal of manual labor that is no longer necessary: filling and cleaning lamps; carrying coal, tending fires and emptying ashes; heating water for baths and carrying it upstairs; baking bread, preserving fruit, making almost all meals from scratch; going on foot to do daily marketing and other errands; taking rugs outside to clean by beating; boiling water for laundry (and wringing it out by hand); and so forth. Servants' wages seem absurdly low to us, but the servant also got room and board and some of her clothing; her meals were almost certainly more plentiful than when she lived in her parents' cottage.

A few sample prices will suggest what some commonplace things cost:

The standard quartern loaf of bread (a large, dense loaf which weighed just over 4 1/4 lb.) cost 8 1/2d. in the 1840s, 7d. in 1875, 6d. in 1887, 5d. by 1895. Because North American grain made bread so much cheaper, working-class people had more money available for other food.

At midcentury cotton stockings cost from 4 1/2d. to 4s. 11 1/2d. a pair, depending on the quality. At the end of the century, silk stockings could be had for 5s. a pair and a ready-made woman's suit for £1. A woman's riding habit made to measure cost a minimum of 10 guineas, and it might come to a great deal more.

A pair of workingman's boots cost 11s. A workingman's shirt could be bought for 1s. 4d. and his socks for 9d.; he probably wore a second-hand coat purchased for about 4s.

The usual London cab fare inside a 4-mile circle with its center at Charing Cross was 1s. for any distance under 2 miles and 6d. a mile thereafter.

A bicycle in the 1880s could be had for £4–£5. By the end of 1890s, cheap newspapers advertised factory-refurbished second-hand cycles at £1.

Books were expensive. A new hardbound novel in three volumes cost 31s. 6d. (i.e., more than an inexpensive woman's dress or a second-hand bicycle); people joined private libraries for a subscription of a guinea a year instead. Dickens and other popular writers issued their books in paper-covered installments at 1 shilling a month, which brought the total price down to £1 and spread it over almost two years.

Working-class schooling until the 1890s (when it became free) typically cost 1d.–4d. a week for each child. Fees for a middle-class boy at a moderate boarding school came to £100–£150 a year. One year at an Oxford or Cambridge women's college towards the end of the century was £105. Expenses for a man, who expected to drink wine and have a more luxurious standard of living while he attended the university, ran two or three times that much.

The daily newspaper sold for 7d. early in the period. Once the stamp
tax and paper duty were repealed and cheap paper was invented,
newspapers fell to a penny and then to a halfpenny.

The cost of an adult's burial, even at the most minimal standard, was
between £4 and £5.

Annual Income and Standards of Living

One good way to get a sense of relative prices is through looking
at household guides that suggest how people should live and what
they can afford at various levels of income. One common way of
putting the question was to list how many servants a family could
employ. A single woman with an income of £100 a year or a married
couple with £150–£200 could afford a young maid-of-all-work. At
£300, the family could afford a maid-of-all-work and a nursemaid
to look after the children, although the woman of the house would
still be doing much of the daily labor, including some cooking.

If the income was £500 a year, household manuals said, there
should be three servants: cook, housemaid, and nursemaid. (If
no children were at home, the nursemaid would be replaced by a
tweenie, whose job was to help both cook and housemaid as needed,
or by a boy for cleaning boots, running errands, carrying heavy
loads, and doing outdoors work.) At £750, the servants should
include cook, housemaid, and nursemaid, as well as a boy; at this
level, the woman of the house exercised supervision but no longer
did household work herself.

An income of £1,000 a year marked a significant dividing line.
At that figure, a family could afford four women (cook, two housemaids, nurserymaid) plus a coachman and stableboy; thus they
could keep one or two horses and a carriage. They no longer had to
depend on public transportation to get around. Above £1,500 a year
the number of servants rose rapidly, including a variety of specialists to tend the larger house and grounds. A family with £5,000 a
year, one manual suggested, could employ 11 women and 13 men:
housekeeper, cook, lady's maid, nurse, two housemaids, laundry
maid, stillroom maid, nurserymaid, kitchen-maid, scullion; butler,
valet, house steward, coachman, two grooms, one assistant groom,
two footmen, three gardeners, and a laborer. (Servants' duties will
be explained in chapter 3.) At over £10,000 a year there would almost
certainly be both a London house and country estate. Most servants
would move with the family from one to the other, but additional
estate servants such as gamekeepers would remain in the country.

Another common way of putting the question, for Victorian writers, was to ask how much income a man must have in order to marry. Single men and women, it was assumed, could maintain their class status even if they lived in an eccentric way, but a married man needed enough to set up housekeeping and provide the proper class background for his children. (Children were born soon after marriage, because there was no effective birth control.) The numbers presented in the table entitled "Typical Annual Incomes" are useful markers for interpreting Victorian daily life.

The 250 wealthiest aristocrats had incomes of more than £30,000 a year. These men owned landed estates in several counties (which is why newly rich city merchants could sometimes find an impressive property to rent) and a mansion in a fashionable part of London such as Grosvenor or Belgrave Square, Park Lane, or Piccadilly.

TYPICAL ANNUAL INCOMES	
Wealthiest aristocrats	£30,000
Other aristocrats	
Wealthy merchants, bankers, manufacturers	£10,000
Smallest landed gentry	
Some clergymen, physicians, barristers, businessmen	£1,000–£2,000
Most of the middle class: doctors, barristers, solicitors, civil servants, senior clerks	£300–£800
Lower middle class: clerks, head teachers, journalists, shopkeepers	
Highly skilled mechanics and artisans	£150–£300
Skilled workers, including cabinetmakers, typesetters, carpenters, locomotive drivers, senior dressmakers	£75–£100
Average earnings for semiskilled working men and for skilled women in factories and shops	£50–£75
Seamen, navvies, longshoremen, some domestic servants	£45
Farm laborers, soldiers, typists	£25
Lowest ranked shop assistants, domestic servants, needleworkers	£12–£20

The figure of £10,000 a year was generally seen as the lower limit for an aristocrat's establishment. There were perhaps 750 families with incomes between £10,000 and £30,000. Not all of them were aristocrats, but it is fairly safe to assume that anyone with a title had at least £10,000 a year. In addition to maintaining his country estate and London town house (and the staff of servants these two establishments required), the peer spent at least £600 a year on his horses. He was advised to put aside £150 a year for each son, from the day of his birth, in order to send him to Eton, and to save £100 a year for each daughter to cover the expenses of her social debut.

By the end of the period, leading bankers and industrialists were also likely to be earning £10,000 a year. Although that did not make an industrialist a member of the upper class, he could afford a country estate, send his sons to Eton, and arrange a proper debutante season for his daughters. Some of his sons and daughters might thus marry into the aristocracy.

Upper-class incomes were often stated in terms of land rather than money. The rule of thumb was that land brought in £1 per acre per year. Thus when an earl was said to have 20,000 acres, his income can be estimated at about £20,000 a year. Landed estates were almost always protected by wills or deeds requiring them to be passed to the eldest son (a system known as *primogeniture*). In addition, there were often further deeds of entail, which restricted what a landowner could do with the property he inherited. Entail ensured that the estate would be passed on intact to the next generation. It was quite possible to be land poor—in bad times, when farm rents fell, the owner of an entailed estate could not sell any property or even mortgage it to raise money. There might also be charges on the estate as a result of other legal agreements: support for the previous landowner's widow, specific capital sums or large allowances to maintain younger sons, marriage portions for daughters, debts contracted in previous generations. Sometimes the income a landowner could actually use for himself and his family was less than half of the money he received from the tenant farmers' rents.

These restrictions affected the landed gentry as well as the aristocracy. The exact conditions of primogeniture and entail differed, depending on what was written in the deeds. In some cases, daughters inherited if there were no sons. In other cases the entail required that the property be passed to a male relation. That is the case in Jane Austen's novel *Pride and Prejudice:* the Bennet family has five daughters but no sons and therefore will have very little income after Mr. Bennet dies and his landed estate goes to a distant relative.

Upper-class people who were not themselves landowners generally lived on the investment income produced by money they had inherited. Safe investments that provided a steady income were the *funds* (government bonds returning about 5% a year) or *consols* (a kind of annuity that was more stable and secure but paid only 3%). The word *fortune* meant inheritance, not income. Thus if a widow had a fortune of £10,000, put into safe investments, her income was at most £500 a year (5% of £10,000). That provided a comfortable life, but was entirely different from an income of £10,000 a year. The fortune, however, remained intact to be inherited by someone else. When reading Victorian novels, it is important to keep this distinction in mind—and also to realize that any Victorian investment that paid more than 7% was probably unsafe. The character who was tempted to put all of his money into mining shares, Brazilian railway stock, or some other speculation that promised a high return was very likely to lose his fortune and be plunged into poverty.

For the landed gentry, £1,000 a year was judged to be the smallest income that would permit life as a country squire (i.e., the squire's estate had to include 1,000 acres of farmland that produced rent). A thousand pounds a year was also an income that would support a solid upper-middle-class life for a professional man and his family or for a successful banker or merchant. On that figure, a man could afford to live in a house with 10 or more rooms and a garden; he could provide a governess for his daughters or a reasonably good (if not elite) school for his sons. He could also keep a horse, which not only required feed, stabling, and wages for a manservant, but also made him liable for the luxury tax that was imposed on carriage horses but not on working horses.

Although a successful barrister or a doctor with a fashionable practice might earn between £1,000 and £2,000 a year, a comfortable (if horseless) middle-class life for a businessman, a less prominent professional man, or a civil servant was possible on an income of £600–£800 a year. One magazine's sample budget suggested a semidetached house (called a twin or duplex in the United States), a private neighborhood day school for the children, a daily supply of wine with meals, and an annual holiday in seaside lodgings or a Swiss hotel.

In the 1860s, a London *Times* debate on the causes of late marriage proposed that the smallest possible sum on which a middle-class man could support a wife was £300 a year. On that income, the family would live in a three-story semidetached or row house and have one general servant in addition to a young nurserymaid. The wife would sew her own clothes after they had been cut and fitted by a professional dressmaker. They would worry a lot about school fees if there were many children and if the man did not get promotions that raised his income.

Later in the century, educated single women who taught in good schools, worked in social services, or wrote for the press earned between £75 and £125 a year. A single middle-class woman could live comfortably in ladies' chambers, which were two-room apartments with a small kitchenette. Cleaning services were provided and there was a restaurant in the building, so a woman with a full-time job did not need to cook her own meals or employ a servant. Her salary would allow her to buy the good clothing she needed, go to concerts, and travel to the Continent with a group of friends during her summer vacation.

For men of the lower middle classes, an annual income of £150 was the minimum needed for marriage. Some London banks dismissed any tellers who married before their salary reached that amount, on the grounds that a respectable man who tried to raise a family on less would be too tempted to steal from the cash drawer. In addition to bank clerks, others who typically earned £150–£200 a year were head teachers in board schools (equivalent to the neighborhood public school in the United States), senior clerks in business offices, reporters on metropolitan papers, and minor civil servants such as sanitary inspectors, poor-law administrators, or police inspectors. Many shopkeepers and small businessmen also fell into this range of earnings.

A magazine article on expenses suggested that if the number of children was not large, the lower-middle-class London family could afford a two-story row house in a cheaper suburb such as Clapham, Wandsworth, Walthamstow, Kilburn, or Finsbury Park. A monthly rail ticket would enable the man to commute into the city for work. He would have to spend some money on his clothing, because he needed a businesslike appearance. (A skilled mechanic, whose income would be similar, did not have this expense.) His wife would do her own dressmaking and remake hand-me-down clothes for the children. Her only servant would be a young maid-of-all-work or an occasional cleaning woman. The children would be sent to board schools.

Similar gradations existed in the working class. The most highly skilled workers in essential trades such as shipbuilding and steelmaking could earn between £100 and £200 a year. Their standard of material comfort was similar to many clerical workers in the lower middle class, although they tended to live in different neighborhoods—indeed, in different cities, because the industries that employed the most highly paid manual workers were concentrated in the midlands and the north of England.

The labor aristocracy of skilled artisans in regular employment earned 30–40 shillings a week (i.e., £75–£100 a year). The group included cabinetmakers, typesetters, jewelers, scientific instrument makers, carpenters, locomotive drivers, and the mechanics who made and repaired factory machinery. To enter these trades, a boy was generally apprenticed after he left school at age 12. By age 20 he was established in a good job that he got through family connections or his father's union (in much the same way that young men in a higher station got desirable posts in the church or diplomatic service). He married in his middle twenties or later, after saving money to furnish a house; the woman he married would have been accumulating linens and housewares with her earnings. Thus prepared, they could anticipate a reasonably comfortable life with an adequate diet, a carpet in the front room, and a seaside excursion in the summer. Their children would be sent to board school. The boys would leave at age 12 for an apprenticeship, but the girls might stay on as pupil teachers to prepare for an independent career of their own.

The lower ranks of skilled workers and large numbers of men in semiskilled occupations earned between 20 and 30 shillings a week. In common speech, the rule-of-thumb lower limit for a tolerable standard of living was set at a pound a week, or about £50 per year. A survey of wages in 1867 reported that hatmakers, glassworkers, upholsterers, skilled seamen, and butchers' and bakers' men earned 28–30s. a week. Hairdressers, dockyard workers, gas workers, tanners, blacksmiths, hosiery workers, and lacemakers earned 25s. Railway workmen, postmen, miners, chemical workers, textile workers, millers, coalheavers, and boot and shoe workers were paid 21–23s. In jobs of this sort wages were sometimes brought up by overtime, but they could also fall short if work was slack or weather was bad.

On wages of 1 pound a week, reasonable comfort could be achieved only if the family was very small or if more than one person was earning. About 60 percent of adult male workers averaged under 25s. a week. But although wages stayed relatively stable during most of the Victorian period, the cost of living fell dramatically in the latter part of the century. Cheap food from Australia and North America, cheap clothing and shoes owing to factory production, and cheap coal as transportation improved meant that late-Victorian workers could spend more of their income on housing and could keep their children in school longer.

Towards the end of the century, social scientist Charles Booth determined that the poverty line was 18s. a week (£45 a year). That was about the usual wage for ordinary seamen, fishers, police constables, quarrymen, longshoremen, and stable hands. After food prices had declined, a small family that could depend on 18s. a week in regular income could make ends meet, though just barely. If earnings fell much below that amount, however, malnutrition and ill health would soon make it impossible to do a day's hard physical labor even if work could be found.

At the bottom of the earning scale for adult male workers, farm laborers, and some general laborers earned between 10s. and 14s. a week (£25–£35 a year). A wage that small could not support a family. However, farm laborers generally had a chance to grow some of their own food; rural women and children could earn extra money at planting and harvest season. General unskilled laborers were almost inevitably single men or had wives in full-time work. Some seamstresses earned as little as 7 or 9 shillings. Unless they were contributing to a family's income, they could not support themselves on that sum; they would almost certainly suffer from malnutrition.

3

WORKING LIFE

GENERAL CONDITIONS

Most Victorians—men, women, and even children—worked long and hard at jobs that required more physical labor than present-day occupations. There were few laws to regulate hours, wages, safety, job security, or working conditions. Workers generally had no contracts, no pensions, and no fringe benefits. Trade unions developed slowly, although by the end of the period the concentration of workers in some fields and the weakening of laws against *combination* allowed labor to organize and to make some significant improvements, especially in hours and working conditions.

The work day and the work week were extremely long. In agriculture, labor from sunup to sundown during the busy summer days was not unusual. Other outdoor jobs (building, hauling, dock work) followed the same pattern: long days in summer, when it was light, and short hours (which also meant short wages) in winter. Retail shops stayed open—with the same employees on duty–for 14 or 16 hours a day. Needleworkers stitched almost constantly, day and night, when trade was busy and were laid off (without pay) between seasons. Domestic servants got up before the rest of the household, went to bed last, and were on call any moment during the day—although there were slack times when they could read or relax in the kitchen.

For most workers except servants, Sunday was a day of rest. Saturday, however, was not; people worked six days a week. Later in the period, *short Saturdays* became customary: Saturday work ended in midafternoon instead of early evening. Domestic servants usually had a half-day off on Sunday, but they were expected to use part of it attending church services. Servants also had some other regular time off, depending on their employer—perhaps one evening a week or one full day every month.

The regularity of factory work, which required rigorous scheduling and timekeeping, could actually be better for workers than the variable day in other jobs, even though factory hours were long. If the machines ran day and night, there were two 12-hour shifts for workers. Even if there was only one shift, the usual factory day was 6 A.M.–6 P.M. or 7 A.M.–7 P.M. Workers had a half-hour breakfast period in midmorning and an hour for dinner in early afternoon. They brought a snack of bread or cold potatoes for the morning break and went home for their midday meal. Factory workers typically lived only a short walk away; the factory whistle was sounded to get them up and on the job in the morning. In the 1870s, unionized factory workers were able to reduce their week to 54 or 56 hours (10 hours a day for five days, plus a half-day on Saturday); by 1900, miners and some other well-organized workers were getting close to an 8-hour day or 44-hour week. For most occupations, however, 50 or 52 hours was usual. Domestic servants and those in other unorganized and unregulated jobs still had extremely long days and very few holidays.

At the beginning of the Victorian period, the largest single employment was agriculture: there were well over a million farm laborers and another 364,000 indoor farm servants (including the dairy maids who milked cows and churned butter). More than a million people worked as domestic servants. The other major occupations for women were nondomestic service (in inns, institutions, and so forth), textile manufacturing, and sewing. Men's principal jobs, in addition to farm work, were found in the building trades and in heavy manual labor.

Over the course of the century, the number of agricultural workers shrank and the number in industry and other occupations expanded. In the 1851 census, 13.3 percent of all employed people were domestic servants and 21 percent were in agriculture. By 1871, with the decline in farming and the growing number of people in middle-class occupations (who, consequently, could afford to employ at least one servant) the proportions had shifted:

15.8 percent of the working population were in domestic service and only 14.2 percent in agriculture. There were also far more workers in industry, mining, building, and transportation. It was partly this concentration of workers into factories and towns that made unionization possible. Isolated workers in small shops—and domestic servants in private homes—remained impossible to organize.

The most significant change in employment during the Victorian period was the great expansion of middle-class and lower-middle-class occupations: teaching, surveying, accounting, drafting, and especially clerical work and retailing. By most estimates, about 15 percent of all workers were in these occupations at the beginning of the period and perhaps 25 percent at its end. Yet although these jobs were relatively clean and required literacy, they did not necessarily provide more security than manual labor. Indeed, with the growth of unions, manual workers in the 1890s might well have a shorter work day and greater protection against sickness and unemployment than white-collar employees.

CHILD LABOR

Twenty-first-century readers are shocked by accounts of the Victorian children—some of them very young—who worked long hours under terrible conditions. However, child labor was not invented by the Victorians. Children in pre-industrial societies had always worked. Most took some part in their parents' labor, whether in agriculture or in producing goods at home. Their work was entirely unregulated—English law was extremely reluctant to intervene in family affairs, even to protect children against parental abuse—but it tended not to be seen by outsiders. What the Victorians did "invent" was concern for working children, and ultimately the legal means to protect them. Victorian reformers made child labor visible and thereby did a great deal toward bringing it to an end.

In the early years of the industrial revolution, the birth rate was high and many people died before middle age. More than half the population were children and many were without parents. Meanwhile, the owners of textile mills had discovered that children (because of their small size) were especially suited to some parts of the work. There were other factory jobs that children could do as well as adults, because machines supplied the strength and skill that would otherwise have been needed. Millowners made agreements with the local authorities in impoverished areas to take orphan children as young as age seven off their hands. They were lodged in dormitories and worked in shifts, 12 hours at a time, day and night. Other children came into the factories with a parent or older sister, doing the finicky bits of work that required a small body and small hands. In coal mines, children worked underground in small dark spaces opening and closing the traps that provided ventilation.

Because it became obvious that protection was needed, Parliament began investigating child labor. In 1802 the first Factory Act was passed. The government was reluctant to interfere with the freedom of employers and workers to come to their own agreements about wages and working conditions, even when this freedom meant that

---

CHILD LABOR IN 1843

1. That instances occur in which Children begin to work as early as three or four years of age; not infrequently at five, and between five and six; while, in general, regular employment commences between seven and eight; the great majority of the Children having begun to work before they are nine years old, although in some few occupations no Children are employed until they are ten and even twelve years old and upwards.

2. That in all cases the persons that employ mere Infants and the very youngest Children are the parents themselves, who put their Children to work at some processes of manufacture under their own eyes, in their own houses; but Children begin to work together in numbers, in larger or smaller manufactories, at all ages, from five years old and upwards.

4. That in a very large proportion of these Trades and Manufactures female Children are employed equally with boys, and at the same tender ages: in some indeed the number of girls exceeds that of boys; and in a few cases the work, as far as it is performed by those under adult age, is carried on almost entirely by girls and young women.

19. That in some few instances the regular hours of work do not exceed ten, exclusive of the time allowed for meals; sometimes they are eleven, but more commonly twelve; and in great numbers of instances the employment is continued for fifteen, sixteen, and even eighteen hours consecutively.

31. That in all these occupations, in all the districts, some of the Children are robust, active, and healthy, although in general even these are undersized; but that, from the early ages at which the great majority commence work, from their long hours of work, and from the insufficiency of their food and clothing, their "bodily health" is seriously and generally injured; they are for the most part stunted in growth, their aspect being pale, delicate, and sickly, and they present altogether the appearance of a race which has suffered general physical deterioration.

Second Report of the Commissioners on the Employment of Children.

employees had to accept extraordinarily difficult terms in order to get a job. But when large numbers of young children without adult guardians were gathered in factories, Parliament had to pay attention. The Factory Act of 1802 applied only to orphans under the age of twelve who worked in factories. It required that they work a maximum of twelve hours a day and that the millowner provide them with some education. The factory acts were not effectively enforced until 1833, when the first inspectors were appointed. The 1833 act also prohibited the employment of children under nine in textile mills, and it limited the work of children between ages nine and twelve to forty-eight hours a week. In 1842, coal mines were added to the list of regulated industries: work underground was prohibited for all women and girls, and for boys under the age of ten.

A pattern for increasing intervention was set. Novelists or journalists or philanthropists would publish terrible stories about exploited children. Then Parliament would conduct an investigation and make new regulations. In 1840, for example, chimney sweeps were forbidden to use climbing boys inside the chimneys. As the years passed, more and more jobs were added to the list of prohibited employments. A minimum age for full-time work at one trade after another was established, and then raised, and then raised again. Hours were shortened, night work was banned, regular breaks were required. By the last year of Victoria's reign, children under twelve could not be employed in any factory or workshop. They could still work, but only part-time, in agriculture, retail trades, and domestic service.

Even in 1900, most young people were in full-time employment by the age of thirteen or fourteen. And many younger children throughout the period did the kind of work that was less visible than factory labor. The worst conditions were probably in home industries. Tedious handwork of all sorts (e.g., box making, toy-making, painting Christmas cards, coloring fashion plates, assembling artificial flowers, putting matches in boxes, sewing buttons on cards, doing embroidery, knitting, lacemaking) was done at home by women and paid for by the piece. Mothers who did this work generally made their children help—both to keep them occupied and because their assistance was useful. If there was no other source of income, a woman and her children might have to keep steadily at work for fourteen or sixteen hours a day in order to survive. Children were trained for some of these crafts at dame schools, which also served as *childminding* institutions while mothers earned a living. Girls and boys as young as three or four would be put to work braiding straw (for hatmaking) or making baskets and given some instruction in reading. The work they produced paid for their schooling.

A more visible kind of child labor was done on city streets, especially in London. Because streets were crowded with horses and horse droppings, a child with a broom who cleared a path for a well-dressed man or a woman wearing long skirts could hope to get anywhere between a farthing and a penny as tip. Both girls and boys swept crossings. Flower girls went to Covent Garden in the morning to get the leftovers that were given away or sold very cheaply after the regular business was done. Then they made *buttonholes*, or small bunches of flowers, which they could sell. Girls also sold matches and watercress. Boys earned small tips by holding horses, fetching cabs, and carrying parcels. Before telephones came into service toward the end of the century, boys waited outside business offices hoping someone would have a message to be carried a few streets away. Some of these young workers demonstrated their responsibility and moved into regular employment.

The illustration from 1871 shows a family making matchboxes in their home, which probably had only one room. Work of this kind was paid by the piece and required both adults and children to labor long hours in order to earn enough for food and heat. Courtesy of The Granger Collection, New York.

WOMEN'S EMPLOYMENT

One of the persistent errors people make about nineteenth-century life is to claim that women did not work. This applies only (and even then not entirely) to middle-class and upper-class women; the person who says "Victorian women led idle and luxurious lives" has forgotten about the other three-quarters of the population. In addition to their role as domestic servants and seamstresses, women worked in laundries, retail shops, textile mills, and other factories. Once machines supplied the strength, women's fine-motor skills made them the preferred workers for needlemaking, pengrinding, and many other industrial processes that required quickness and neat work habits.

All in all, women made up about one-third of the regular paid labor force. Poor and working-class women did many jobs that were hard, dirty, and dangerous. Although the Mines and Collieries Act of 1842 ended the practice of using women underground to haul sledges of coal, women continued to work above ground in sorting and loading coal. They worked in brickmaking, chainmaking, and collecting trash from city streets. It was not unusual for women who did heavy and dirty work to wear trousers and appear almost indistinguishable from men in the same trades.

Aside from the major employments—domestic service, factories, and needlework—there were dozens and dozens of other ways for women to earn a living. Some of those listed in the census of 1841 include actor, agricultural implement maker, artist, auctioneer, author, baby linen dealer, baker, basket maker, bead maker, blacksmith, boat woman, bonnet maker, bookbinder, brazier, brewer, brick layer, brush and broom maker, butcher, butter dealer, button maker, cap maker, carpenter, carrier, chair maker, charwoman, china dealer, clock maker, clothes dealer, coffee-house keeper, draper, farmer, fish monger, flour dealer, flower maker, gardener, glove maker, greengrocer, gunsmith, haberdasher, hairdresser, hatter, keeper (in a lunatic asylum), lace dealer, laundry worker, leech dealer, livery stable keeper, lodging house keeper, map maker, midwife, milk seller, music seller, nail manufacturer, net maker, newsagent, optician, paper hanger, pastry cook, pawnbroker, pen maker, perfumer, pig dealer, pipe maker, pottery maker, printer, provision dealer, quill cutter, rag dealer, ribbon manufacturer, ropemaker, sack and bag dealer, schoolmistress, scissors maker, shopkeeper, shroud maker, stationer, stay and corset maker, sugar baker, tailor, tape manufacturer, tavern keeper, tobacconist, toll collector, whip maker, wool dealer, yarn manufacturer, and yeast merchant.

In 1885, domestic service remained the largest employment for women and girls, but clerical work and shop work had moved into second place. There were still large numbers of needleworkers and factory workers, but not nearly so many women as in the 1840s were doing agricultural labor.

The true number of women workers was even larger than the census shows, because many married women earned money in ways that went unreported. When a census taker asked for occupation, a married woman generally classified herself as *wife* even if she also produced income by keeping lodgers, childminding, nursing sick people, taking in laundry, mending, ironing, doing piecework at home, working in the fields during harvest, or doing irregular day work as a cleaner. For married women in the working classes, bringing in some money was an expected part of the housewife's role.

Even in much of the middle class, women contributed to their husbands' success in trade, shopkeeping, or a profession. Except for the most socially prominent physicians, for example, the doctor's wife was often called on to serve as his assistant or to give advice to patients who stopped at the office when the doctor was away on a house call. The scientist's wife might act as note taker and laboratory assistant. The farmer's wife was responsible for the dairy; she supervised the indoor farm servants who made butter and cheese, which often provided a major part of the cash income. In trades and small businesses, the wife might tend shop while the husband saw to production, packing, ordering, and dealing with wholesalers; once they were prosperous enough that she no longer served in the shop, the woman was often the more literate partner and did the bookkeeping and correspondence.

MAJOR AREAS OF EMPLOYMENT

Agricultural Labor

In 1851, one-fourth of all employed males worked in agriculture, although by the end of the century there were only half as many. The average wage in the 1850s was about 11 shillings per week for an adult man; agricultural labor had the lowest pay of any job held by significant numbers of men. Women were paid from sixpence to a shilling a day; children about a shilling a week. The more fortunate agricultural workers, however, had a *tied cottage* (that is, a cottage that went with their employment) at a low rent, and a piece of ground where they could grow some of their own food.

Some agricultural laborers had lived in the same place for generations and were descended from peasants who had worked the same fields during the Middle Ages. Others were hired at an annual fair in the nearest market town. Annual hiring was usual for the unmarried farm servants. They were often boys and girls in their teens who got board and dormitory-style lodging plus a very small wage. The hiring fair, sometimes called a *statute fair* or a *mop fair*, generally took place at Michaelmas (the end of September) or around Lady Day (March 25). Workers in search of a job carried a sign of their specialty: a shepherd's crook, a milking apron, a scythe, a horsewhip, a mop (for indoor servants). After agreements were made, the farmer gave new workers a small payment to bind the deal, and everyone spent the rest of the day enjoying the fair's games and stalls and sideshows. Even if they weren't looking for a new job, farm workers went to the fair to have a holiday and see old friends.

Outdoor farm work was physically demanding, but not equally heavy all year round. A variety of skills were involved: plowing, tending animals, digging ditches, mending hedges and fences, planting, weeding, hoeing, and harvesting. Women did regular field labor early in the period, although this was less common by the 1870s. Children picked up stones before the ground was plowed, scared birds away from newly planted fields, and watched animals that were grazing in unfenced areas. Much of the children's work was part-day labor when needed. Even after education became compulsory, schools in farming villages did not expect very many children to attend during the busiest weeks at planting and harvest time.

Getting in the harvest when the grain was ripe was an annual drama, a race against time and weather that required virtually everyone to work from dawn to dusk. Men with scythes cut the crop; women gathered the sheaves together; children prepared the bindings; strong youngsters loaded the wagons and drove the horses; elderly people and little children followed behind to pick up any grain that remained. Once the stalks were cut they could not be left on the ground, and once the sheaves were gathered they had to be threshed before they lost their grain. Everything had to be kept dry or it would begin to rot or sprout. When the last load was brought in, the triumphant cry of "harvest home" echoed over the fields. Then the farmer and his family put on a grand dinner of celebration for all who had brought the year's work to a successful conclusion.

In actuality, farm work had to be done, although less intensively, for much of the year. After the highly perishable grain was in, there were root crops to dig: potatoes for human consumption and turnips to feed cattle. From the 1860s and 1870s, steam-

An 1884 watercolor painting by Miss E. D. Herschel shows agricultural laborers of all ages working to bring in the harvest. Courtesy of The Art Archive/Bodleian Library Oxford, shelf mark Top Oxon b 249 No 9 whole.

powered threshing and mowing machines slowly came into use. In the 1880s, when cheap grain poured in from North America, English farmers turned increasingly to dairying and grazing sheep. A smaller number of farm workers, year round, were needed for tending animals.

Until very late in the century, farm laborers were identifiable by their traditional clothing: a loose smock which came below the knees and was worn over breeches. The country air and country food made people strong and healthy—laborers' daughters were the preferred domestic servants, and laborers' sons were the best tall soldiers for guards regiments. But much of the work on farms was done outside in rain and mud and cold; many farm laborers were disabled by rheumatism by the time they reached middle age. Moreover, they received no pay for workless days in winter. If they did not have children to support them, they would almost certainly become paupers in their old age.

Domestic Service

Domestic service was the largest single category of work for women and girls. In the 1890s, one-third of all girls between the age of 15 and 20 worked as domestic servants. There were also significant numbers of men in service, primarily in wealthier households and on large estates. With the rising standard of living and the growing number of people who could afford servants, the total increased steadily until almost the end of the period. In 1851, 13.3 percent of the employed population were in domestic service; in 1881, 15.9 percent. By the last years of Victoria's reign, however, a change had come: better wages and conditions in other occupations diminished the supply of women willing to work long hours in private homes, and the demand lessened as domestic appliances began to reduce the physical labor of housework.

For many girls from the laboring class, life as a servant in a respectable middle-class household had significant benefits. The food and living conditions were more comfortable than in a rural cottage, and the servant learned about town life as well as cooking and household management. Although wages were low, room and board were included; a girl could save money toward her future. Her chances of making a good marriage increased, because she could meet apprentices, tradesmen, and male servants in addition to the farm laborers she knew at home.

Servants of the aristocracy and gentry worked in large establishments with an elaborate and formal *downstairs* life. There were servants' halls for meals and recreation, specialized duties, opportunities for advancement, and good companionship. At the head of the indoor staff were a butler, a housekeeper, and a cook. The butler supervised the footmen, boot-boys, pages, and watchmen. Under the cook were assistant cooks, kitchen-maids, scullery-maids, and a stillroom-maid (in charge of making preserves, liqueurs, tea, and coffee). The cook kept the keys to cupboards and storerooms, where supplies were locked up until needed. The housekeeper had responsibility for parlourmaids, nurserymaids, housemaids, laundry maids, and other female indoor servants. She was also often the general manager, who hired and fired staff and oversaw the accounts. Outdoor servants such as gardeners, grooms, and coachmen were usually supervised by a steward or agent, but sometimes they had their meals in the servants' hall. Servants in a large establishment could hope to be promoted up the hierarchy from scullery-maid to kitchen-maid to (eventually)

LEAVING HOME.

To her first place poor Jenny goes,
Wondering what life may now disclose
Of sharp or sweet, of good or ill,
Mid faces strange, hearts stranger still.

She "like a woman" heard it said
She must go forth for daily bread ;
Even heard it with some pride,
And strove all doubts and fears to hide.

She'd learn, aye, all that could be learned,
Send home to mother all she earned.
Bright hopes, thank heaven! give rainbow gleams
Even to poor plain Jenny's dreams.

So bustling talk and cheerful face
Bade brave good-bye; she'd not disgrace
Her fifteen years with sigh or tear,
Though leaving all to her most dear.

But the train moves, and now, alack!
The child's heart yearns. Would she were back!
The lessening view and farms upstart
Bigger to her—they fill her heart.

She "has her feelings." Who has not?
And tearful eyes strain for the cot
Where rough but happy youth was spent,
And nights were calm and days swift went.

Oh, "misuses," if Jennys come
Across the threshold of your home,
Adrift from theirs, give kindest heed
To ignorant faults, to ignorant need.

You have the 'vantage ground ; you stand
'Twixt toiling Marthas and the Hand
That beckons nearer angel wings,
To raise you both to higher things.

L. G.

The October 10, 1885, issue of *The Girl's Own Paper,* an inexpensive weekly magazine for older girls and young women, printed this illustrated poem about a country girl leaving home to become a domestic servant.

cook; from nurserymaid to nurse; from page boy to footman to butler. Ladies' maids generally started out being apprenticed to a dressmaker rather than rising from the ranks of housemaids.

The majority of domestic servants, however, were in households that employed between one and three servants. A girl age 12 or 13 would begin either on the lowest rung of an estate or as maid-of-all-work in a tradesman's family, where she would work alongside the woman of the house and learn how to perform her duties. Sometimes she was treated almost as a daughter. In other cases her work was extremely burdensome: she did virtually all of the housework and child care, was on duty for 17 or 18 hours a day, and slept on a pallet on the kitchen floor.

The most typical middle-class urban household had three female servants: cook, housemaid, and nursemaid. The cook was in charge; she conferred daily with the woman of the house about what meals to serve, what special cleaning or other chores to accomplish, and what supplies to order or bills to pay. In a three-servant household, the mistress would share some of the work. She might, for example, give the older children lessons in the morning while the nursemaid cleaned upstairs and washed out clothing and diapers.

RULES FOR GOOD SERVANTS

Always move quietly about the house, and do not let your voice be heard by the family unless necessary.

When meeting any ladies or gentlemen about the house, stand back or move aside for them to pass.

Should you be required to walk with a lady or gentleman, in order to carry a parcel, or otherwise, always keep a few paces behind.

Do not smile at droll stories told in your presence, or seem in any way to notice, or enter into, the family conversation, or the talk at table, or with visitors; and do not offer any information unless asked, and then you must give it in as few words as possible. But if it is quite necessary to give some information unasked at table or before visitors, give it quietly to your master or mistress.

The Ladies' Sanitary Association, *Rules for the Manners of Servants in Good Families* (London, 1901).

She probably cooked the meals on washday so that both cook and housemaid were free for the burdensome chore of boiling, rubbing, rinsing, wringing, and hanging the clothing and household linens.

Almost all female servants were unmarried. The cook, who was generally older, was usually called *Mrs*. Sometimes she was a widow, though more often the title simply marked her higher status in the household. Other servants were called either by first name or by last name—that is, a maid could be *Mary* or *Johnson* but it seems to have depended on the employer, rather than on any regular custom. Young servants disliked it when the mistress insisted that there be *no followers*, which meant "no boyfriends." But servants did have a chance to meet tradesmen and delivery boys and to make other acquaintances while they were going to church or taking children to play in the park. Sensible mistresses understood that secret meetings were a bad idea, so they let servants invite a friend into the kitchen from time to time for a snack and a cup of tea.

Household manuals describe the duties of specialized servants in large households. A butler was an emblem of status. He supervised the other male servants and was responsible for formal rooms: he saw that fires and lamps were tended, curtains were open or closed as they should be, and books and newspapers were in order. The butler announced visitors and supervised the serving of meals. He was responsible for the wine and the silverware; he kept all of the keys and made sure that everything was locked up at bedtime. He also looked after the master's wardrobe and personal effects if

A SERVANT'S DIARY
(SATURDAY 14 JULY 1860)

Opened the shutters & lighted the kitchen fire. Shook my sooty things in the dusthole & emptied the soot there. Swept & dusted the rooms & the hall. Laid the hearth & got breakfast up. Clean'd 2 pairs of boots. Made the beds & emptied the slops. Clean'd & wash'd the breakfast things up. Clean'd the plate; clean'd the knives & got dinner up. Clean'd away. Clean'd the kitchen up; unpack'd a hamper. Took two chickens to Mrs. Brewer's & brought the message back. Made a tart & pick'd & gutted two ducks & roasted them. Clean'd the steps & flags on my knees. Blackleaded the scraper in front of the house; clean'd the street flags too on my knees. Wash'd up in the scullery. Clean'd the pantry on my knees & scour'd the tables. Scrubbed the flags around the house & clean'd the window sills. Got tea at 9 for the master & Mrs Warwick in my dirt, but Ann carried it up. Clean'd the privy & passage & scullery floor on my knees. Washed the dog & clean'd the sinks down. Put the supper ready for Ann to take up, for I was too dirty & tired to go upstairs. Wash'd in a bath & to bed.

Liz Stanley, ed., *The Diaries of Hannah Cullwick, Victorian Maidservant* (New Brunswick: Rutgers University Press, 1984), 106–107.

there was no valet. The butler did not wear livery; his *uniform* was the ordinary clothing of a gentleman. The family called him by his last name and the other servants addressed him as *Mr*. His was a position of trust and responsibility—and in addition to his wages, he had the opportunity to collect tips and commissions from wine merchants and other major suppliers of household needs. Traditionally, the butler retired with enough savings to open a pub or a seaside boarding house (and sometimes he married the cook or housekeeper to secure a partner in the enterprise).

Footmen did a combination of indoor and outdoor work. They delivered messages, did errands, carried luggage, and reserved railway seats. Indoors, they tended fires, trimmed lamps, answered the door, washed glass and silver, acted as valet for younger gentlemen of the house, carried trays from the kitchen to the serving pantry, brought in the tea service with its urn of boiling water, and did other heavy lifting. When the master or mistress went out (either on foot or in the carriage), the footman went along to provide an escort, carry parcels, knock on doors. Footmen were often hired on the basis of their physical appearance—in grand houses they wore traditional livery, with knee breeches and stockings that showed a fine pair of legs. They might be called by conventionalized names rather than their own names: Charles, James, John, John Thomas. Service as a footman was good training for a young man who wanted to become a butler or to manage a school or college lodging. The pageboy was a sort of junior footman, hired at the age of 12 or so, who ran general errands and cleaned all of the boots and shoes, including those of the servants.

The valet was a gentleman's personal servant. His duties were to take care of the master's clothes, carry bath water, and wait on his master at table. Married men did not generally have valets. They worked primarily for single men (who might live in lodgings or a gentlemen's club instead of keeping a house with a staff of servants) and for men who were elderly. One reason that menservants were employed only in substantial households, aside from their higher wages, was that the government imposed a luxury tax for keeping a male servant. However, an exception was made for disabled military or naval officers, who could keep one manservant tax-free. The valet to a disabled or elderly man also rendered personal help as needed and generally slept either in his room or just outside his door.

Among women servants, the housekeeper had the role of executive manager. She was usually a mature woman, often a widow, and sometimes came from a higher social class than the other servants. In large households, her duties were almost wholly executive: she had *orders* from the mistress only rarely, and she was responsible for all of the purchasing, planning, and the managing as well as hiring and supervising of servants. A housekeeper might also be employed in a modest home if the woman of the house had died. In that case she would supervise the children and do other work, helped by a servant or two. Her title of housekeeper recognized her status as manager and demonstrated her respectability, even though she was an unmarried woman living in a house with an unmarried man.

The cook prepared meals and ordered the necessary supplies. A *plain cook* prepared ordinary food for a modest household; a *professed cook* was a specialist who worked in an establishment where there were elaborate dinners and frequent guests. Although the jobs with highest prestige went to men, most professed cooks and virtually all plain cooks were women. The cook learned her trade by working as assistant in a large household or by taking lessons from the cook in a smaller house where she worked as maid. Because virtually everything was made from scratch—including bread, preserves, pickles, soups, and confectionery—she kept a notebook of recipes from the moment she began learning. Like butlers, cooks had certain accepted perquisites, including the right to sell any left-over tallow and dripping from the kitchen.

When there were only two or three servants, the cook cleaned the kitchen and dining room and swept the outside steps; she might also look after children for part of the day. In larger establishments, kitchen-maids did the preparation, cleaning, and unskilled work. If there was a separate scullery-maid, her status was even lower: she scrubbed floors and pots and did the other wet and dirty kitchen chores.

Housemaids swept, dusted, and cleaned. If there were no men-servants, the housemaids carried coal and tended fires; and even if there were menservants, housemaids would be responsible for the fires in bedrooms used by women and children. They also carried water upstairs, saw to baths, emptied slops, and looked after lamps. The parlourmaid was a high-status housemaid who took on some of the duties that would have been done by a footman in a larger household. She answered the door, waited at the table during meals, and brought tea into the parlor. Most servants were expected to be as invisible as possible, but because the parlourmaid was seen by guests, employers preferred that she be attractive and well-spoken.

The lady's maid was also expected to be pretty and literate. Like the valet, she was a personal servant: she kept her mistress's wardrobe in order and laid out her clothes; did spot-cleaning, mending, and some dressmaking; washed lace and fine linen; did hairdressing; brought bath water; swept the bedroom and made the bed; tidied and picked up; and looked after her mistress's dog or cats. The lady's maid was generally given her mistress's cast-off clothes; she would remake some garments for her own use and sell the rest. A married woman or a single woman who was *out* in society probably had a lady's maid if her social position was high enough to require dressing well. The term *schoolroom maid* was sometimes used to describe a kind of lady's-maid-in-training who looked after one or two younger teenagers.

Because servants' age and working conditions varied so greatly, it is difficult to generalize about wages. The table entitled "Typical Annual Wages for London Servants, 1861," taken from a household guide, suggests appropriate annual pay in or near London. The wages appear low, but because room and board were provided, servants did not have many expenses. Sometimes they had to pay for their own laundry; in other cases their clothing was washed with the family's. Women servants might have an extra allowance to buy their own sugar, tea, and beer. The idea was to keep them from being wasteful in using the household's supplies, but if a servant was careful she could save some additional money from her allowance.

The standard outfit for female servants consisted of a washable cotton dress (usually of striped or printed material) with a

TYPICAL ANNUAL WAGES FOR LONDON SERVANTS, 1861	
Men	
House steward	£40–£80
Valet	£25–£50
Butler	£25–£50
Cook	£20–£40
Gardener	£20–£40
Footman	£20–£40
Under butler	£15–£30
Coachman (livery supplied)	£20–£35
Groom	£15–£30
Under footman (livery supplied)	£12–£20
Page or footboy	£8–£18
Stableboy	£6–£12
Women	
Housekeeper	£20–£45
Lady's maid	£12–£25
Head nurse	£15–£30
Cook	£14–£30
Upper housemaid	£12–£20
Upper laundry-maid	£12–£18
Maid-of-all-work	£9–£14
Under housemaid	£8–£12
Stillroom-maid	£9–£14
Nursemaid	£8–£12
Under laundry-maid	£9–£14
Kitchen-maid	£9–£14
Scullery-maid	£5–£9

Isabella Beeton, *The Book of Household Management* (London: S. O. Beeton, 1861).

full-length apron and a white cap, which was worn in the morning while cleaning. Servants who might be visible in the afternoons wore a black dress with a fancier cap and apron. Providing her own outfit was sometimes difficult for a young girl looking for her first place. She might take a rougher job, perhaps as farm servant, in order to save money, or she might get help from her godmother, from aunts or sisters who were already in service, and from the wife of the local squire or clergyman who took an interest in laborers' daughters. Once she was in service, it was customary for her employer to give her a length or two of material suitable for working dresses at Christmas time.

Male servants (except for butlers and valets) were provided with uniforms. (The term *livery* was used for a manservant's uniform.) A coachman generally had rooms over the stable or a rent-free cottage; he might therefore be married. All other servants were expected to be without family responsibilities. In addition to wages, most servants made extra money in tips and gifts. Houseguests who stayed for any length of time, for example, left a small sum for the maid who looked after their room. Running unusual errands or undertaking extra work would earn a tip. Gifts were given to servants on special occasions such as family weddings.

When the family was away for a visit or holiday, some of the servants stayed in the house. They were given extra *board wages* to buy their food. The time was often used for extensive cleaning or redecorating—but the servants could organize the work as they wanted and make time for pleasures of their own. Servants were also given a week or two for a summer holiday, which they traditionally spent going home to visit their families.

Industrial and Factory Work

Factory work was done in a broad variety of industries by the middle of the century. In addition to early processes such as spinning and weaving, increasing numbers of consumer goods and foods such as jams, canned fruits and vegetables, pickled meats and fish, breads, and cakes were factory-made as the century went on. Factories grew larger; machinery became more complex; the work was routine and regimented; and the workers' pace and actions were controlled by the speed of the machines.

In many industries, the majority of factory workers were female. Society at large often saw *factory girls* as rough and disreputable, probably because of their independence and their relatively high

A clean and well-lighted factory in Birmingham used mass-production methods for making steel pen nibs. This drawing from the *Illustrated London News* for February 18, 1851, shows women at work in the room where a slit was cut into each nib to improve the flow of ink. Courtesy of The Library Company of Philadelphia.

wages. Unlike servants or shop workers, factory hands did not live under their employer's supervision. Their workdays were long but defined—and their free time was entirely their own. Another appealing element of factory work, for some workers, was the group spirit that developed when large numbers of people were engaged in the same occupation.

Factory work had many advantages, but (as with all manual labor) conditions could be brutal. Workers' health was damaged by regular repetitive movements, by cotton dust or metal fragments in the air, by heat, by damp, and by crippling chemicals such as the lead in pottery works and the sulfur in matchmaking. As in the case of child labor, however, it was partly the concentration of workers in one place that made the ill effects visible. Although agriculture and domestic work could be equally harmful, in factories the evil was seen and publicized. Workers as well as government investigators took actions to demand better health and safety. The so-called matchgirls of Bryant and May's, in London, conducted the first successful strike of unskilled workers in July 1888. They won not only higher wages but also sanitary arrangements that gave them some protection from the dangerous chemicals.

The textile industry, which gave rise to the Industrial Revolution, grew rapidly. Massive multistory mills with thousands of workers dotted the landscape in Lancashire and Yorkshire. As the spinning and weaving machinery grew more complicated (and laws curtailed child labor), the workforce in textile mills was made up primarily of women between age 14 and 25. Textile workers tended to marry later than other women of the working classes, probably because their wages were so high. By the mid-Victorian period, large factories had become centers of social and cultural life, with musical societies, bands, sports clubs, reading rooms, and other organized recreations. In many towns it was customary for the factories to close for a week or two every summer. Maintenance work was done on the machines—and the workers went off in large groups for holidays at the seashore.

The iron and steel industries were primarily located in the midlands, where Birmingham and Sheffield were traditional homes for the metal trades. Most of the fabrication and craftwork (nailmaking, needlemaking, pen grinding, chainmaking, and production of other metal goods) was done in relatively small factories. Steel mills themselves grew very large in the latter part of the century. The work was hot, heavy, dangerous, and done almost entirely by men.

The skilled portion of the factory work in these industries was done by *engineers*. The word had multiple meanings in the nineteenth century. It was used for patternmakers and metalsmiths, for the men who repaired and maintained machines, for shipbuilding workers, for locomotive drivers, and for factory hands in the manufacturing plants that increasingly produced the machinery that was being sold abroad as other countries industrialized. Probably because it had its origin in crafts where boys had served a formal apprenticeship, almost all engineering work was done by men— although by the mid-nineteenth century most of them were trained on the job. (The more educated and scientific varieties of engineering were increasingly professionalized. Men doing that work distinguished themselves as civil engineers, mechanical engineers, mining engineers, and so forth. Someone called simply an *engineer* was likely to be a skilled worker rather than a professional.)

Mining was another essential industry: coal fueled the steam engines that drove locomotives, ships, and factories, as well as heating houses and (late in the century) powering the generators that made electricity. Over a million men worked as miners by

the 1880s. Until 1842, boys and girls opened and closed the vents
that controlled the supply of air underground. (Most of these children came into the mines with their father or some other relative.)
Women, along with older girls and boys, hauled wagons of coal
along the shafts, and carried it up ladders to the surface. After the
Mines and Collieries Act prohibited underground labor by women
and children, machinery was increasingly used to ventilate the
mines and transport the coal.

Mine work, however, remained difficult and dangerous. About
a thousand miners died in cave-ins and other accidents every year.
When the coal seams were narrow, miners worked on their knees
all day long. It was also dark underground; they wore safety lamps
that provided very little illumination. (Any open flame might cause
an explosion, since natural gas is found along with coal.) The workday was 11 or 12 hours.

Miners had a masculine and independent culture. Most coal
was found in hilly country, where miners and their families lived
in isolated communities. The men were small, muscular, and hardworking; they went to the mines at age 12 or 14, and most were too
disabled from arthritis or lung disease to continue work after the age
of 40. They were well paid in comparison to other workers and often
had free housing as well as free coal. (If coal wasn't given to them
as a perk, their children could easily pick up all that was needed
for family use from the scraps overlooked in slag heaps and along
the loading platforms.) Because coal was so essential and because
the communities were isolated, miners were able very effectively to
unionize and gain greater control over the conditions of their work.

Other Manual Labor

Despite the invention of machinery for factory production, a great
deal of other heavy labor was still done by muscle power. The word
navvy came into use in the 1830s to describe the laborers who did
excavation and construction for canals, railways, embankments, and
roadways. The navvy used pick and shovel and wheelbarrow to do
the work now accomplished by bulldozers and other heavy equipment. Although the work itself was not new, the appearance of large
gangs of navvies who moved through the countryside scooping out
cuttings and banking grades for the rail works of the 1840s marked
them out as members of a significant occupation. Railways required
gentle grades, well-banked turns, and cuttings and tunnels and
bridges to span obstacles. In 1845 there were perhaps 200,000 men

working as navvies. Most were recruited from England's unemployed farm laborers and from famine-stricken Ireland.

Navvies worked in gangs under a foreman or a subcontractor who hired and housed the gang himself. They lived communally in temporary huts that were moved along to follow the project under construction. Each man was expected to shift many tons of earth a day, often working in slippery mud. Worse yet were the tunnels dug and blasted through rock. Reformer Edward Chadwick calculated that 3 percent of the workers were killed and 14 percent injured in the construction of one tunnel on the Sheffield-Manchester rail line.

The hard work, danger, and communal living attracted—or created—a distinctive breed of worker. Navvies wore gaudy waistcoats and heavy trousers of a thick cotton twill that was known as *moleskin*. Many had colorful nicknames. Navvies ate huge quantities of meat and bread, spent most of their wages on drink, and worked off their reckless energy in fighting and rowdiness. Many became perpetual rovers, unattached to women or families, following in the wake of the British engineers and contractors whose expertise brought rail lines to every continent.

Skilled Trades

The terms *skilled worker, craftsman, artisan,* and *tradesman* were used in senses that overlap. All describe people with specialized training in the skills needed for a particular kind of work. Some of them produced goods that they sold from their own premises (e.g., bootmakers, saddlers, hatmakers, jewelers, glassblowers); others (e.g., typesetters, bookbinders, wheelwrights) were employed to do one part of the production in a business that required a variety of skilled workers. Still others were factory hands who had become experts in some complex part of the process and could thus command high wages and steady employment. Skilled workers in the building trades (e.g., carpenters, masons, plumbers, painters, plasterers, glaziers) were also referred to by one or another of these terms.

In earlier times, workers entering crafts or skilled trades usually served a formal apprenticeship. A boy or girl was indentured or articled at a fairly early age, generally between 10 and 14. The child's parents or guardians paid a fee to the master craftworker and signed a legal agreement. The apprentice was bound to obey the master and to keep the trade secrets; the master was bound to provide food and lodging and to teach the trade to the apprentice.

Excavations, grading, and tunnels for railway lines were done without any heavy machinery. The illustration of navvies at work in a railway cutting was published in *The Pearl of Days* for December 1884.

Five years and seven years were common terms of apprenticeship. Although some apprentices were still bound or articled in the Victorian period, the system was not as universal or formal as it had been. However, most skilled work was still learned through a period of doing unpaid or very low-paid work with an expert; and a premium (fee) was generally involved. A highly reputable master craftworker in a well-paid field would be able to ask for a substantial fee to take an apprentice or learner.

Boys and girls learning skilled trades tended increasingly to live with their parents, rather than with their masters. The time to be served varied greatly, depending on the craft; the ordinary range was between two and seven years. The young learner would begin by doing the least skilled part of the work (and also by making tea or fetching beer for the older workers, sweeping up, and running errands). As they grew proficient, learners were trained in more advanced skills. Some traditional crafts still observed formal transitions to journeyman and then master craftsman, with examinations and initiation ceremonies. More often, however, learners who became proficient were simply offered an adult job at adult pay, either in the shop that trained them or elsewhere. Many craftworkers, especially in the newer factory-based skilled trades, remained employees (journeymen) for their entire lives. Others became masters—that is, they set up in business for themselves, employed workers, and began training learners.

In the London construction trade, for example, there were in the 1830s about one thousand master painters and three to four thousand journeymen. A still larger group of men and boys—six to eight thousand—worked in painting either as learners or as irregularly employed casual labor doing the least skilled work. The master painters might be in business for themselves or they might be subcontractors hired by builders or decorators. Many of the journeymen worked for a master but others were independently employed.

The building trades and clothing trades provided work for the largest number of artisans and craftworkers, but there were hundreds of other skilled occupations. The most successful masters—who set up as producers or independent contractors, or who sold goods from their own shops—could become quite prosperous. At that point, that line between the labor aristocracy and middle class becomes less clear.

Needlework

The needle trades were (after domestic service and factory work) the third major source of employment for women. In the strictest sense, dressmakers produced dresses, milliners made hats and other accessories, seamstresses worked on anything made out of cloth, tailors cut and sewed men's clothing, and lady's tailors made garments such as riding habits. The terms tended to be used loosely, however, along with some older words such as *mantua-maker*.

To become a quality dressmaker or milliner, a girl first served an apprenticeship of two or three years beginning at about age 14. The premium could be quite high, and she earned almost nothing during her apprenticeship. She would then work as an *improver*, at modest wages, for several more years while she learned to cut and fit. When she reached senior status in a good house and was supervising younger workers her wages could be as high as £80 a year. She might then set up on her own. Because fashionable clothing during most of the Victorian period was closely fitted and intricately cut—and because there were very few paper patterns— skill at interpreting designs and fitting bodices to the individual customer were the master dressmaker's most important assets. She employed apprentices or less-skilled seamstresses to do long hems and seams for the elaborately trimmed full skirts. Even in smaller towns where not many people could afford expensive clothing, a skilled dressmaker with a good class of client could earn a comfortable income.

Women who sewed for a living thus included some of the most prosperous women workers and the most impoverished. The trade was seen as more genteel than domestic service or factory work, so middle-class women who were left without income turned hopefully to needlework. It could be done at home (while looking after children) and by invalids or elderly women. However, because virtually all girls had at least the basic ability to handle a needle, the oversupply of qualified workers kept wages very low in the less-skilled branches of work.

Many seamstresses worked in warehouses where they hemmed sheets and towels or made plain underwear, men's shirts, or military uniforms. Their workday was typically between 12 and 15 hours, and their wage as small as 7 shillings per week—not enough to survive on unless they shared lodgings and income with other people. Other rough work—often called *slop work*—was done under sweat-shop conditions. Cheap workingmen's shirts, canvas pants worn by fishermen and miners, coal sacks, mailbags, and similar items were cut out and handled by a subcontractor. The workers went

The seamstresses shown here are at work either in a department store or for a dressmaker who employs both apprentices and experienced workers.

to a depot to pick up the materials, did the sewing at home (which meant paying for their own light, heat, needles, and thread) and then brought the completed work back, hoping they would be paid promptly and get the full price they had been promised.

Department stores and shops that specialized in clothing had workrooms on the premises. The customer chose a design and picked out a fabric; her measurements were taken; and then the dress was cut and made for her. Seamstresses in fashionable London shops were thought to have a glamorous life—but they, too, worked long hours, sometimes in rooms with inadequate light and ventilation. During the height of the social season, when customers ordered many elaborate new dresses, seamstresses might be kept steadily at work for several days in a row, with only short breaks to rest and have a cup of tea. At other times of the year, when work was slack, they were laid off.

Needlework was done in other settings as well. Some girls who served a dressmaking apprenticeship became lady's maids. Very large estates and institutions such as children's hospitals might employ two or three full-time sewing women. Gentry and upper-middle-class families had a seamstress come to stay for a few weeks once or twice a year to do household sewing, make children's clothes, and do the long seams and finishing work on dresses that had been cut and fitted by a quality dressmaker. Country towns had a range of millinery and dressmaking establishments, sometimes including a specialist in mourning wear. Factory production made textiles cheaper, and rising disposable income meant that women paid attention to changes in fashion. After the 1860s,

---

NEEDLEWOMEN: INQUIRY BY DR. ORD

Thousands of girls and young women can only earn about nine shillings per week; and Dr. Ord concludes, after careful inquiry, "that girls living alone, and without other means of support, cannot obtain proper nourishment upon nine shillings a week. Many, without doubt, find means of increasing their earnings, mostly by taking work home, or by taking in work on their own account, or by less praiseworthy means; but in all cases encroaching on their hours of rest. The position of girls going home late at night—say nine, ten, or eleven P.M.—is full of discomfort. If they can afford fuel, they light their fire, and cook what is often the only real meal in the day; and after that they have their own needlework to do."

"Labour, Food, and Morals," *Wesleyan Methodist Magazine* 11 (December 1865): 1085–89.

sewing machines made the plain seams and hems less laborious, but not many women wore wholly ready-made garments before the twentieth century.

Shop Work

When the Victorian period began most retail shops were small. Many shopkeepers were craftworkers who sold goods produced on the premises. Even when goods were bought from wholesalers, the shopkeeper had to do much of the processing. Grocers, for example, blended tea, roasted coffee, ground sugar, and packaged dry foods. Most of the selling was done by members of the shopkeeper's family or by an apprentice (usually male) who was learning the trade so he could open his own shop. Urbanization, railways, and factory production significantly changed the retail trades. Shops grew larger; more of the preparation and processing were done elsewhere. A new kind of employee became common: the shop assistant. Because the job required at least an elementary education (to read labels and make change), increasing numbers of women went into shop work. Young women who were neat, responsible, well spoken, and literate were willing to work at relatively low wages for a few years between school and marriage; young men with similar qualities had access to jobs that offered more upward mobility than serving in a shop.

Self-service stores were virtually unknown. Goods were kept in drawers, boxes, bins, and storerooms. Customers stood or sat in front of a counter and explained what they wanted; the shop worker, behind the counter, brought things out for the customer to see. When decisions had been made, the assistant wrote up a bill. Sometimes she also took in the money. Many stores, however, had a separate cashier in a well-protected location—Victorian cities were by no means crime-free, and goods were paid for in cash, not by check. (Shops that served prosperous customers offered credit; purchases were recorded in account books, which were sent for payment once a month or even once a year.)

Shop assistants' pay varied greatly, depending on the kind of shop and its location. Senior women workers in fashionable shops might earn £1 a week; junior assistants as little as £10 a year. However, as much as half of their pay was deducted for board and lodging. In big clothing, dry-goods, and department stores in London and other cities in the latter third of the century, almost all employees except married men were required to live in. Separate quarters were provided for men and for women, either on the store's upper floors on in nearby lodging-houses. If the employer was considerate, shop assistants slept two to a room, had meals in a pleasant dining room, and were provided with magazines, a piano, and space for recreation. Because shops were open very long hours, young workers did not have to walk home in the dark or sleep in a room where the fire had been out all day. Although the system could be exploited by mean-spirited employers, living in had many advantages, especially since the majority of shop assistants were between the ages of 16 and 22.

PROFESSIONAL AND CLERICAL OCCUPATIONS

The training and conditions of work for most of the professions will be discussed in other chapters: teachers, governesses and professors in chapter 8; medical workers in chapter 9; the clergy in chapter 11; naval and military officers in chapter 13.

The Legal Profession

The legal profession had two major divisions. Barristers (also called *advocates* or *serjeants*, depending on where they worked) argued cases in court *(before the bar)*. Solicitors (also called *attorneys*) did almost all other legal business: they took statements and affidavits and otherwise prepared cases for the barrister who would appear in court; wrote wills and contracts; and dealt with land titles, leases, trusts, apprenticeship papers, guardianships, and other family matters. Barristers were concentrated in London. Court sessions in other towns were held quarterly; a barrister would come in from London when he had a case. Solicitors, however, were found throughout the country.

Barristers were the gentlemen of the legal profession. In order to qualify, they had to attend one of London's four Inns of Court: Lincoln's Inn, Gray's Inn, the Inner Temple, and the Middle Temple. They often had a university education as well, though it was not required. There was no formal curriculum or qualifying examination. Men who were reading for the bar had to eat a certain number of dinners in the hall of their Inn over a period of three years. They studied statutes and old cases, got advice (if they were serious) from respected mentors, and talked with senior barristers who judged their character and competence.

Progress in the profession came through contacts, reputation, and family connections. Barristers could not practice in partnership, although they could share chambers (and informal referrals) with other barristers. Chambers—in or near the Inns of Court—were suites of one to three rooms that served as the barrister's office. A barrister could also live in his chambers if he hired someone to clean and bring in meals. A mature and successful barrister, however, certainly had a substantial house elsewhere; his social status was high and his income could reach several thousand pounds a year.

It was not uncommon, however, for young men of good family to study law and live in shared chambers without ever intending to practice. Attending one of the Inns of Court was a good excuse to spend a few years living in London and a way to meet influential people who might help one obtain a government post. A rather large number of Victorian novelists and journalists had, at least in theory, also studied for the bar. Women were not permitted to practice law until the 1920s.

Solicitors had a lower social status, although their earnings could be substantial. (The wives of barristers were eligible to be presented at court; the wives of solicitors were not.) The solicitor was trained by apprenticeship. He paid a premium and served five years as articled clerk to a practicing solicitor. He needed a reasonably good secondary education but probably had not attended university; he usually began his apprenticeship at about age 16.

Solicitors could (and generally did) form partnerships. In addition to those in London—who did a great deal of ordinary business and also worked with barristers to prepare cases for court—every town of any size had several solicitors. As well as taking care of wills, contracts, real estate transfers, and so forth, solicitors served as clerks for local justices of the peace (who rarely had legal training) and acted as election agents. Some of them worked as *man of business* for a landowner: overseeing property, arranging loans, giving advice, and drawing up any necessary legal papers. Although the social status of London solicitors was fairly low—compared to all the other professional men in the city—a respected solicitor in a country town could be among its most influential and prosperous residents.

Clerical Work

At the beginning of the nineteenth century, agriculture was still central to the economy. At midcentury, industry ruled. By the century's end, however, commerce was gaining fast. The growth of business, banking, insurance, the civil service, and other nonfactory employment led to a vast increase in the proportion of workers engaged in clerical and managerial jobs. Almost every office worker would be called a *clerk* (which, in England, is pronounced to rhyme with *park*), although many of them had functions that included accounting, administration, and management. Clerks were considered middle class because their work required some education and didn't involve manual labor, but in many cases the pay was lower than a skilled laborer's. However, clerks expected their pay and status to rise steadily throughout their working lives; relative poverty in their twenties would be balanced by substantial respectability when they reached age 50.

The rapid growth of commercial occupations brought significant changes. The number of clerks (mostly male) doubled during the 1860s and continued to explode during the next decade. There were 130,000 men in commercial occupations in 1861 as compared to 449,000 in 1891. Meanwhile—and especially after the typewriter and telephone were invented in the 1870s—office work was increasingly subdivided. Women flowed into the clerical workforce. The Post Office began employing large numbers of women in 1876; in 1881 the government established a new civil service category of woman clerk, with a separate entrance examination—and a lower pay scale. By the time of the census of 1901, some 60,000 women were in clerical occupations. In 1851, clerks were about 0.8 percent of the total labor force; by 1901, it was 4 percent.

Early in the period, an office boy typically began at 14 or 15, after passing a test in handwriting, arithmetic, and general knowledge. At first, he might have no wage at all while he ran errands, delivered messages, and got acquainted with the business. If he proved alert and responsible, he would be made a junior clerk and earn a modest salary for copying letters and addressing envelopes. Later his work would become increasingly more responsible. Some boys attended night classes for shorthand and bookkeeping and some were formally apprenticed, but most of them simply learned on the job. Young male clerks were sent to docks and warehouses and made responsible for counting and weighing goods. Even the owner's son often started as errand boy and junior clerk to learn the business. A responsible and hardworking young man could expect to advance to a post as senior clerk (where the work was essentially managerial) and could even hope to eventually be brought into the business as partner.

The hours and pay depended on the type of employer. Many business offices had a 10-hour day; hours in banking and civil service were shorter; insurance offices usually worked from 9 A.M. to 6 P.M. However, clerks—who had an annual salary rather than an hourly wage—often did unpaid overtime. A barrister's junior clerk, probably age 17 to 21, earned £35–£45 a year, which was below average even for working-class male income. But with some experience, he could look for a place as sole clerk to a young barrister, where his annual salary would be £75–£100. His fortunes would rise with his employer's; by middle age he might be chief clerk to a barrister with a large practice and earn as much as £800 a year. He would manage the office, oversee several junior clerks, confer with solicitors, and be responsible for the most confidential parts of the barrister's activities. His working hours would be from 10 A.M. to 6 P.M., with a 4 P.M. closing on Saturdays and several vacations or very short workdays when the courts were in recess.

Career patterns like this remained possible throughout the century; but as the number of clerks increased, the proportion who could expect to rise to the top diminished. In addition, compulsory education provided many more boys with the skills needed to enter commercial occupations. The segmenting, subdividing, and feminizing of the clerical workforce further reduced the average pay and created a number of dead-end clerical occupations in which promotion was unlikely.

Young women took up typewriting and shorthand at age 15 or 16, usually by attending classes at a business college or evening school. The beginning pay for a qualified typist in the 1890s was about 10 shillings a week (£25 a year)—not enough for a woman to live decently on her own. Since there was an adequate supply of girls living at home who were eager to do the work, wages remained low. Typists and secretaries were expected to leave when they married. If they did not marry, employers frequently replaced a woman in her mid-twenties with a girl straight from school.

Women also found work as telephone operators. They were hired at age 16 or 17 after they passed an examination in reading, dictation, and arithmetic and were tested for hearing and general health. Their speaking voice, according to the regulations, was required to "be free from pronounced local dialect." After six or eight weeks of training and practice, the operator would take her place at a switchboard. In a typical end-of-century telephone exchange, each operator was responsible for answering and connecting the calls of about two hundred subscribers. They worked 45 hours a week, in 8-hour shifts, with one meal break in the middle of a shift. After about five years their salary would be in the vicinity of £50 a year.

By the last quarter of the century, the path into skilled work of all sorts was becoming more regularized. Apprenticeship or on-the-job training was replaced by vocational schools and evening classes; government jobs were obtained by competitive examinations and formal training rather than through family contacts and personal influence. Families were beginning to realize that middle-class as well as working-class girls should have a means of earning a living. New semi-professions emerged, with schools that offered a year or two of training: librarianship, pharmacy, photography, bookkeeping, physical training (also known as *medical and educational gymnastics*). There was, however, a wage difference between women and men even when their work was exactly the same. In the Post Office, for example—a government employment, with a standard and published pay scale—a first-class woman telegraphist at the end of the century earned just under £100 a year, while a man with the same qualifications and experience earned £160.

4

TECHNOLOGY, SCIENCE, AND THE URBAN WORLD

The new technologies of the nineteenth century dramatically changed the conditions of people's daily lives. Because of the link between technical innovation, industrial success, and economic prosperity, the men who developed new ideas became popular heroes. A series of books by Samuel Smiles—*Self-Help* (1859), *Lives of the Engineers* (1862), *Men of Invention and Industry* (1884)—showed what could be accomplished through initiative and hard work, and they made self-educated and self-made men into models to emulate.

Science, as well as invention, had an effect on both material conditions and the way people thought about the world. Victorian scientific and technical achievements altered daily life in ways both large and small: vaccination against smallpox; chloroform for surgery; photography, suspension bridges, sewing machines, and safety matches; glass bottles and rubber nipples that could be sterilized to safely feed infants when nursing was impossible; the telegraph, telephone, and typewriter; railways, steamships, bicycles, buses, trams, subway trains, and (finally) automobiles; kerosene lamps, gaslights, and then electric lights; canned and frozen foods, rayon, X-ray photographs, and safety razors.

Inventions fed on one another. In 1856, for example, Henry Bessemer developed a process that allowed iron to be cheaply turned into steel. Because steel is stronger and lighter, whole new vistas of shipbuilding were opened and the construction of more powerful steam engines followed. Long steel bridges carried rail lines across rivers and gorges that had previously formed impassable barriers.

Urban life was dramatically altered. For example, most cities became crowded with small houses. Before there was inexpensive transportation, people had to live where they could walk to work. Broad streets and lawns would make the distance impossibly long. When one factory employed thousands of people, the housing jammed close to it was inevitably narrow, cramped, overcrowded, and insanitary.

Technology brought new patterns of life. As public transportation developed, rings of suburban housing were built along bus routes and subway lines. New construction permitted the dwellings near factories to be more adequately ventilated. Water was brought from a distance and piped into homes instead of being fetched from a pump; by 1876, for example, 80 percent of the dwellings in Manchester had their own water supply and flushing lavatories were becoming available. As cities grew prosperous, public interest led to the construction of schools, hospitals, parks, and other civic amenities.

GETTING PLACES AND MOVING GOODS

Coaching

Illustrations on Christmas cards and novels by Charles Dickens have created an impression that coaches were used for Victorian cross-country travel. In fact, many books by Dickens and other popular novelists are set in the days of their childhood, earlier in the century. The golden age of coaching was quite short. It began about 1800, when new surfaces improved major roads, and ended in the 1840s (except for short trips in rural areas distant from the railways).

Coaches were enclosed vehicles pulled by teams of horses that were changed about every 10 miles. The coach lines maintained stables at staging points along the route. On some heavily used roads near London they kept as many as five hundred horses. Coach routes were also served by inns where passengers stopped for food and rest. Even at its best, however, coach travel was expensive and uncomfortable. The coach bounced and swayed; it covered, on average, no more than 10 miles in an hour. On long trips, almost everyone who could afford it chose to break their journey at night to get a decent rest in an inn.

A mail coach moved faster and carried only a few passengers (along with the fast mails). It could cover 100 or 120 miles in a day, but the fare was about 10 pence a mile for an inside passenger. Passengers who rode outside, where they were exposed to the weather, paid five pence a mile on a mail coach. The ordinary stage coach charged about half as much: five or six pence a mile for inside passengers, two or three pence for those outside. At that rate, even a journey as short as the 80-mile trip from Dover to London would take a full day and (for an inside passenger) cost at least £1 13s.— considerably more than the average working man's weekly wage. The same journey by rail was far cheaper (less than 7 shillings at the most inexpensive fare) and three or four times as fast.

Railways

The first rail lines, used for hauling coal and other heavy freight, were built in the mid-1820s. Liverpool and Manchester were connected in 1830 by a regularly scheduled service that carried both people and goods. The great expansion, however, came in the 1840s, when passenger lines connecting most of England's towns and cities were built over a span of less than 10 years. The term *railway mania* is often used to describe the period between 1844 and 1848. It was virtually a gold rush: lines were projected, rights-of-way secured, shares issued, construction begun—and then, depending on the circumstances, the owners and stockholders either grew rich or lost all of their money when the line encountered some problem that kept it from being finished.

The hero engineers of the early railways were George Stephenson and his son Robert. In 1829 they developed the locomotive known as the *Rocket*. Robert Stephenson went on to supervise construction of many rail lines. Another important developer was Isambard Kingdom Brunel. Brunel built tracks 7 feet apart, so the locomotives and cars could be wider and steadier. Stephenson's lines had rails 4 feet 8 1/2 inches wide, which allowed him to lay out tighter curves and build narrower bridges and tunnels. Since the track width determined the distance between the wheels on cars and locomotives, equipment could not be switched between the two. Passengers had to change trains and freight had to be unloaded and reloaded when moving between lines of different gauges. In 1846 Parliament standardized rails at the narrower Stephenson gauge, although the last wide-gauge lines were not eliminated until the 1890s.

The first railway journey in England took place in September 1825, when a locomotive invented by George Stephenson pulled 22 open cars loaded with passengers and six wagons of coal at a top speed of 12 miles per hour, according to the account published with this picture in the children's magazine *Chatterbox*. The rapid spread of practical rail transportation began soon after Victoria took the throne in 1837.

The first comfortable passenger cars looked like three horse-drawn carriages hooked together on a flatbed wagon. The fancy painting and imitation coachwork were soon abandoned, but until late in the century first-class cars continued to have private compartments that carried six or eight passengers on two facing seats. There was no aisle or corridor. Doors from each compartment opened to the outside of the train; passengers could enter or leave only at a station. Some trains had separate ladies' compartments, which made it safer for women to travel alone. Many of the passengers who traveled first class would be accompanied by a footman, ladies' maid, or other servant, who would ride in the second-class cars. When the train stopped at a station, servants would rush up the platform to see if their employers wanted food to be fetched from the restaurant or a shawl brought from the luggage, which had been put into a baggage car.

Gentry rode first class. Tradespeople and the gentry's servants rode second class, in carriages which had reasonably comfortable seats and an interior aisle as well as doors leading out to the platform. Third class was initially a single large car with open windows and wooden benches; sometimes it did not even have a roof. The 1844 Railway Act required each line to run at least one train a day each way that had a fare of one penny a mile. These were often called *Parliamentary trains*. The name is misleading; it sounds impressive but actually describes the cheapest way to travel—which would also be the most uncomfortable and inconvenient.

Second class was eventually eliminated, but third-class carriages were improved. Until 1879, when the first dining car was put into service, all railway passengers carried their own food or bought something from stalls on the station platform while the train was stopped to replenish its steam engines with a new supply of coal and water. Passengers also had to go into a station if they needed to use restroom facilities.

The speed and extent of the transformation brought by rail travel was truly astonishing. In the late 1820s, many people laughed at the idea of railways. Twenty-five years later, railways had completely altered many aspects of daily life. Before the railways, most people never traveled more than 10 or 20 miles from home; all their work, shopping, and recreation were done within walking distance. Rail travel was dependable, fast, and cheap; relatively comfortable (though not first-class) accommodations could generally be had for twopence a mile. Passenger service was remarkably frequent; in 1888, for example, there were 29 express trains daily between London and Manchester. When the track was new and ran through countryside that was not yet built up, travel on many routes was faster than it is today. Townspeople and country dwellers went into the city for a day's shopping; middle-class urbanites could spend weekends in the countryside. Servants and factory workers made quick visits home to see their relatives and took day trips to the seashore on holidays. Even the most ordinary aspects of daily life were changed: fresh milk, for example, could be brought daily from the country to city doorsteps; and fresh fish, quickly transported inland, made fish and chips the most popular fast food in working-class neighborhoods.

Shipping

Ocean transport was also utterly transformed during Victoria's reign. Wooden sailing ships reached their highest peak of achievement with the clippers built during the middle years of the century. Using design features that originated in the United States, British dockyards developed a ship that was longer and narrower than earlier vessels. With its beautiful square rigging carrying a vast breadth of canvas, a fast clipper moved more quickly than steamships of the same period. Although their narrow wooden hulls did not leave much space for bulky cargos or comfortable passenger accommodations, clipper ships continued to be used through the 1850s and 1860s—especially on long Pacific routes where it was hard for steamships to carry enough coal for their engines. *Cutty Sark,* the most famous of the fast clippers that brought tea from China, can still be seen at dry dock in Greenwich, on the eastern outskirts of London.

In the 1830s, however, ships made of iron and powered by steam began to replace sailing ships for many uses. Two paddle steamers raced across the Atlantic in 1838; it took them just under 20 days. The breakthrough in technology came during the next decade with the shift from paddle wheels on the side of the ship to propellers underwater. In the 1840s, propeller-driven iron ships of the Peninsular and Oriental Steam Navigation Company started carrying mail to Egypt and India, and a line owned by Samuel Cunard began regular transatlantic passenger service. By 1855, a nine-day Atlantic crossing was standard.

New technologies, including the fabrication of massive steel plates and improvements in engine capacity, let steamships grow bigger, faster, and (for first-class passengers) far more comfortable. Although wooden sailing vessels continued to be used for certain long routes and for coastal cargos, steamships were more important than sailing ships by 1865. The first luxury liner, the *Oceanic,* was built in 1871 for the White Star Line's passenger service to Australia. During the last quarter of the century, a number of companies competed to create ships that would make Atlantic crossings or the passage to India a memorable experience for first-class travelers. These adventurers enjoyed comfortable cabins with beds, constant supplies of food and drink, and elegant evening entertainments in gracious ballrooms.

Urban Transportation

Although only the well-to-do could afford to keep their own carriage, a private coach could be hired from a livery stable by making arrangements in advance. It was much more common, however, to use a cab for door-to-door transportation in town. (If a cab had not been ordered ahead of time, a servant or a boy who was standing around looking for errands to run was sent to the nearest stable or cabstand to fetch one.)

Four-wheeled hackney carriages were used by large groups or if there was a lot of luggage. The hallmark of Victorian cities, however, was the Hansom Safety Cab, a two-wheeled vehicle patented in 1834. The hansom was light and maneuverable for quick journeys through crowded streets. The hood and apron protected passengers from the weather, and they had a good view since the driver sat behind rather than in front. Although fares were published, a bit of negotiation was generally carried on. A hansom cab journey within central London cost a shilling for any distance under two miles and sixpence a mile thereafter. It was slightly disreputable for an unaccompanied woman to take a cab, although less so if a servant fetched it for her and a respectable person came out to meet her at her destination.

Cabs were too expensive for most people's ordinary daily use. Omnibuses pulled by teams of two horses, which first appeared in

Various models of double-decker bus pulled by teams of horses were designed during the second half of the century. The London omnibus shown here was patented in 1860. In later models the outside passengers sat in rows instead of back-to-back. Courtesy of The Granger Collection, New York.

1829, were more affordable although there was some concern about the safety and cleanliness of sharing close spaces with so many other people. Buses typically charged about a penny a mile. Several thousand buses were in service by 1850. In 1851, the crowds of people traveling to the Great Exhibition prompted the development of double-deckers, which carried 12 passengers inside and another 8 to 12 on the roof. Some omnibuses were built with a second roof, so the outside passengers stayed dry when it rained. Pulling loads of that weight was extremely hard on horses—the typical working life of an omnibus horse was no more than two or three years. Rails for horse-drawn trams were installed on some streets in the 1860s, but although they made the work easier for horses, they never became common in England. In 1901, at least 400,000 working horses pulled passengers and loads on the streets of London.

Motor buses and electric trams were introduced at the end of century; by 1911 there were only half as many horses in London as there had been in 1901. More dramatic, however, was the development of the underground railway system, which took place much earlier than most people realize. Work on it began in 1854. The first routes—the Metropolitan, District, and Circle lines—were built through *cut and cover* construction: deep trenches were dug and then covered over with brick archways; on top of that the earth was replaced and the street relaid. The Metropolitan Line conducted several test runs in 1862 and opened for regular passenger service on January 9, 1863.

The underground revolutionized the speed and cost of urban transportation. Although fare structures were initially complex and first-class tickets could be expensive, by the 1870s both second-class and third-class tickets were usually cheaper than the omnibus. Before long, most lines had special workmen's trains at a fare of 2d per day return (round-trip) for any distance. And avoiding the congestion of horse-filled streets made trips across town fast and simple. The underground thus was central not only to the commercial and industrial development of London but also to the growth of suburban residential areas. The lines were constantly extended further and further out as the city expanded. The earliest to use tube construction (with deep tunnels wholly underground) and electric locomotives instead of steam engines was built in 1890.

THE URBAN ENVIRONMENT

In the early Victorian years, most cities had no paving, no sewers, and few public buildings. The essential physical features of twentieth-century urban life were largely designed and created by nineteenth-century engineers and civic reformers.

London, the world's largest city and most important commercial center, developed in astonishing and complex ways. The name *London* actually has three meanings. The City of London (usually called *the City*) is the financial district. It is located where the Romans settled; it covers about one square mile. Bordered on the south by the Thames, it stretches from the Temple to the Tower of London; its other familiar landmark is St. Paul's Cathedral. Already the location of the Bank of England, the City became increasingly public and commercial during the nineteenth century. Massive new buildings were constructed for the Royal Exchange, the General Post Office, and the headquarters of other banks, insurance companies, and businesses. Very few people, any longer, lived in the City; four railway stations and the Metropolitan underground brought tens of thousands of black-coated workers daily from all parts of town and from the surrounding suburbs.

The other boroughs, villages, and new developments that had become part of the urban area were consolidated in 1888 under the administration of London County Council. This wider city is what most people mean when they use the word *London*. It grew enormously during the course of the century—from perhaps one million people in 1800 to five million by 1900. Docks, warehouses, light industry, and vast tracts of working-class housing spread east of the Tower of London (the East End); luxurious shopping precincts, residences for the wealthy, theaters, and cultural institutions filled the West End. The names of villages and boroughs that had been swallowed up remained to label dozens of other neighborhoods, each with a distinctive reputation and character. Much of Victorian London is still visible: Kensington's fine bay-windowed row houses with the railed areaways that give light to the rooms below ground level, the iron and glass technology of stations such as Paddington, the graceful engineering of Albert Bridge and the Tower Bridge, the impressive Gothic Revival architecture of Parliament and the Royal Courts of Justice.

In addition, by the end of the century, suburban rail lines promoted development in an even wider area covering parts of Middlesex, Essex, Surrey, and Kent, which lie close to London and are known as the *home counties*. Another two million people lived in this greater London area. The families of men in senior business or public positions (who had a short workday and could afford a longer commute) enjoyed pleasant new neighborhoods with spacious houses, green lawns, and new amenities such as tennis clubs.

Similar expansion took place in Manchester, Birmingham, Leeds, Liverpool, and other industrial cities. There was constant building and rebuilding. Older areas became slums and were then cleared away for new commercial buildings or the construction of rail lines. More and more workers were needed not only in factories but also for clerical, administrative, and commercial jobs. Rings of new brick houses spread into the surrounding countryside. Civic officials recognized the need for open spaces and designed the typical layout of walks, shrubberies, play areas, and athletic fields still found in most urban parks.

Prosperous cities invested in town halls, law courts, universities, museums, concert halls, libraries, schools, and other substantial building projects. The preferred style for public buildings was Gothic Revival, an architecture consciously intended to express the seriousness, reverence, and importance inspired by cathedrals in the Middle Ages. (Visualize, for example, Big Ben and the Houses of Parliament, which most people imagine are extremely old, though they were actually constructed in the 1840s and 1850s.) Gothic Revival (also called *Victorian Gothic*) was used for London's Law Courts and Manchester's Town Hall, for the new parish churches in expanding cities and suburbs, and also for hundreds of schools, workhouses, and administrative offices.

Nineteenth-century civil engineers soon had to tackle the problems that came with densely populated urban areas. Roads were seldom adequately paved; traffic sent up clouds of dust in dry weather and stuck in the mud when it rained. Streets were jammed with horse-drawn vehicles; sheep and cattle were herded through them to urban slaughterhouses; milk cows were kept in sheds in residential areas. The coal used for virtually all domestic cooking and heating as well as for the steam engines that drove industry and transportation polluted the air, stained stonework and brickwork, and left soot and cinders on surfaces inside and out.

Sewerage and water supplies were another massive problem. Piped water inside houses was rare; even Windsor Castle did not have a bath supplied with running water until 1847. Without running water there could be no flush toilets. The Public Health Act of 1848 (largely a response to cholera epidemics in the previous decade) recommended that all dwellings "have a fixed sanitary arrangement of some kind, namely an ash-pit, privy or a water closet." The fact that such a recommendation had to be made reveals that it was still common, in city slums as well as rural areas, for there to be no toilet facilities at all—sometimes not even a shared privy at the end of a street. The very best neighborhoods still dumped household waste into cesspools or sent it untreated into the nearest river.

In 1855, London established a Metropolitan Board of Works under chief engineer Joseph Bazalgette, who was soon nicknamed *the sewer king*. Over the next 20 years, hundreds of miles of sewer pipe were put down. All new buildings were required to have drains that fed into the sewer. Bazalgette also constructed the embankment that runs along the Thames from the City west to Chelsea. The embankment not only provides handsome parks, landing stages, and public walks but also protects against flooding at high tide in stormy weather and deepens the channel so the current runs more swiftly.

In the last quarter of the century, virtually all municipalities built reservoirs, provided adequate water supplies, and established sanitary drainage. Indoor toilets became common once water mains and sewers were available. The Public Health Act of 1875 required municipalities to collect trash and garbage on a regular schedule. Streets were paved—although it was difficult to keep them clean so long as horses were the chief means of hauling goods. And coal smoke remained a serious problem in most English cities until the 1960s. (Coal smoke was responsible for the dense and killing fogs, which could be so thick people would lose their way while trying to cross a narrow street.)

One early technological improvement in urban safety was the development of gas lighting. Some cities built municipal gasworks (which burned coal to produce the supply of gas) during the first twenty years of the century. In 1842 there were at least 380 London lamplighters to light the streetlamps in the evening, put them out in the morning, and clean the panes of glass. Most cities were well lit by midcentury, which may have had something to do with the diminishing crime rate. In the country, the dim illumination provided by an oil lantern made driving at night quite dangerous: carriage accidents and collisions with farm carts are staple plot events in novels of the period. The gentry planned large evening events for nights when the moon would be full; even so, guests who came from any distance were generally invited to spend the night.

Early gaslights were simple tubes for burning a flame, like a gas stove or a Bunsen burner; they consumed too much oxygen for indoor use except in very large spaces where high ceilings provided plenty of air. Interior gaslights were used in the new Houses of Parliament built in the 1840s and in other public buildings, factories, and large shops. Later in the century the invention of an incandescent mantle made indoor gas lamps safe and cheap; gas lighting was installed in most homes built after the mid-1880s.

Although Michael Faraday had discovered electromagnetic induction in 1831, electricity was slow to affect everyday life. Not until the late 1870s was an effective light bulb invented (independently but at nearly the same time by Joseph W. Swann in England and Thomas A. Edison in the United States). Electric lights were installed at once in large buildings: the machine rooms of the London *Times* in 1878, the Royal Albert Hall and the British Museum Library in 1879, Victoria Station in 1880. Public electric generating plants were built in the early 1880s to supply power for trams, streetlights, and some manufacturing operations. Country estates—which were not connected to municipal gas lines—sometimes installed their own electric generating systems. Not very many homes, however, used electricity before the twentieth century.

The principle of electromagnetic induction had also been harnessed, earlier, to pass signals along telegraph lines. In England, as in the United States, the telegraph network spread along railway lines for sending signals. During the 1850s, the use of telegraphy for commercial and private messages developed rapidly. In 1851 a cable to France provided links to the Continent; the War Office—as well as the London *Times*—used it extensively during the Crimean War. The Atlantic cable was completed in 1866. A dependable link between London and Bombay, in 1870, greatly enhanced England's ability to govern its distant Empire—and also made life less anxious for people with relatives living or working overseas.

The Post Office took over the domestic telegraph system in 1870, creating an efficient monopoly and ensuring that lines were run to remote rural post offices so that messages could reach (or be sent from) all parts of the country. In cities, telegraph lines served every fire station and linked police precincts to street corner call-boxes. Large offices and commercial firms had their own telegraph equipment. Branch post offices in most neighborhoods had messenger boys on duty to rush incoming telegrams off to householders as soon as they arrived. Although telephones were invented in the mid-1870s, they were not much used at first, partly because the telegraph links were so good. Even in the 1890s, telephones were installed primarily in larger businesses and in wealthy urban homes. People in the countryside still depended on the Post Office telegraph.

The postal system was superb. Fast cheap mail service had been one of the earliest Victorian triumphs of technological expertise combined with governmental intervention. Early in the century letters had been very expensive; even within London they cost twopence or threepence apiece. They were priced by the sheet. Outside London, letters were carried by fast mail coach but charged by weight and distance. In order to save expense, people would write across the page from side to side and then, turning it ninety degrees, carefully continue the letter by writing across from top to bottom. (A crossed letter can be hard to read, but if the handwriting is small and the letters carefully made, it is not impossible.) To avoid the weight of an envelope, letters were folded and sealed with wax or a sticky wafer. The address was added in some spot that had not been covered with writing. Postage was not prepaid; recipients had to pay before the letter was put in their hands. This could be very troublesome if the charge were high, particularly when the letter was unexpected and the sender and contents were not known.

In 1840 all this changed. Parliament established a uniform mail service which became known as the *penny post*. All domestic letters—no matter how far they traveled—cost one penny per half-ounce. The postage was paid by the sender; adhesive postage stamps were introduced for the purpose. Rail service moved the mail quickly to all parts of the country; clerks in mail cars on the train sorted it ready for its destination. Rural carriers made deliveries in surprisingly remote places, although in most villages it was usual for people to call in at the post office (generally a counter in one of the village shops) to see if they had letters. Estates and country houses kept a post bag in some central location; mail was locked in the bag, and a servant made regular trips to the nearest post office on a rail line. City dwellers had several mail deliveries daily, with the first post always arriving before breakfast; mail deposited in London letter boxes before 8 P.M. was delivered anywhere in the city or suburbs by 8 A.M. the next day. By 1888 London had hourly deliveries between 10 A.M. and 7:45 P.M. to all addresses within three miles of the General Post Office at Charing Cross; most letters were delivered within three hours of the time they were mailed. In many parts of London it was thus possible to mail an invitation in the morning, receive an answer in the afternoon, and have time to make preparations for dinner the same evening. Night mails from London left the General Post Office at 8 P.M. and reached Edinburgh, Glasgow, Dublin, and other important towns in time for morning delivery.

SCIENCE

Most of the technological innovations that so dramatically changed the nineteenth-century world were made by men who worked with their hands—skilled craftsmen or practical inventors—rather than as a result of deliberate research. The word *science*, however, took on its present meaning during the course of the century. It had previously described wisdom or skill in any field. When the physical world was studied as part of a university curriculum it came under the heading *Natural Philosophy*. By 1900 people generally used the term *science* to mean a systematic body of knowledge about the natural world, as developed and verified through the research of academics or professionals. Indeed, the term *scientist* is apparently a Victorian invention.

By the time universities gave science degrees in the latter part of the century, the generalists who took all of nature as their field had been largely replaced by men (and a few women) who worked on a fairly restricted subject: botanists, biologists, chemists, geologists, physicists. Specialized journals published experimental and theoretical papers that could be understood only by those with advanced knowledge of the field. The division between science and technology was greater in England than in the United States; practical subjects such as engineering were not taught in universities but continued to be learned through apprenticeship or in trade schools. (Scientists search for general laws; technologists develop practical applications.) Cambridge began to offer degrees in natural science during the 1850s but did not build its first laboratory until 1871.

The growth of scientific knowledge had a major impact on the way people thought about the world. Information about new discoveries was written up for popular magazines. Many skilled workers and men and women of the middle class had scientific hobbies: collecting shells or fossils, propagating ferns, keeping aquariums, classifying insects or plants. These self-educated amateurs provided evidence that was useful to professional scientists. Their carefully catalogued and labeled specimens showing variations within a single species can still be seen in local collections and—most impressively—in the vast glass cases of London's Natural History Museum in South Kensington. Amateurs also gained the expertise to conduct sound archaeological work on the Roman and prehistoric finds that were frequently unearthed by local builders or farmers.

By the middle of the century, the general spread of scientific awareness had cast doubt on the biblical account of creation by revealing the great age of earth and the late appearance of humankind. Geological evidence that the planet was very old could be accommodated by interpreting the seven days of Genesis as seven eras. A greater difficulty lay with what was called the *argument from design*. As science demonstrated the predictability and regularity of the physical world, many people were confirmed in their belief that the universe had been constructed by an intelligent designer with a rational purpose. However, other explanations were also possible. Intelligent laypeople were sufficiently engaged in this debate to make Charles Darwin's *On the Origin of Species by Means of Natural Selection* an immediate bestseller when it was published in 1859.

Darwin himself was an example of the self-taught amateur; he studied both divinity and medicine but took up neither as a profession. His work in natural science was based not on his education but on close observation and careful thought. The idea of evolution, in general terms, was already in the air; many people who had been

---

ON THE ORIGIN OF SPECIES: CONCLUSION

It is interesting to contemplate an entangled bank, clothed with many plants of many kinds, with birds singing on the bushes, with various insects flitting about, and with worms crawling through the damp earth, and to reflect that these elaborately constructed forms, so different from each other, and dependent upon each other in so complex a manner, have all been produced by laws acting around us. These laws, taken in the largest sense, being Growth with Reproduction; Inheritance which is almost implied by reproduction; Variability from the indirect and direct action of the external conditions of life, and from use and disuse; a Ratio of Increase so high as to lead to a Struggle for Life, and as a consequence to Natural Selection, entailing Divergence of Character and the Extinction of less-improved forms. Thus, from the war of nature, from famine and death, the most exalted object which we are capable of conceiving, namely, the production of the higher animals, directly follows. There is grandeur in this view of life, with its several powers, having been originally breathed into a few forms or into one; and that, whilst this planet has gone cycling on according to the fixed law of gravity, from so simple a beginning endless forms most beautiful and most wonderful have been, and are being, evolved.

Charles Darwin, *On the Origin of Species by Means of Natural Selection* (London: John Murray, 1859).

collecting fossils or cataloging the regional variations in a living species were grappling to explain what they found. Darwin did not introduce a dramatically new concept (indeed, when his findings were first presented at a scientific meeting in 1858 another paper on evolution, by Alfred Russel Wallace, was also read). What Darwin provided was a theory to explain why species evolved and a great deal of physical evidence from the fossil and living record in many parts of the world to support it. Plants and animals changed, Darwin argued, in adaptation to their environment. The alterations could initially come from chance or mutation, but ultimately those organisms whose physical makeup gave them some advantage would live longer and have more offspring to inherit their traits. Those who were not so adapted would die out. Thus new species evolved, and their physical form was a result of natural selection (survival of the fittest), rather than evidence of God's care in designing each animal for the surroundings in which it was placed.

Of course Darwin's work aroused controversy—but the immediate widespread comprehension of both his theory and his evidence (even by those who vehemently disagreed) indicates the extent to which people's mental outlook was being changed by the habit of scientific thought. Rather than depending on argument or authority, science was now seen to require careful method: hypothesis, observation, measurement, experiment, revision, retesting, a weight of evidence that could be accepted as proof. By the end of the century, most of the theoretical and experimental sciences had become too complicated for people without training to understand; the division between the amateur hobbyist and the professional scientist was well established. At the same time, however, people in general had great confidence in scientists' ability to create knowledge and solve problems.

5

OFFICIAL LIFE: GOVERNMENT AND THE LAW

NATIONAL GOVERNMENT

Great Britain (the political unit made up of England, Scotland, Wales, and Ireland) is, officially, ruled by a sovereign with the advice of Parliament. Parliament, like the United States Congress, has two branches. The upper house is the House of Lords, which during the nineteenth century was almost entirely based on heredity. Members of the House of Commons are elected. The British government differs from that of the United States in having no absolute separation of powers between its legislative, executive, and judicial branches. The prime minister and the cabinet are members of Parliament; the House of Lords has ultimate judicial authority and operates (although only rarely) as the highest court of appeal.

England has no written constitution, although the term *British Constitution* is used to describe the accumulated laws and traditions that determine how the government operates and define the relationship between individuals and the state. In the early nineteenth century, the central government was primarily limited to foreign relations, defense, and justice. Its powers and activities grew rapidly during the Victorian period as it began to control domestic affairs and take responsibility for citizens' health and safety.

By 1837, the monarchy had taken its modern form. Formally, the queen selected the prime minister—but in actuality, her choice was determined by Parliament's political leaders. She was always kept informed of government business but she no longer had any real power except for the moral and symbolic influence she was able to exercise.

The prime minister, usually the leader of the political party with the most seats in the House of Commons, was the effective head of government. He could be a member of either House, although he was increasingly apt to be a commoner rather than a peer. As a member of Parliament he represented a single constituency; unlike the president of the United States, the prime minister is not elected by the country as a whole.

The prime minister selected a cabinet to advise him on specific issues, provide political leadership in Parliament, and take responsibility for the major administrative departments of government. The number of men in the cabinet varied but was usually about 14; the cabinet included a chancellor of the exchequer (treasury), a foreign secretary, a home secretary, a colonial secretary, and a secretary of war. Members of the cabinet were chosen from both houses of Parliament; the foreign secretary, by tradition, was usually from the House of Lords. The cabinet was bound by a principle of collective responsibility. When they debated in private, each cabinet minister could argue for his own position, but once they made a decision, all had to support it or resign. Even the prime minister could lose an argument in the privacy of a cabinet meeting. He would then faithfully promote the policy that the cabinet determined.

An English peer automatically became a member of the House of Lords when he inherited his title (as duke, marquess, earl, viscount, or baron) and reached the age of 21. The House of Lords also included representatives from the Scots and Irish peerage, the archbishops of York and of Canterbury, and a set number of bishops from the Church of England. The size of the House of Lords varied, because titles were sometimes inherited by minors who could not yet take their seats and new peers were created from time to time. The range in the Victorian period was between 421 and 577. Many aristocrats attended sessions only on ceremonial occasions; the ordinary business in the House of Lords was done by a small group of peers who had strong political interests.

The number of seats in the House of Commons was 658 until 1885, when it was increased to 670. Members are referred to as Member

GENERAL ELECTIONS

A general election does not, as in America, take place on one day, but is spread over several weeks. The purpose of this prolongation is to permit those persons who possess votes in different parts of the country . . . to cast them, for one man may have as many different votes as he has a property qualification in different places, and can vote once for as many different candidates.

An American Resident in the United Kingdom, *"Good Form" in England* (New York: D. Appleton and Company, 1888).

of Parliament, abbreviated MP (usually with no periods; for example: John Bright, MP). They are elected but—in another crucial difference between British and U.S. government—need not live in the district they represent. In theory, a young man interested in politics would make his ambitions known to landowners and other influential people in a district and they would invite him to *stand* (rather than *run*) for a seat. In practice, the national political parties came to exercise a great deal of control by suggesting which candidates should be adopted to stand for election in which districts.

Until 1858, everyone elected to the House of Commons was required to have a certain amount of property. There was no pay for MPs until the 1880s. Political service was viewed as a duty for men of substance whose private income was such that they would not be influenced by economic or other obligations. Membership widened during the century. Following the removal of religious qualifications, the first Jewish member was seated in 1858; the atheist Charles Bradlaugh was seated in 1888. Socialists and working men were elected in the latter part of the period.

Elections were not as predictable as in the U.S. system. Until 1911 elections were required at least once every seven years, but could be called at any time. The prime minister and cabinet usually resign whenever they are defeated in an important vote in the House of Commons. Although this is called the fall of a government, it is a regular part of the political process, and not necessarily a major crisis. Because it means that the prime minister's party no longer controls enough votes to pass legislation, a new election is held. Political parties were changing and unstable during the nineteenth century; there were several small factions, and it was not unusual for an MP to switch parties. Members of the government—that is, the prime minister and cabinet—usually belonged to the same party, although some coalition governments included men from several factions.

Victorian elections were disorderly. Crowds tossed eggs and vegetables and shouted so candidates could not be heard. Political agents bribed voters with liquor and other treats. Until 1872 there was no secret ballot. A voter simply went to the polling place and announced his choice out loud to a clerk. This made it very hard for him to vote for anyone except the candidate supported by his landlord or employer.

Parliament itself could also be rowdy. Neither chamber is big enough to hold all of the members. In the Commons, they sit not at separate desks looking towards the speaker (as in the U.S. Congress) but elbow-to-elbow on crowded benches. The benches face each other across an aisle—and seem to encourage shouting during a heated debate. Parliamentary sessions began at 4 P.M. and continued until very late at night or into the early morning hours.

During the course of the century, Parliament became increasingly active in regulating economic conditions, public health, education, and other aspects of national life. Therefore the civil service—the paid government employees who run agencies, sit on commissions, collect taxes, enforce regulations, and so forth—became much larger and more professional. In 1837 almost all posts were filled by patronage. A man got a government job—whether as a minor tax clerk or as a colonial governor—not because of his qualifications but through the influence exerted by his family or friends. Although reforms were often proposed, not until 1870 was there a professional civil service with entry through competitive examination. The examination for beginning jobs that would eventually lead to senior posts in domestic or colonial service was put together so that it favored men from prestigious schools and universities. Examinations that required specific skills (e.g., accounting or chemical engineering) led to more routine jobs. Later in the century a separate women's examination for clerical posts was added.

LOCAL GOVERNMENT

Many Victorians paid little attention to Parliament, since it was remote from their daily lives. Local government was more visible. The basic unit of local government was called the *parish*, although it no longer necessarily had the same boundaries as a Church of England parish. In the traditional system dating from medieval times, the parish was responsible for policing and mending roads.

Each parish was also obliged to look after its own poor, which it did well or badly in a great variety of ways depending on local needs and available resources. The New Poor Law of 1834 was intended to reform the welfare system and will be discussed below under a separate heading.

Many functions of local government were carried out by justices of the peace appointed by the county's Lord Lieutenant. (The other duties of the Lord Lieutenant, who was almost always a peer and county's biggest landholder, were largely ceremonial.) Justices of the peace had to own land and belong to the Church of England. In the countryside, the local squire was almost certain to be a justice. Clergymen could also be appointed. The justice was an unpaid amateur; he did not need to have any training in law or administration. Serving as justice was a gentlemanly obligation—and a remaining vestige of the paternal authority that upper-class men exerted over the lower orders.

Justices of the peace supervised the paid parish officials who managed poor relief and fixed roads. They also served as magistrates: for petty criminal offenses, the local justice heard the case, passed judgment, and pronounced the sentence. In more serious matters, he ordered that the suspect be bound over for trial before a judge.

The old system of local government was largely superseded during the Victorian years. As the interlocking and widespread nature of many social and economic problems became clear, Parliament began to create agencies that covered larger areas. Highways, hospitals, sewers, prisons, workplace safety, the inspection of slaughterhouses, and similar matters could not be funded and managed by individual parishes. A succession of local government acts created new administrative units with elected officials. Justices of the peace lost most of their powers in 1889, although they continued to serve as magistrates.

During the 1870s, women became eligible to serve on school boards and some other local government agencies. When voting was a right reserved for landowners with a stake in the country, women were almost necessarily excluded. After successive reform bills enfranchised middle-class and then working-class men, however, women's lack of landed property was no longer a reason to keep them from voting. Late-Victorian legislators began to accept the idea that women should have a voice in the matters that seemed to fall within their own special "sphere of expertise"—matters such as education, welfare, and health. By the end of the century, women could vote in most municipal and county elections. National affairs such as defense and foreign policy were still reserved for men. In 1897, various local suffrage organizations joined forces as the National Union of Women's Suffrage Societies with Millicent Garrett Fawcett as president. The dramatic campaign of disruption and civil disobedience led by Emmeline Pankhurst began soon after 1900, although women did not win the parliamentary vote until 1918.

THE NEW POOR LAW: THE WORKHOUSE

Societies need some way to look after people who can not take care of themselves and have no family to do it. The system used in England before 1834 dated from the time of Queen Elizabeth I. Each parish had to provide for its own poor by means of taxes or *poor rates* paid by residents who owned or rented property over a certain value. The system was not only inefficient but it varied widely from place to place, depending on the capability of local officials and the amount of money they could collect. Since parishes did not want to spend their funds on people who were not, strictly speaking, their own responsibility, poor people who had been born in some other parish were often simply told to move on.

The Poor Law Amendment Act of 1834, commonly called the *New Poor Law*, entirely reorganized the administration of welfare. The 15,000 or so individual parishes were combined into 643 *unions*. Each union was to build a workhouse. Under the New Poor Law, *outdoor relief* in the form of money and food for people who stayed in their own homes was available only for the elderly and disabled. It was meant to provide a supplement that would help their families look after them. All other persons who needed public assistance were to enter the workhouse, where they would do suitable labor in return for their food and housing.

Despite its horrible reputation, the New Poor Law workhouse was in some ways better than the earlier system. A single parish, before 1834, might put all of the people who could not care for themselves in one place—orphans, unemployed adults, the elderly, the sick, the disabled, and the mentally incapacitated were all mixed together and for the most part left to tend each other. In a union workhouse, where there were far more people, the various groups could be given separate lodging and appropriate treatment.

The other core principle of the New Poor Law was, however, the concept of "less eligibility." Administrators (known as *poor law guardians*) were ordered to be sure that people in the workhouse had a "less eligible" standard of living than the poorest working people outside. The idea was to make the workhouse so unpleasant that people would take any job at all rather than ask for relief. People were put into separate wards by age and sex. Families were split up, elderly couples divided from each other. In the earliest years, parents did not have the right even to see their children. People could not leave the workhouse during the day and come back at night; those who claimed public assistance went "into the house" and stayed there until they had some way to support themselves outside. Most workhouses required everyone to wear coarse clothes of some distinctive and uniform color. Smoking and drinking were forbidden. Outsiders could visit only during limited hours and in the presence of a matron or master. The New Poor Law union workhouse was often the first large public institution to be built in a town; it loomed on the outskirts as a massive, high-walled, and forbidding presence.

The inmates, under supervision, did the labor of running the workhouse. Women cooked, cleaned, sewed. People who did nursing and certain unpleasant jobs such as burying the dead were paid with a ration of tobacco or alcohol. Finding enough work for able-bodied men was a problem. Most workhouses assigned them to boring and laborious tasks such as breaking up stones to make gravel for roadmending. Old people were set to picking oakum, which involved teasing apart matted ropes so the hemp could be used by the Navy for caulking ships.

This labor did not train people for employment: it was simply deterrent, designed to make people think twice about claiming relief. Yet it was soon evident that Parliament was wrong in

---

THE ECONOMY OF AN ENGLISH WORKHOUSE

All the inmates, except the sick, the aged and infirm, and the young children, are required, between the 25th of March and the 29th of September, to rise at six o'clock, breakfast between half-past six and seven, begin work at seven o'clock, dine between twelve and one, leave off work at six o'clock, sup between six and seven, and retire to bed at eight o'clock; and during the other part of the year, the hour of rising is an hour later. The Master of the Workhouse is empowered . . . to fix such employment for the aged and infirm and children, as may be suitable to their respective ages and conditions.

The Penny Magazine, July 6, 1839.

assuming that there were a lot of loafers who had to be discouraged from going on public assistance. Only about one-fourth of the pauper population, it turned out, were able-bodied adults. The separate wards of the workhouse began to develop into separate institutions. By the end of the century, there were public hospitals for the chronically ill; asylums for the mentally handicapped; schools for blind, deaf, and disabled children; homes for the elderly; and other appropriate public institutions for people incapable of self-support.

Orphanages and children's homes were among these new institutions. They took in both children whose parents were dead and children whose parents could not support them. Boys were taught a trade such as carpentry or shoemaking; girls were prepared for domestic service. There were also training ships to supply naval recruits. Indeed, pauper children had more schooling than many outside the workhouse system. Overseers of the poor felt they needed an extra boost to become self-supporting adults. They were not sent out on their own until they were 15 or 16 years old, although children outside the workhouse often worked full-time starting at the age of 12.

In fact, despite the official tenet of "less eligible," most workhouse administrators did not allow the paupers in their charge to be as overworked and malnourished as the poorest laborers. They wanted able-bodied people to obtain jobs and stop living on the public dole, which meant they had to be healthy enough to work. Before going into the workhouse, people were supposed to exhaust their own resources, which included selling everything they owned. This rule was not enforced, especially when breadwinners were ill; they were allowed to keep the tools and clothing they would need to go back to work when they recovered. Local authorities also discovered that providing outdoor relief briefly in cases of temporary unemployment was much cheaper than housing whole families in the workhouse.

But although the New Poor Law never worked as uniformly as intended, the stigma attached to going into the workhouse was deliberate. It was designed not only to discourage loafers but also to encourage prudence. To avoid the workhouse, women would marry before having children. Poor families would avoid having more children than they could support. People would save money to provide a cushion when they were ill. Grown children would make sacrifices to look after their elderly parents.

The workhouse was especially hated for dividing couples who had been married for many years. (Most people thought it was a good idea to separate younger residents by sex so women would not be victimized by men. Even in the case of married couples, the reasoning went, if they could not support the children they already had, why should they be allowed to produce more?) Another source of loathing was the fear of dissection: by law, medical schools could have the body of anyone who died in the workhouse unless it was promptly claimed by relatives who could provide a burial. Most of all, perhaps, people feared the workhouse because of its disgrace.

Some historians believe that the New Poor Law did help diminish pauperism—people who had any other recourse avoided the workhouse at whatever cost. In addition, there was an expanding market for unskilled labor in the mid-nineteenth century, and several organizations helped able-bodied poor people emigrate to Australia and North America. The workhouse was a terrible idea, however, for dealing with people who were temporarily unemployed because of illness, layoffs, or family problems. And the lingering stigma of the workhouse created a sense of humiliation among people who needed to ask for help.

Two other aspects of the workhouse system need to be mentioned. Its infirmary served as a public hospital or nursing home for people with long-term illnesses. There were hospitals run by charities and medical schools that treated poor people at little or no cost, but most of them only admitted patients who were likely to be cured. Very few hospitals took patients in the last stages of tuberculosis, which was the most frequent cause of death in the period. The workhouse infirmary was a hospital for the poor and a hospice for people who had no family available to do the nursing.

The workhouse also had (often in a separate building) a *casual ward*, which gave food and lodging for one night (or, in some cases, three nights) to people with no money and no fixed place of residence: tramps, poor people walking to another part of the country to seek work, seasonal labor, seamen who had spent their pay and were heading back to port for another ship, navvies moving from gang to gang. The casual ward also served as an occasional shelter for the kind of urban homeless who did not want to claim relief because they preferred to live on the streets. They would take a night's lodging once in a while when they wanted to escape bad weather and get a morning meal.

CRIME AND PUNISHMENT

Crimes and the Crime Rate

In 1800, there were about two hundred types of capital crimes—crimes for which the punishment was execution by hanging. Many reforms in criminal law took place between 1808 and 1838. People convicted of offenses such as shoplifting, theft, housebreaking, forgery, and burglary were no longer sentenced to death. In 1841, 11 capital crimes remained on the statute book, but the only criminals actually executed were those convicted of murder. For other capital offenses, the judge would pronounce the death sentence and then recommend that it be commuted to transportation or imprisonment. By 1861, there were four capital crimes: murder, piracy, treason, and setting fire to an arsenal or dockyard. (Fire was equivalent to terrorism at a time when naval ships were constructed of wood and loaded with gunpowder.)

It is very difficult to measure changes in the crime rate, because standards of reporting differ so much. Historians do, however, generally agree that there was less crime in England during the Victorian era than in earlier times, and that the crime rate diminished even more as the period went on. In addition, crime became less violent. About 90 percent of the cases serious enough to go to trial were crimes against property. Riots, brutal robberies, and murders became uncommon. In London in the 1890s, with a population of five million people, there were only about 20 homicides per year.

The falling rate of criminal behavior had many causes: less poverty, better lighting, educational and other measures that kept children and teens off the streets, professional police forces, the temperance movement, and restrictions on the sale of alcohol. These and other broad changes made society much more orderly. Early in the nineteenth century, the English lower classes were seen as naturally rowdy. Drunken riots at sporting events were common in the 1840s but newsworthy in the 1880s (because by then they were rare). The public was much less tolerant of fighting and cruelty. There was very little of the casual violence that now makes cities unsafe.

The common crimes were such things as theft, stealing from shops or street-sellers' stands, pick-pocketing, and burglary. Property was at risk in the country as well as the city, especially as urban policing grew better. People of any substance did not generally leave houses unattended. Even when the family went to church on Sunday, one or two servants remained at home. Certain elements of Victorian architecture, such as heavy wooden shutters, iron gratings, and high walls topped with broken glass, are a reminder that there never was a golden age of honesty when everyone could be trusted.

Because there was a market for used clothing, one crime that parents feared was the abduction of a well-dressed child. The motive was not to collect ransom (which is terribly risky for the kidnapper); the child would soon be turned loose in its underwear and brought home crying by the police. This was one reason why middle-class and upper-class youngsters were accompanied by a nursemaid even when walking across a square to play with friends, and why women and teenaged girls brought a servant along when they went to do errands. Etiquette manuals advised ladies that when paying calls on foot, their clothing must "not be gay or have anything about it to attract attention." Silks, plumes, jewelry, and lace should be worn only when going out in a carriage.

In the countryside, poaching was a widespread crime. Game birds and wild animals, according to the law, could be killed only by landowners. However, hungry rural laborers found it hard to resist trapping rabbits and edible birds. Aristocrats and the gentry employed gamekeepers whose job was to make sure there was good shooting on the estate during autumn; they looked after the game, protected breeding grounds—and hunted down poachers. Although the brutal mantraps (concealed pits, sometimes with spikes set in the bottom) that had been used earlier were outlawed by Victorian times, the gamekeeper carried a shotgun. Furthermore, the magistrate who tried and sentenced accused poachers was usually the local squire—that is, a major landowner.

Children over age seven were considered to be morally responsible beings. They were sentenced to the same prisons as adults and were executed for capital crimes. As late as 1839, a boy nine years of age was hanged for setting a building on fire. People worried a lot about juvenile crime, because the dislocations of industrialization created a relatively large population of orphaned, homeless, and runaway youngsters. After the middle of the century, reformatory and industrial schools began to provide education and vocational training for young offenders, and magistrates were given more leeway choosing an appropriate sentence for children under 14. In the latter part of the century, juvenile crime as well as adult crime diminished.

Trial and Punishment

The system known as *common law* arises from precedents and decisions made by earlier judges. English law is complex because of its very long history. By 1837, however, many of the important principles had also been codified in laws passed by Parliament. Common law covers all criminal cases and most civil disputes. In London, three courts were involved: the Queen's Bench heard criminal cases; Common Pleas decided civil cases over matters such as contracts, ownership of land, injuries, and so forth; and Exchequer settled cases involving money owed to the national treasury. (Chancery, which will be discussed below in the section entitled The Law and Private Life, took up additional civil matters.) Judges from the London courts also went "on circuit" to visit county towns to preside over assizes (i.e., court sessions in provincial towns), where they tried the cases which had come up since their last visit.

There were two categories of crime: indictable (which in the United States would be called felonies) and summary (misdemeanors). The serious crimes, which led to indictment and trial by jury, included murder, armed robbery, burglary, larceny, fraud, rape, and significant violations of public order. Summary offenses included petty theft, poaching, vagrancy, drunkenness, vandalism, and taking part in minor disorders. Prostitution was not against the law, but prostitutes were often charged with misdemeanors such as annoying passers-by or public drunkenness.

Summary (minor) offenses were tried by the local justice of the peace or, in cities, by a police magistrate. He heard the charges, questioned the prisoner and witnesses, made a decision, and passed sentence. There was no jury, and ordinarily no lawyers were involved. The justice, who seldom had any legal training, was the local squire or clergyman or some other man of substance—a man who had enough standing in the community so that people respected him, and enough money that he was not likely to take bribes. The justice could sentence guilty prisoners to a few weeks or months in the local house of corrections, impose fines, or require public work such as roadmending. Whipping was a common sentence for boys found guilty of vandalism or petty theft, and for men who assaulted women or children. By Victorian times, female prisoners could no longer be whipped, but they were otherwise treated much the same way as males.

When the crimes were serious, the justice would have the accused bound over to be tried at the quarter sessions, held four times a year, when all of the justices in a county met together to decide cases. The most severe cases went to the assizes, which took place once or twice a year in various larger towns. Judges came from London and cases were tried in front of a jury.

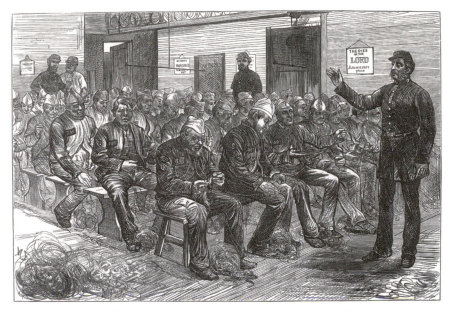

Prisoners at the Clerkenwell House of Correction in 1874 are preparing oakum for caulking ships, a boring task also assigned to elderly inmates in the workhouse. Courtesy of The Granger Collection, New York.

Trials were perhaps less fair than they became in the twentieth century. People accused of crimes could not take the stand in their own defense until 1898. There was no public defender to give advice to prisoners who could not afford an attorney; indeed, sometimes the accused was not allowed to have defense counsel at all. On the other hand, judges intervened to ask questions, and juries tended to be lenient. When stealing a horse was a capital crime, for example, a jury might decide to find the accused guilty of stealing a bridle. (The horse just followed along because the bridle was fastened around its head.)

The use of long-term imprisonment to punish criminals began in the Victorian period. People convicted of minor crimes had generally been sentenced to 30 days or three months in the local house of correction (often called the *bridewell*). The gaol (pronounced "jail") held people awaiting trial. The most famous was Newgate, the goal for prisoners who would be tried at London's central criminal court (known as Old Bailey). In Newgate, as in most local goals and bridewells, prisoners did not have separate cells but were crowded together in large rooms where they slept on the floor. There was no segregation of children from adults (though the sexes were kept separate). Newgate did, however, have secure cells for prisoners who had already been tried and were sentenced to death.

Executions took place two or three days after the sentence was handed down. Until 1868, the prisoner was hanged in public. When a crime was particularly notorious (e.g., a woman found guilty of killing her lover, or a multiple murderer) the crowds were enormous. People took their children to see the criminal executed and learn a moral lesson; souvenirs were peddled; and pickpockets made themselves very busy, undeterred by the example that public hangings were supposed to provide. After 1868, executions took place behind prison walls. A black flag was raised to let the waiting crowd know when the criminal was dead.

Criminal transportation was an alternative to hanging; the death penalty was often commuted to a sentence of transportation for 7 years or 14 years. Penal settlements in Australia were established in 1788, when prisoners could no longer be sent to the American colonies. At first the prisoners built roads, cleared land, and made harbors. Women convicts cooked, cleaned, and did laundry for the other prisoners and for guards and government officials. Educated convicts did clerical work and other minor governmental tasks. After Australia began to attract emigrants (and was no longer simply a penal colony), prisoners were assigned to do contract labor for free settlers.

Children as well as adults were sentenced to transportation. In the 1840s there was a separate penal settlement for boys at Point Puer. (*Puer* is Latin for "boy.") Young convicts were generally given some schooling and taught a trade. Before transportation came to an end, about 140,000 convicts had been sent to Australia. They could return to England after their sentence expired, but passage back was not provided; they had to pay for it by having money sent to them or earning it as free laborers. Most of them chose to stay in Australia, where work was plentiful and wages were high. The sentence of transportation was abolished in 1857, although some criminals with long sentences continued to be sent to Australia instead of being housed in English prisons. The last convict ship sailed in 1867.

In the 1850s, when sentences of penal servitude replaced transportation for serious crimes, true prisons began to be constructed: massive secure buildings where convicted criminals could be confined in cells. These were not, in England, called *penitentiaries*—the Victorian penitentiary was a charity, usually run by women, designed for penitence and reform. Prostitutes, unmarried pregnant women, runaways who had been sleeping on the streets, and other girls or women would enter a penitentiary voluntarily (although often, no doubt, under pressure from a justice of the peace). After spending a year or two in healthy living, prayer, and vocational training, the penitent would be helped to emigrate or to find a suitable job in England.

The Police

Some of the improvements in public safety during the nineteenth century were brought about by the development of efficient police forces. In pre-industrial times, all citizens were supposed to take turns of duty as constables: preventing crime, maintaining order, presenting criminals in court. The system worked only in small communities where everyone knew everyone else. By the eighteenth century, most towns of any size had paid constables, but there were no laws governing them. The system was inefficient and often corrupt. When there were riots or other serious dangers, the army was brought in to keep order.

The Metropolitan Police Act of 1829 created a full-time paid police force in London. The city was divided into 17 districts. Each district, headed by a superintendent, had 4 inspectors and 16 sergeants. Under each sergeant were nine constables; eight patrolled beats and the ninth was on reserve in the station house. The police district that was located in Great Scotland Yard also had the commissioner's staff, clerks, and additional reserves. The first mission of the police was to establish social control. Their job was to prevent riots, break up fights, curb public drunkenness, restrict begging, and stop street crime.

When Victoria's reign began, London's police had already demonstrated their effectiveness. Legislation encouraged other towns to establish professional forces. By midcentury, there were competent police in cities such as Birmingham and Manchester, but many other areas still had no regular force. In 1856, national standards for organization and training were established.

To become a London Metropolitan Police constable in the 1850s, a man had to be 5'8" tall. Because most people were shorter than nowadays (owing to poor nutrition), constables had a meaningful physical presence. Most of them were former soldiers or sailors. They had two weeks of training. Unmarried police constables lived and ate in barracks. They were not well paid, but they could legally earn extra money when hired to watch the crowd at theaters or knock on doors in the morning to wake people who had no clocks.

The London police constable's overcoat, helmet, and "bull's eye" lantern are shown in the frontispiece of a book entitled *Police!*, which was published in 1889. It was written by police officer Charles Tempest Clarkson and journalist J. Hall Richardson.

Police in the countryside often spent most of their working life as the sole constable in a village. The county superintendent retained the right to give permission for marriage, because the constable's wife became his backup and assistant. The telegraph was used in both country and city for communications between headquarters, police stations, and (eventually) outdoor call-boxes, which constables could open with a key.

The Metropolitan Police Detective Department was established in August 1842 with two inspectors and four sergeants. Its headquarters was in Scotland Yard—a name that has stuck although the actual physical location has been moved several times. (In 1878 it was reorganized as the Criminal Investigation Department, or CID, which remains the official title.) From the beginning, detectives not only investigated crimes but also had anticrime duties, such as working in disguise to spot pickpockets in a crowd. By the end of the century the CID had 800 members. Their education, training, prestige, and pay were higher than that of other police. Howard Vincent, a barrister who reformed the CID and was its director from 1878 to 1884, developed a uniform criminal record system, produced a manual of criminal law for the police to use, and established the Special Branch (originally the Special Irish Branch), which has the duty of protecting royalty and keeping track of political extremists.

THE LAW AND PRIVATE LIFE

Marriage

Marriage law determined who could marry and how marriages were conducted. In addition, the act of marriage affected a woman's legal status in significant and profound ways.

In England before 1836, a legal marriage could be performed only by a clergyman of the Church of England, although of course other Protestants, Roman Catholics, and Jews who married in their own religion considered their ceremonies legitimate. The 1836 Marriage Act recognized marriage as a contract regulated by the state rather than the church. Roman Catholic and Nonconformist marriages became legally binding. (The meaning of these religious terms is discussed in chapter 11.) In addition, people could take out a civil license and be married by a registrar instead of a clergyman. Nevertheless, the great majority of couples continued to marry in the Church of England, even though they might worship elsewhere. In England and Wales in 1844 there were 120,000 marriages celebrated in the Church of England, 2,280 Roman Catholic ceremonies, 6,515 in other religious denominations, and 3,446 civil marriages.

For a Church of England wedding, a couple visited the parish clergyman and had him announce their intent to marry during the regular Sunday service for three weeks in a row. This was known as *crying the banns*. People who wanted to be married in some other parish or with less publicity could obtain a special license, although it was quite expensive and also involved a waiting period. Public notice was also given for civil marriages. No marriage in England could take place behind closed doors; the church or registrar's office had to be open to anyone who chose to enter. This was an old requirement intended to make sure that people were not forced into marriage against their will.

A man or woman who was under age 21 needed consent from a father or guardian. The Church of England (and, consequently, English law) allowed marriage between first cousins, but a widow or widower could not marry someone who was brother or sister of the spouse who had died. This sounds like an unimportant issue; but when a young mother died, her unmarried sister often moved in to look after the children. In these situations, the law that prevented her from marrying the children's father could be a real hardship. Some people (including the artist Holman Hunt and his second wife, Edith Waugh) had a church marriage abroad and lived in England as husband and wife, although the law did not accept the union as legal.

In Scotland, a binding marriage required only that a couple acknowledge one another in public as husband and wife. They could do this by making a pledge in front of witnesses or even by signing a hotel register as, say, "Mr. and Mrs. John Martin." Eloping couples who wanted to be married quickly without anyone's knowledge could slip across the border. The town of Gretna Green was especially popular. After 1856, however, the law was changed so that at least one of the two people had to have lived in Scotland for three weeks, and Gretna Green elopements were no longer common.

A woman's civil status was dramatically altered when she married. In the famous phrase written by the eighteenth-century jurist William Blackstone, husband and wife were "one person, and that person was the husband." Once married, a woman had no independent legal existence. Everything she owned or inherited or earned was her husband's; she had no right even to spend her own income for her own needs. A wife had to live with her husband wherever he chose. She could not sign a contract or make a will. She had no standing before a court in any legal action because, in the eyes of the law, she had no separate existence. She also had no right to control or custody of her children; their father could train or educate them in any way he wished. Furthermore, the father's right to custody of his children was inalienable—any agreement he made that gave them to his wife (in the case of a friendly separation, for example) was legally unenforceable. If he died before the children were grown, his will had to appoint a guardian or they became wards of the court; he could name their mother as guardian but he had no obligation to do so. If a woman was not named as her children's guardian, she could lose them entirely.

Wives gradually acquired some legal standing between 1839 and the end of the century, but unmarried women still had far more rights than married women. After several sensational cases and a great deal of public pressure from well-organized women's groups, married women gained control of their own earnings in 1870. A further Married Women's Property Act in 1882 secured possession of all other property they held or inherited. But even the law can not really shield a woman from the emotional and physical pressure exerted by a husband who wants to get his hands on her money. Both before and after passage of the Married Women's Property Acts, well-to-do men arranged marriage settlements to protect their daughters.

A deed of settlement was a contract signed by the bridegroom before marriage that set aside a sum of money for his wife. A marriage settlement thus ensured that a woman had some independent income. The money not only gave her protection from her husband (if the need arose) but also could support her if he died or went bankrupt. (Assets guarded by a marriage settlement could not be seized to pay a man's debts.) Settlement deeds let a woman make her own will—when younger sons inherited property it was generally by way of their mother's marriage settlement.

The money usually came from the bride's family. Sometimes the groom also made a contribution. The funds were placed in a trust; if the woman were widowed, the trustees would help arrange her financial affairs. Although a guide to everyday law published in 1864 explained that "no prudent woman should marry without this provision," settlements were usual only when there was extensive property: among the aristocracy, the gentry, and the wealthy middle class.

A dowry is not precisely the same as a marriage settlement, though the terms often overlap. A dowry is the money or property that a bride brings into marriage; but if the dowry was substantial, the woman's father or guardian would certainly demand that it be protected by a settlement. Dowries were customary among well-to-do people. The money (referred to as a woman's *portion*) was often the amount which a bride would otherwise inherit; it was settled on her when she married instead of coming to her after her parents died.

Among aristocrats, dowries of £10,000 to £30,000 were common. Late in the century, gossip reported that titled men with narrow incomes married American heiresses who could bring dowries of £100,000 and even £500,000 into the union. Working women were also expected to bring something to marriage, although they had no settlements. A working woman's portion might be the household linens or a sewing machine that enabled her to earn money at home.

Divorce

Before 1857, divorce was difficult, expensive, and rare. The Church of England granted what was called a divorce *a mensa et thoro* ("from bed and board") in cases of adultery, extreme cruelty, or desertion. This was actually a legal separation; neither person was allowed to remarry. The Church also granted divorce *a vinculo*, or annulment, which did permit remarriage. Annulments were given only when the marriage was not valid in the first place, usually because one of the partners was found to be underage, mentally incompetent, or already married to someone else.

To end a valid marriage with the right of remarrying required a special act of Parliament. Parliamentary divorces were sought when a man had substantial property, could prove that his wife had committed adultery, and wanted to be certain that the son who inherited his property was indubitably his own child. The man first went to the ecclesiastical court for a divorce a mensa et thoro. Then he brought suit in civil court against his wife's lover for what was called *criminal conversation.* Finally, with this evidence in hand, he would get a member of Parliament to introduce the special act that ended the marriage and allowed him to take a new wife. In the first 50 years of the century, fewer than 10 bills of divorce per year passed through Parliament. In only three cases was a parliamentary divorce granted to a woman.

The Divorce and Matrimonial Causes Act of 1857 set up a civil divorce court in London that could grant both judicial separations and divorce decrees. The grounds for divorce were not the same for men and women. A man could get a divorce if his wife committed adultery. For a woman to sue for divorce, her husband's adultery had to be aggravated by physical cruelty that was greater than "ordinary chastisement" or by other extreme circumstances.

Divorce was still very expensive; only about 150 per year were granted. It was easier, especially for working-class women, to get a separation order. The grounds for legal separation were adultery, cruelty, or desertion. Although a separation did not permit remarriage, it did give a woman control over her money so the husband who had deserted her could not reappear and seize her income and furniture for his own use.

Divorce was thought to be shameful, not so much because it ended a marriage and broke up a family but because the grounds for divorce were so limited. A woman's adultery or a man's cruelty had to be proven by evidence supplied to the court. Divorce cases were regularly reported, in full, in the newspapers. Yet some middle-class women were divorced and still retained their reputations, including actresses Fanny Kemble and Ellen Terry; some well-known men (such as novelist Robert Louis Stevenson) married divorced women. On the other hand, the political career of Charles Parnell was ruined in 1889 when he was named in divorce court as the lover of Captain O'Shea's wife Katherine, although men earlier in the century had routinely committed open adultery and remained in Parliament.

Married couples did separate—and sometimes took other partners—without going through the courts. There also remained in some parts of the country the rural custom of *wife sale*. This was a legendary (if not legal) form of divorce: a man sold his wife, often for a very small price, to the man with whom she was already having an affair. The so-called sale might be intended to humiliate the wife, but sometimes it was more a public announcement that her (former) husband accepted her new union.

Children, Orphans, Guardians

Children were minors until they reached age 21, after which they were free to marry, control their own property, and conduct their own affairs. Twenty-one was the voting age for men who qualified, and the age at which an aristocrat who inherited his title while still a minor could take his seat in the House of Lords. Legal contracts involving people under 21 had to be made by a father or guardian. The money earned by children belonged legally to their parents. Parents were only required to provide support, however, until children reached age 16; and even after reform schools were established, the criminal courts treated youngsters as adults from the age of 14 or 16.

Until 1886, fathers were legally, in all circumstances, the guardians of their children; if a father died before a child was 21, it was necessary for his will to name a substitute guardian. A guardian, like a father, had a right to the physical custody of children and a right to chastise them. He determined their education and religious training, could give or refuse consent to their marriage, had control of their estate or earnings, and had what was called "the right to enjoy their services" (which meant that children could be kept at home to do unpaid work in the house or the father's trade until they were 21).

In actuality, however, the law took notice of children only if they were orphaned and property was involved. When a working-class father died without a will, no one questioned the right of the child's mother to act as guardian; although if a contract had to be signed— an apprenticeship agreement, for example—the mother had to get approval from some legal authority, usually the local justice of the peace. If mothers and children could not earn enough to support themselves, they had to go into the workhouse; the mother was put in the women's ward and the children sent to a poor-law school or a separate orphanage.

When a will established someone as legal guardian, the child was called his *ward*. Property that a minor inherited was put in the hands of trustees. The guardian was not necessarily one of the trustees. The trustees might be, for example, a banker and a reputable solicitor whereas the guardian might be an older male relative whose high social status would help the child get a good start in life. The child might live with yet another person or a couple to whom the guardian assigned physical custody.

English law had no provision for legal adoption until the 1920s. Orphaned or deserted children were informally adopted; a friend or relative or neighbor simply took them in. Unofficial fostering was also fairly common: among families of any social class, relatives might take one or two children to raise as their own. None of these arrangements could be made legally binding; they depended on good will and mutual agreement.

Orphaned children were sometimes provided for by sending them to training schools or charitable institutions that would prepare them for a career. Soldiers' sons, for example, could be sent to a military school until they were old enough to enter the army. The daughters of clergymen or naval officers could be educated at special boarding schools so they would be able to support themselves as governesses. When a child's inheritance was small—a few hundred pounds, say—the trustees and guardian often agreed it would be best spent by paying the fees for some such institution.

If orphans who had some property were left with no guardian, the court of Chancery (in London) was supposed to protect their interests. Chancery also heard other cases involving trusts, estates, and the care of people (such as the insane) who could not look after their own affairs. The court operated under cumbersome rules, and cases could drag on for year after year. Several nineteenth-century reforms ultimately eliminated Chancery as a separate institution.

When children were not orphaned, English courts were very reluctant to interfere with parents' absolute authority. Not until 1889 were poor-law officials authorized to assume full parental rights even over children who had been abandoned. In the 1890s the law finally began to provide mechanisms that made it possible to remove children from the custody of parents who abused them.

Wills and Inheritance

A will could be made by most men and single women over 21. Until the property acts of the 1870s and 1880s, a married woman's will could only include the property reserved for her use in a marriage settlement. Wills could not be made by minors, by people who were mentally incompetent, or by people who could not hear and speak unless it was proved that they understood written material. A convicted felon could not make a will. The wife of a transported convict could make a will and otherwise be treated like a single woman, although she could not remarry.

Among aristocrats and the landed gentry, wills and entails (i.e., legal restrictions) kept the estate and most other property in the hands of the eldest son. The will usually directed that support or marriage settlements be provided for daughters and that pensions be paid to a few servants who had been on the estate for most of their lives. An aristocrat's widow often moved to a *dower house* that was (by will or by marriage settlement) legally set aside for her use; the son who succeeded to the title took possession of both the manor house and the London residence.

Middle-class people were more likely to divide their property equally among their sons. The most prosperous son was expected to make a home for his widowed mother or any unmarried sisters. Since it was only landed estates that were protected by entail, nothing prevented a middle-class man from leaving his business to a daughter if he believed she would be the best manager. Several well-known Victorian women successfully owned and ran iron works, breweries, banks, and other enterprises they had inherited.

Debt and Debtor's Prisons

Credit was generously allowed to people of any substantial background. They were not expected to carry large amounts of gold around to make purchases. Much of their ordinary shopping was done for them by servants. Smaller tradesmen such as butchers submitted accounts monthly; those with more operating capital, who dealt in expensive luxuries, sent bills only once a year. Financial liabilities were not very well regulated. Young men (in particular) could borrow large sums of money at high interest on their *expectations* of an inheritance that would be coming when an elderly relative died. Tradesmen such as tailors and saddlers enhanced their reputation by having fashionable men as customers, and they felt certain that a young man's family would eventually pay his debts.

If investments failed or the inheritance did not come through, and the bills could not be paid, a man was declared bankrupt. Everything he owned was sold so that creditors could get at least part of the money owed to them. (Remember, except for the property protected by a marriage settlement, a married women did not own anything; even the clothes she bought with her private income belonged to her husband. Until 1882, the phrase *everything he owned* included all of his wife's personal possessions, although if she did have a marriage settlement, the property held by her trustees remained safe.)

When the man who owed money did not have much to sell, or in other cases of unsecured debt, the creditor could take out a writ to have the debtor imprisoned. People arrested for debt were sent to special debtor's prisons. Imprisonment was not punishment for a debtor—rather, it was security for the person he owed. A creditor brought suit because he was afraid that someone would run away to France or Canada and leave his bills unpaid.

People in debtor's prison were not treated like ordinary prisoners. They had separate quarters where they could be joined by their families; they could have visitors and tobacco and get meals sent in from restaurants. If the debtor's children were old enough to work, they could sleep in the family's prison room and go out every day for their jobs. The debtor was freed as soon as he paid the money he owed. Imprisonment for debt was abolished in 1869, although people who were able to pay their bills and refused to do so could still be arrested.

6

THE MATERIAL SUBSTANCE OF PRIVATE LIFE: HOUSE, FOOD, AND CLOTHES

Like almost everything else in Victorian times, people's houses, furniture, food, and clothing depended on their class and income—but changes in transportation and technology affected everyone. In particular, a distinctive and substantial middle-class way of life developed during the period.

HOUSES AND FURNISHINGS

The Middle-Class Ideal

Except for aristocrats and the gentry, who inherited their country estates, people did not usually own houses. Most middle-class town dwellings were leased for a term of three, five, or seven years. The tenant took care of the furnishing and decoration; the landlord was responsible for major renovations.

City houses were narrow (because land was expensive) but several stories tall. The most desirable homes were on a square rather than a street. One row of houses faced each side of a parklike garden. The square was enclosed by a railed iron fence; each householder had a key to the gates. Other rows of new houses were built along streets in towns and suburbs.

The bottom story of the house was about halfway below ground level. In the front, a space was dug out and paved so the basement could have full-sized windows. This space, known as the *area*, was protected at street level by railings with a locked gate. Steps leading down to the area provided a service and delivery entrance. The basement was servants' territory: it contained the kitchen, pantry, scullery, and (if the house were large) a sitting-dining room for the servants. The scullery was supplied with water from mains or a pump; washing and wet chores were done there.

The front entrance to the ground floor of the house was several steps above street level. On the ground floor were an entrance hall, a dining room, and a room set aside for the man of the house. This room was called the *library, study,* or *office*. Some professional men, including physicians, saw most of their clients or patients in the office on the ground floor of their residence.

From the entrance hall, a broad stairway led up to the floor above. (In England it is the first floor; in the United States it is the second floor). The most elegant rooms of the house were on the first floor, well above any noise that might come from the street or kitchen. Most of the floor was taken up by the drawing room, although (depending on the space and the architecture) it might be divided into two or three rooms with archways or folding doors between them. These rooms could be given names such as *music room, gallery,* or *conservatory*. When guests came to the house, a servant let them in, took their coats, and showed them up the stairs to the drawing room. The hostess welcomed them at the top of the stairs. Later, the guests went down to dinner—to the ground floor, where the dining room was located.

The floor or two above the drawing room had family bedrooms. Depending on the size and design of the house, the master bedroom might be flanked by separate dressing rooms for both wife and husband, which allowed them private space for their clothing and personal possessions. For children, there was a day nursery (where they ate and played) and a night nursery with beds for all the younger children and their nursemaid. Children over eight or so shared a room with siblings of the same sex; youngsters did not usually have private bedrooms until they were grown. In larger houses there was a schoolroom where a governess gave lessons to the girls and the younger boys. Later in the period, when both girls and boys were more likely to go to school, the *schoolroom* was the children's living room, where they worked on projects, entertained their friends, and had meals separate from their parents.

The top floor (called the *garret* or *attics*) had storage space and servants' bedrooms. Besides the formal front stairs, which reached the first and second floors, back stairs ran from the cellar to the attic. Servants used the back stairs to go up and down with water, food, and coal, as well as to reach their own bedrooms.

For an upper-middle-class family with children, the smallest appropriate house had 10 rooms: kitchen, dining room, drawing room, library; three family bedrooms; a nursery (which would become the schoolroom when children grew older); and two servants' rooms. A household guide published in 1881 suggests the ideal furniture and decoration. The entrance hall should have a stone floor, Oriental rugs, an umbrella stand, and one or two plain high-backed chairs. In the dining room, a round or oval table with a center leg would let everyone be comfortably seated. Leather chairs were best, since velvet attracted dust and dragged at the delicate fabrics of women's dinner dresses. A sideboard should display silver serving dishes and good china; it should have locked cupboards for liquor. A dumbwaiter connecting a serving pantry outside the dining room to the kitchen on the floor below would make servants' work easier.

Unless the house were grand enough to have a separate morning room, the drawing room was essentially a ladies' room. It was furnished with comfortable couches and chairs, a piano, and a substantial center table (often round) covered with a tablecloth. (It is partly this table that gives pictures Victorian rooms such an overcrowded appearance.) At tea time, servants put the urn on this table; people pulled chairs up or had cups handed to them by the parlourmaid. The table was used for doing needlework and crafts, for looking at photograph albums and heavy books, for working puzzles and playing cards or games. Women generally had a *desk*, which was not a piece of furniture but rather a portable wooden box with a slanted lid where writing materials were kept. A woman would fetch her desk and put it on the drawing-room table to write. (Men worked in their office or study, where they used a library table or a *partners' desk* with drawers.)

The drawing room generally had light walls or patterned wallpaper. The floor might be painted dark brown, with a flowered or Indian rug in the center. Ideas about furnishing and decoration abounded in books and magazines. Middle-class people had more money to spend, and keeping the house up-to-date was an appropriate interest for women. Japanese decoration was all the rage for a while; so were styles influenced by the Middle East and by classical Greece. The most long-lived furnishing style was Gothic or antique: heavy, dark wood with carved decoration. New ways of making springs allowed chairs and sofas to be more rounded. Mahogany, walnut, oak, and elm were the popular woods. Interior decorators (known as *upholsterers*) and furniture dealers brought pattern books to help customers make their choices.

Rooms were crowded with plants, fire screens, embroidery frames, bird cages, decorative china and glass, paintings, family pictures, collections of seashells or souvenirs. The cluttered and crowded appearance results partly from the casual arrangement *(romantic disorder)*, a distinct contrast to the formality of eighteenth-century rooms where delicate furniture was symmetrically lined up along the walls.

Bedrooms were more sparsely furnished, even in prosperous homes. After the middle of the century, people began to understand the need for ventilation. Four-poster beds with curtains and piles of dust-catching pillows were replaced by brass or iron bedsteads. (Victorians made a distinction between the *bedstead*—that is, the frame—and the *bed*, which lay on top. The bedstead generally held a straw or horsehair mattress, topped by a bed stuffed with feathers.)

A healthy modern bedroom, according to Victorian decorating manuals, should have rugs which could be shaken every day, a wardrobe to hold clothing, a dressing table with mirror, and a washstand. On the dressing table was a *set* consisting of a tray, a ring-stand, and some cut-glass bottles and china containers for homemade toilet water and hand cream. There was also usually a *tidy*—an embroidered bag for disposing of hair-combings. (Tidies, like penwipers, needlebooks, and pincushions, were gifts that girls made for their mothers and aunts.) A chamber pot or slop pot was kept in a closed bedside cabinet or under the washstand. Although most bedrooms had a fireplace with a grate, the fire was seldom lit except in cases of illness—bedrooms were for sleeping and dressing, not for spending private time during waking hours.

Some Others Ways of Living

As urban rail transportation became fast and cheap, more and more versions of a somewhat smaller basic dwelling were built, either in rows along new streets or as three-story semidetached houses (*twin* would be the term used in the United States). The basic floor plan hardly changed from 1860 to 1960: ground floor with entrance, drawing room, dining room, and kitchen/scullery;

first floor with three or four bedrooms and a bath; upper floor with small rooms for servants and storage. Many dwellings were *dressed up* with picturesque details such as mock half-timber or lattice windows to echo the rage for Gothic architecture.

Most suburban developments were strictly commercial. The tenants did not own the houses but had very long-term leases, usually for 99 years. The house changed hands when the remainder of the lease was sold; the new tenant bought the right to move into the house and pay rent to the landowner. Although most Victorian suburbs were built close to the outskirts and quickly merged with the city, the landowner's control created a uniform social atmosphere. No industry was permitted; shops were strictly segregated from houses. The most exclusive areas had private roads with a gatekeeper to control access and keep beggars and street vendors out of the neighborhood.

The oldest areas of cities were grim slums. Whole families lived in single rooms in run-down houses. During the eighteenth century, when cities expanded, buildings had been jammed into every yard of open space. Courts and warrens of interconnected alleys virtually excluded fresh air and prevented adequate policing. In common lodging houses, people of both sexes and all ages slept on beds or pallets jammed into open rooms. A fire with a grate allowed lodgers to fix a meal.

There were also vast neighborhoods of working-class housing. Early in the Industrial Revolution, workers' houses were built in back-to-back rows. Each dwelling shared its back wall with the house behind and its side walls with the houses on either side. The only windows were in front. Houses typically had one room upstairs and one downstairs. Furnishings were minimal: a table with wooden chairs; a few hooks on the wall and a small tin or wooden trunk (called a *box*) for keeping clothes; one bed for the parents and one shared by all of the children. The kitchenware—a kettle and two or three pans plus some knives, forks, spoons, and plates—was kept on a shelf over the fireplace.

Middle-class housing had space for privacy and family life, but in poorer working-class houses, there might not be room for a table big enough for the entire family to eat together. Workers used the streets and the pubs for their social life; this encouraged group solidarity but diminished the emphasis on individual families. It was not uncommon for some children to be sent elsewhere to sleep (perhaps with an older couple whose family was grown) so that teenagers of opposite sexes would not have to share beds.

In the countryside, laborers' cottages often had only one or two rooms. The floor was dirt (packed tight) or paving stones. The cottage was furnished with chairs, a table, a few shelves, a cupboard, and one or two beds. Food was cooked over an open fire in a large fireplace and all of the eating and living and sleeping were done in the single room. Sometimes there was a curtain that could be pulled to allow some privacy.

By the 1860s and 1870s, back-to-backs had been outlawed and other health and building codes, as well as rising prosperity, improved the general standard of working-class housing. From midcentury onwards, houses for both the working and the lower-middle class were built in single rows, with one entry in front and another in back. The back door led to a small paved yard with a brick wall around it where trash bins were kept, clothes were dried, and a few plants could be grown. On the ground floor were a kitchen and a parlor, and on the upper floor were three bedrooms (one for parents, one for sons, one for daughters).

By the 1860s, artisans and respectable workers planned to have at least £10 saved up for furniture before they got married. They bought some of their household goods secondhand and added other things in the first year or two of marriage, before children came. The front room on the ground floor was called the *parlor* and kept for best. It had a sofa, chairs, a carpet, a few books, and sometimes an upright piano. The back room on the ground floor (usually called the *living room*) was for cooking, eating, and most family activities. In addition to an oilcloth-covered wooden center table and some benches or stools, it had one or two comfortable chairs beside the fireplace. A wooden cupboard held plates and crockery.

The houses in lower-middle-class neighborhoods and working-class neighborhoods were virtually the same, although their size might be slightly different. Setting aside a separate and formal parlor, however, marked a class difference. Middle-class people thought it was silly to have an entire room that was rarely used, especially when space was tight. Among the lower-middle class, the front room was for family living (and the maid-of-all-work probably slept on a cot in the kitchen). A working-class household with much the same income did not have a maid in the kitchen. The parlor was for kept for special visitors and for Sunday dinner, when the entire family sat down together.

MUD AND DUST OF LONDON

The 300,000 houses of London are interspersed by a street surface, averaging about 41 square yards per house, and therefore measuring collectively about 12 1/4 million square yards, of which a large proportion is paved with granite. Upwards of two hundred thousand pairs of wheels, aided by a considerably larger number of iron-shod horses' feet, are constantly grinding this granite to powder, which powder is mixed with from two to ten cart-loads of horse-droppings per mile of street per diem, besides an unknown quantity of the sooty deposits discharged from half a million smoking chimneys. . . . The close, stable-like smell and flavour of the London air; the rapid soiling of our hands, our linen, and the hangings of our rooms, bear ample witness to the reality of this evil, of which every London citizen may find a further and more significant indication in the dark hue of the particles deposited by the dust-laden air in its passage through the nasal respiratory channels. To state this matter plainly, and without mincing words, there is not at this moment a man in London, however scrupulously cleanly, nor a woman, however sensitively delicate, whose skin, and clothes, and nostrils are not of necessity more or less loaded with a compound of powdered granite, soot, and a still more nauseous substance. The particles which today fly in clouds before the scavenger's broom, fly in clouds before the parlour-maid's brush, and the next day darken the water in our toilet-basins, or are wrung by the laundress from our calico and cambric.

"Mud and Dust of London," *The Working Man's Friend and Family Instructor* (August 23, 1851): 222.

Cleanliness was very important to the respectable working class—and not easy to maintain, what with unpaved streets, horse traffic, and coal fires everywhere. Because hard shiny surfaces were easiest to clean, floors were generally covered with linoleum. Varnish protected the furniture and woodwork. Lace curtains in the parlor windows were washed frequently. The front step leading into the house was scrubbed and whitened every Saturday by one of the children.

At the other end of the spectrum, the country houses of aristocrats and the landed gentry had clearly defined areas for separate activities. There were perhaps three or four thousand families in all of England who lived in grand style. Prosperous aristocrats modernized and rebuilt the Elizabethan or eighteenth-century mansions they had inherited. Other wealthy men commissioned the period's leading architects to construct suitable country residences set on large private grounds with stables, outbuildings, greenhouse, and gardens.

Nineteenth-century building and remodeling provided additional space for special functions. A new children's wing might have nurseries, a schoolroom, rooms for the nurse and governess, and separate bedrooms for older children. The offices (i.e., the working quarters: kitchens, storerooms, laundry, rooms for cleaning boots and lamps) and the servants' rooms were moved out of attics and basements into another new wing. The family areas of the house showed clear gender divisions in furnishing and decoration: wood paneling, dark colors, and heavy furniture for the library, billiard room, smoking room, and study; delicate patterns and light paint in the morning room, drawing room, and ladies' bedrooms. The drawing room was suitable for large and formal entertainments. The woman of the house had a morning room for ordinary family activities and for receiving daytime callers.

DOMESTIC TECHNOLOGY

Although many people still live in houses built during the nineteenth century, the original systems for heating, plumbing, lighting, and cooking have almost certainly vanished. Victorian domestic technology would be very difficult to cope with today. Bathrooms and central heating were rare, even in wealthy homes. There was seldom any running water above the basement or ground-floor level. Lighting was dim and often unsafe. Not until the Public Health Act of 1875 were all newly built dwellings required to have a privy or water-closet.

The English climate is almost mild enough to manage without central heating. (It became common only in the 1970s.) During most of the year, people who wear heavy clothing and do some physical work can be comfortable indoors in the daytime. On the other hand, evenings (even in summer) can be very chilly. In Victorian times, substantial houses had a fireplace in every room. Sometimes wood was burned—especially in country houses where it could be cut on the estate—but usually the grate was designed for coal. Coal is safer because it does not flare up like wood does, and it burns slowly so the fire needs less tending. In rooms that were regularly used, putting coal on the fire was a job for the housemaid, pageboy, or footman. Having a fire lit in the bedroom was considered a luxury except among the very wealthy. A well-guarded fireplace would heat the day nursery when the children were young. Otherwise, bedroom fires were only for people who were ill.

In the kitchen, a coal fire was kept burning all day long for cooking. Working-class families who used the kitchen for eating, homework, and everything else were probably warmer during much of the year than middle-class people who sat in a larger room with a smaller fireplace. Coziest of all, perhaps, were rural laborers with one room on the ground floor and one above; the heat from the cooking fire would rise into the upper room.

In cottages and in the poorest working-class dwellings, food was cooked over an open fire, which meant that it could be grilled, fried, or boiled. In some neighborhoods, the baker would (for a small

The drawing published in *The Pearl of Days* in 1886 shows a boy bringing the family's Sunday dinner home from the shop where it has been cooked in the baker's oven. His sister has evidently come out to greet him.

charge) put people's roasts or meat pies in his oven on Sunday. The coal-fired kitchen range, however, gradually spread from the well-to-do to the middle classes to working-class people. In addition to burners for cooking and ovens for baking, a good cast iron stove had a built-in tank that kept water hot.

There was as yet no domestic refrigeration. Large country estates might have an ice house dug into a hillside, where ice harvested from a local pond during the winter was protected by layers of straw to use in warm weather. Such an arrangement, however, was rare. Food that needed to be kept cool was put on a marble or stone slab in an unheated larder, but it could not be kept for long. Perishable supplies had to be bought as needed; the butcher, fishmonger, and milkman made daily deliveries.

The water supply was in the kitchen or in a scullery behind the kitchen. If the house had a well, the pump was in the scullery. More often, there was a water tank or barrel; servants (or, in poorer families, children) kept it full by carrying water from a neighborhood pump or standpipe. In urban and suburban areas, middle-class houses had a cistern that was regularly filled by a waterman with a horse-drawn water cart. When piped water became available (in most places, beginning in the mid-1880s), many women thought it was the century's most dramatic improvement—for the first time ever, they could use unlimited water for bathing, cleaning, cooking, and washing.

A middle-class or prosperous kitchen had a stone sink with a wooden or stone drainboard. The floor also was stone. Cutlery and dishes were kept in a kitchen dresser with shelves and drawers. Ordinary eating and cooking utensils were iron (not stainless steel) and had to be very carefully dried so they would not rust. A large wooden center table, used for preparing food and for the servants' meals (unless the establishment was so big that there was a separate servants' hall) was scrubbed with sand and scalded; although doctors had not yet discovered bacteria, women knew that wooden milk pails and kitchen tables had to be washed with boiling water to keep them from smelling sour. There were chairs for the servants and a comfortable cushioned rocker for the cook. Though it was usually below ground level, the stove's constant fire probably made the kitchen the most comfortable room in the house.

Coal stoves and fireplaces meant that rooms got much dirtier than they do now. When a housemaid did the daily cleaning, she first emptied the ashes from the fireplace, coated all of its metal parts with *blacking* (rather like liquid shoe polish) to prevent rust, and laid the fire ready for lighting. Then she swept the rugs with a broom. After that everything had to be dusted and the windows and mirrors rubbed down. She polished any brass trim or knobs and carried lamps to the kitchen for filling. A really thorough spring cleaning was essential. Painted walls were washed, papered walls were cleaned with a kind of eraser-putty; woodwork was scrubbed; rugs were carried outside for beating; all of the curtains and drapes were cleaned and rehung.

Households made most of their own cleaning supplies. Almanacs and other books offered recipes, remedies, and instructions for making stain removers, wallpaper cleaners, and so forth. In between, as filler, they gave advice about etiquette and entertaining, suggested games for children, and reported odd facts. Mrs. Beeton's *Book of Household Management* (1861) was by no means the first such book, but Isabella Beeton did a better job of organizing and explaining her materials than most earlier authors. Nineteenth-century editions, now easily found online (see the Appendix for information), provide a storehouse of general information about the Victorian household.

Laundry was a major disruption. Household books recommended that each bed have six pairs of sheets—it was a great advantage to own so much bed linen and underclothing that washing had to be done only eight or nine times a year. Servants got up early to heat water in the *copper* (a large washtub that could be put on the stove). Soaps were not yet very effective; soiled clothes had to be scrubbed and boiled. Wringing out sheets by hand took substantial physical effort. Outdoor drying depended on the weather; if laundry was dried inside, the rooms might be damp for days. Families that could afford it hired a laundress. Otherwise, doing the wash occupied all of the servants and the wife as well; the family ate cold meals on wash day.

The only artificial light in most houses in the early part of the century was from candles. Expensive beeswax tapers in mirrored fixtures lasted well and provided good illumination, but most people had to use cheaper tallow candles. They not only flickered but also had an unpleasant smell. In one-room cottages, daylight and firelight were made to do. (In paintings of quaint country villages, women are generally seen sitting outside their cottage doors spinning or making lace. They did this not just to look picturesque for the painter, but so they could have the best light for their handwork.)

During the 1840s, oil lamps became affordable. (Whale oil had been too expensive for most people; kerosene was much cheaper.)

Lamps were far safer and brighter than candles, though trimming the wicks, cleaning the glass globes, and filling the reservoir with oil was still troublesome. After effective and clean-burning gas fixtures were invented in the 1880s, new homes were built with gaslights and older houses converted to gas when the mains became available. Gas heaters were sometimes put in the bedroom fireplace; they could be easily lighted for a few minutes to take off the chill. Most people, however, still preferred a coal fire for the main rooms of the house.

Indoor toilets and separate bathrooms were installed in houses built at the end of the century, and added to other houses when they were remodeled after neighborhoods had piped water. Until that time, the toilet was usually just outside the back door. Sewers came before water mains; the toilet was flushed by pouring down a pail of water from the scullery. People who were "delicate" or ailing continued to use a chamber pot and then called a servant to empty it.

Most middle-class and working-class people washed daily with water in a basin on the kitchen table (for the working classes) or in the bedroom (if they had a servant). Working people took a weekly bath in a tin tub placed on the kitchen floor. A kettle, boiled on the stove, warmed the cold water that had been dipped into the bath. Usually all of the children used the same water, one at a time; it was *topped up* with hot for each in turn. Fathers and older daughters (who could afford it if they earned their own money) went to the public baths that had been built in many neighborhoods.

In a house with servants, people washed in their own bedrooms or in the dressing room, if it was separate. The bedroom washstand held a basin and jug, a tooth glass, a soap dish, and a bowl for the sponge. Underneath the washstand was a larger basin or china footbath and also a slop pail. About an hour before breakfast time, the housemaid would knock and enter, bringing in a can of hot water and a jug of cold water for the ordinary morning wash. For a full bath, a tub was brought in, placed in front of the bedroom fireplace, and protected by a screen to prevent drafts. The maid brought water to fill the tub and carried all the water down again by the pailful after the bather had dressed and left the room. The tubs were quite small and oval or round; often people sat on a stool beside them and had a thorough wash rather than actually getting in. A full soak in a long deep bathtub was virtually inconceivable before hot and cold running water became available in the 1880s and 1890s. Wealthy people could have had elaborate bathrooms by the middle of the century—but the wealthy also had lots of servants, and were therefore sometimes slow to install labor-saving comforts.

FOOD

Availability and Preparation

Information about food and eating during the Victorian period can be found in parliamentary and public health investigations that looked at household budgets. In addition, cookbooks were published for people of all classes. Charitable organizations put out recipes to help workers get the best value for their money; commercial publishers found a ready market among middle-class and upper-class women for books to be used by themselves or their cooks.

It is always necessary to look critically at cookbooks—practically any guide on the kitchen shelf contains some recipes that hardly anyone really uses. Nevertheless, the successive editions of best-sellers such as Eliza Acton's *Modern Cookery* (first published in 1845) and Isabella Beeton's *Book of Household Management* (first published in 1861) reveal a good deal of information about the foods that were available. The 1861 edition of Beeton's book, for example, has many pages of soup recipes that use winter vegetables such as turnips, carrots, parsnips, potatoes, beets, dried peas, and onions, but even the summer soups never call for tomatoes as an ingredient. Twenty years later, with improved transportation and greenhouses as well as canned foods, tomatoes were easily obtained and routinely appear in recipes.

People in the working classes got most of their nutrition from bread. The budgets collected by factory commissioners in the 1840s show purchases limited to bread, cheese, butter, sugar, tea, salt, and potatoes. A tiny amount of bacon or other meat might be used for flavoring. Workers' diets were short on both protein and fat. Men from the urban working class were noticeably shorter than upper-class men—although most people believed this was an inherited (so-called racial) difference, rather than a consequence of nutrition.

The staple diet of rural laborers was bread, potatoes, and tea. (Tea was cheaper than beer and safer than unboiled water.) Bacon—usually very fat and more like salt pork than the crisply fried bacon eaten today in the United States—was used in small quantities for flavoring once or twice a week. In prosperous times, farm laborers also had milk and cheese. A medical man in 1863 found that 30 percent of the rural laborers he talked to had never tasted any meat except for bits of bacon used as flavoring. (The people who occasionally poached a hare or grouse from the local woods presumably didn't mention it.) Nearly 20 percent of factory workers in some districts also claimed they had not eaten any meat other than bacon.

Poor people's eating habits reflected their living conditions as well from the expense of food. When everything had to be cooked over an open fire, and when women worked either away from home or at home to bring in some income, elaborate meals were impossible. Bread is always ready to eat; potatoes can be easily boiled. In cities, a frequent meal was *bread and dripping*. Dripping was the fat from roasting meat; household and institutional cooks sold it to dealers. Used instead of butter, dripping gave bread a tasty meat flavor and supplied some needed fat.

Since it was hard to store food (and wages might be paid daily), poor people shopped in extremely small quantities. Young children were sent to do errands, because the shopkeeper might be generous when a child asked for a halfpenny's worth of butter. Adults were sometimes told that the shop didn't sell such small amounts.

In cities, street food could be bought by workers who had no time or place to cook. Stalls and hawkers sold coffee, lemonade, ginger beer, roasted potatoes, pea soup *(pease porridge hot)*, sandwiches, meat pies, pickled eels, smoked herring, fruit tarts, gingerbread, and luxury treats such as oranges, lemons, and pineapples. After railways and ice brought fresh fish to inland towns, fish and chips became popular. Chips, in England, are the same as *french fries* in the United States. A heap of greasy potatoes and a fillet of batter-fried cod or plaice, served in a twist of newspaper and sprinkled with vinegar, made a cheap and substantial meal.

The diet of working people improved later in the century. With cheap wheat imported from North America and the development of technology to ship chilled meat from the Americas and Australia, a typical working-class food budget fell by 30 percent between 1877 and 1889 and could include more meat. Investigators in the 1880s noted that working families had added jam, margarine, eggs, milk, coffee, and cocoa to their regular diet, and also consumed tinned salmon, sardines, and larger quantities of butter and cheese.

As long as there was no oven in the kitchen, a roast of meat remained a rare Sunday treat; it was carried to a neighborhood baker for cooking. Stews and fried meats such as sausages and kidneys could be managed on a fireplace grate or on a small iron stove without an oven. When there was meat, the largest portion went to the man of the family. Sunday's leftovers were added to the bread or potatoes he took for his meal at work. It was almost universal among the working classes to give the best food to men and boys who did physical labor. This made practical sense when the primary income depended on a male wage-earner's strength. Women who moved into the middle class (through marriage or by training as a teacher) remembered finding it odd that women were chivalrously served first. In the homes where they grew up, the mother dished out the meal and stinted herself if the supply was short.

The middle and upper classes could afford a wider variety of food. Not much was accurately known, however, about diet and nutrition; vitamins had not yet been discovered. Moreover, the lack of refrigeration meant that even the meals of fairly well-to-do families were limited by the available local food supply. This is evident in the menu of plain family dinners for August taken from the 1861 edition of *Beeton's Book of Household Management.*

In these August menus, *vegetable marrow* is a summer squash similar to zucchini. *Pudding*, in England, is any boiled, steamed, or sweet dish that is served as dessert. One can have almost anything for pudding, including layer cake or plain fresh fruit. A boiled pudding is an English staple not much known in the United States. A thick batter made of flour, eggs, suet (animal fat), milk, dried fruit, and spices is tied in a cloth, boiled for several hours, and served with a sweet sauce. Puddings come in many varieties, depending

---

PLAIN FAMILY DINNERS FOR AUGUST

Sunday—1. Vegetable-marrow soup. 2. Roast quarter of lamb, mint sauce, French beans and potatoes. 3. Raspberry-and-currant tart, custard pudding.

Monday—1. Cold lamb and salad, small meat pie, vegetable marrow and white sauce. 2. Lemon dumplings.

Tuesday—1. Boiled mackerel. 2. Stewed loin of veal, French beans and potatoes. 3. Baked raspberry pudding.

Wednesday—1. Vegetable soup. 2. Lamb cutlets and French beans; the remains of stewed shoulder of veal, mashed vegetable marrow. 3. Black-currant pudding.

Thursday—1. Roast ribs of beef, Yorkshire pudding, French beans and potatoes. 2. Bread-and-butter pudding.

Friday—1. Fried soles and melted butter. 2. Cold beef and salad, lamb cutlets and mashed potatoes. 3. Cauliflowers and white sauce instead of pudding.

Saturday—1. Stewed beef and vegetables, with remains of cold beef; mutton pudding. 2. Macaroni and cheese

---

Isabella Beeton, *The Book of Household Management* (London: S. O. Beeton, 1861).

on proportions and seasoning; stale bread, rice, and other grains can be substituted for the flour. Among its other advantages, a boiled pudding does not need an oven or require much attention after the batter is mixed, and leftovers put into a covered tin will keep for several days without drying out. The suet makes pudding a heavy and filling dish as well as a sweet ending to a meal.

The family menus in Beeton's cookbook call for a surprising amount of meat. In fact, the English middle and upper classes ate more roasted and cooked meat (and fewer stews or casseroles) than Europeans of a similar class. In addition, cooking two or three different kinds of meat in the same oven at the same time saved fuel and labor. Portions eaten at the table could be small; the cold or reheated leftovers would be used for breakfast and luncheon, for children's nursery meals, and for servants' dinners.

With their ordinary meals, people generally drank beer or ale; working people who could not afford the expense had tea instead. Both beer and tea were safer than unboiled water. Milk was also problematic, even in rural areas, until very late in the century. Before pasteurization was discovered, milk could spread tuberculosis. There were other dangers in the food supply. Bakers added alum and chalk to make bread look whiter; copper salts gave color to pickles; arsenic added tanginess and emphasized the flavor of some prepared foods. Many of these abuses were brought under control in 1872 when Parliament passed the Adulteration of Food, Drink, and Drugs Act.

By the last quarter of the century, the diet of the middle and upper classes (as well as the working class) had improved. Fruits and vegetables from parts of Europe with longer growing seasons were available during much of the year. Packaged foods and trademarked brands—as well as laws preventing adulteration—increased the range and quality of foods available. Thomas Lipton built a chain of grocery stores that became famous for many products besides tea. Imported bananas and chocolate bars became popular new delicacies.

It also became possible to safely feed infants whose mothers could not breastfeed them. Although sending a baby out to nurse with a country woman was still common in some parts of Europe, wetnurses had seldom been used in England except by people of extremely high social position. It was not uncommon, however, for mothers to die in childbirth or get infections that prevented nursing. Cow's milk was apt to be contaminated and needs diluting so babies can digest it; the water was even more likely to be dangerous.

For centuries, milk had been put in an animal horn or a stoneware bottle with a rag stuffed in the end so the infant could suck. This, we now realize, made an ideal environment for germs; no wonder that in some foundling homes 90 percent of the newborns died. Glass bottles and rubber nipples became available in the middle of the century, and the importance of sterilizing the milk, water, and bottle was understood in the 1890s. For the first time, conscientious mothers could consider bottle feeding when it was difficult to nurse.

Meals, Mealtimes, and the Social Rituals of Food

Eating habits changed during the nineteenth century. In addition, there were class differences in the hours and names for meals. During the eighteenth century, prosperous people ate a late and very large breakfast, probably a holdover from the medieval practice of having dinner in the morning. An eighteenth-century breakfast could include cold roast meat, cheese, fish, eggs, steaks, and ale. Lunch—if eaten at all—was a small, cold meal. Dinner was at 5 or 6 P.M.

By the Victorian period, breakfast on a country estate when there were many guests might still be an elaborate meal at 10 A.M. Usually, however, it was less formal. People served themselves from foods set on a sideboard: eggs, hot rolls, toast, perhaps some cold meat. Other foods which might appear at breakfast were fish, tongue, meat pies, ham, mushrooms, bacon, and muffins. A small family ate together; but in larger households and when there were guests, breakfast was available from 8 A.M. on, and people ate when they were ready. (The servant who knocked on the door with hot water first thing in the morning had brought up a cup of tea or coffee and a sweet biscuit to have while dressing.)

Among the middle classes, because breakfast was early and fairly small, the husband generally had a substantial hot lunch at his club or at work. Many businesses, including banks and law offices, had meals brought in for the upper-level employees. A middle-class married woman ate a light cooked meal at home. The children ate with her unless she had guests. The children's cooked lunch served as their main meal; they had a supper of bread and milk or something similar before bedtime. In upper-class households, a hot luncheon or an assortment of cold dishes from which everyone helped themselves was served between 1 and 2 P.M.

The earlier practice among ladies of having cakes and wine when friends came to call evolved into afternoon tea as women began to consume less alcohol. Afternoon tea (between 4 and 5 P.M.) became popular during the 1840s. It was thought of as a ladies' meal, although men were sometimes present. An urn of boiling water was carried into the parlor or drawing room along with teapots and a caddy, which held the loose tea. The lady of the house made the tea and poured it out; servants handed the cups to guests. Small cakes, rolled bread and butter, and other dainty finger foods were offered around. Afternoon tea, in other words, was an occasion for visiting rather than a meal.

As luncheon grew more substantial and afternoon tea became more general, the dinner hour got later. The urban middle classes generally had dinner at home between 6 and 7 P.M. (or later for sub-urbanites who had a long trip). Fashionable people dined at 7:30 or 8 P.M. In lower-middle-class and working-class families, however, dinner was a hot meal served between noon and 2 P.M. It was the main meal of the day, especially when the man of the family was a farmer, artisan, shopkeeper, or other worker who could be at home in the middle of the day. Otherwise, a hot supper was provided for the man when he got home in the evening. On Sundays, everyone except the upper classes had dinner at 2 P.M. It was the week's most substantial meal, eaten after church, by the whole family sitting down together. The rich dined in the evening even on Sundays.

It may seem confusing that the working-class evening meal was increasingly called *tea*, even when it consisted of bread, beer, and something tasty such as kippers or sausage. While father had his tea, the children had bread and water (or weak tea) and some tidbits from his plate. When times grew more prosperous, the worker's evening meal became indistinguishable from what in the United States would be called *dinner*—but it was still generally called tea.

High tea, in good society, was a meal found only in the country or in the suburbs on a Sunday evening, when servants had been given a half-day off after clearing away the Sunday dinner. Originally it was a way to entertain on the spur of the moment when unexpected guests came from a distance. One foreign visitor described a Sunday high tea in the country as a sort of indoors picnic, with an odd assortment of hot and cold food, tea, and wine; guests helped themselves because most of the servants were out. Fashionable late dinners were somewhat unsuited to country life; visitors would have to travel home in the dark or rise early for hunting or shooting. High tea became a late-afternoon or early-evening meal eaten instead of dinner. Fruits, cakes, and hot muffins were on the table with a tea tray at one end and coffee at the other. As at breakfast, more substantial dishes such as cold salmon, meat pies, and roast game birds were available on the sideboard.

Supper, like tea, had several meanings. The name might be used for the evening meal in suburban families where the man ate dinner in town at midday. (The middle-class supper, in other words, was often the same meal as the working-class tea.) Nursery children had supper in the late afternoon and went to bed before their parents dined. A supper was also the very late meal at a ball or an evening party. In that case, it could be almost as elaborate as a society dinner; guests were seated at tables set with a full range of silverware, and served by footmen.

The formal dinner party had become a ritualized event. The hour at the end of the century was 7:30 or 8:30 P.M. Guests arrived punctually; etiquette books said they must be no more than 15 minutes late—except in the country, where a little more leeway was allowed for difficult transportation. Everyone assembled in the drawing room, and the host told each gentleman which lady to escort down to dinner. This would not be his wife—married couples were not seated together but made conversation with others. As soon as all of the guests arrived they went down to eat; there were no before-dinner drinks.

Although formal dinners involved vast amounts of food, no one was expected to eat everything. Servants carried the bowls and platters around; guests had a written menu, knew what was coming, and said yes or no to each dish. The butler offered appropriate wines for every course. Etiquette books told the host and hostess not to insist that guests take wine or urge them to have more food. Properly, no one even mentioned what was served; the conversation was to focus on other topics.

At the end of a dinner, servants cleared everything except the flowers and (using a silver knife) removed crumbs from the tablecloth. Then finger bowls, dessert plates, and fresh wine glasses were put at each place. After offering desserts around, the servants left. (During dinner they remained in the dining room, although they had to act as if they couldn't hear any of the conversation.) After a short time the hostess caught the eye of the lady on her husband's right (the wife of the most important male guest) and stood up. The gentlemen rose while the ladies left the room, and then sat down again for brandy or port and "masculine" conversation. (After cigarettes became popular, they might also smoke, but it would not be acceptable to rejoin ladies with clothes reeking of cigars; a man who smoked a cigar in his study or billiard room would put on a

DINNER FOR 12 PERSONS (MARCH)

First Course
White Soup
Clear Gravy Soup
Boiled Salmon, Shrimp Sauce, and dressed Cucumber
Baked Mullets in paper cases

Entrees
Filet de Boeuf and Spanish Sauce
Larded Sweetbreads
Rissoles
Chicken Patties

Second Course
Roast Fillet of Veal and Béchamel Sauce
Boiled Leg of Lamb
Roast Fowls, garnished with Water-cresses
Boiled Ham, garnished with Carrots and mashed Turnips
Vegetables—Sea-kale, Spinach, or Broccoli

Third Course
Two Ducklings
Guinea-Fowl, larded
Orange Jelly
Charlotte Russe
Coffee Cream
Ice Pudding
Macaroni with Parmesan Cheese
Spinach, garnished with Croutons

Dessert and Ices

Isabella Beeton, *The Book of Household Management* (London: S. O. Beeton, 1861).

smoking jacket.) The ladies were served coffee in the drawing room. The gentlemen should remain (all etiquette books insist) only a *short* time over their wine. Then they joined the ladies in the drawing room and tea was brought in. The guests left at 10:30 or 11:00 P.M.

Dining out socially in hotels and restaurants was done only in the last years of the century. Before then, middle-class and upper-class women simply did not eat in public, even with their husbands, unless they were traveling. In addition to the new restaurants (many of them run by immigrants from Europe) that welcomed respectable couples, department store tea shops and chains such as the ABC began serving modest noontime and late-afternoon meals to women alone or in groups.

TRANSPORTATION

Horses were expensive to buy and even more expensive to maintain: they required food, stabling, and a male servant to look after them. Horses also need regular exercise. A woman who had a horse for her own use made daily excursions to shop, pay a short visit, or simply take a drive in the park. A thoughtful woman arranged for friends to use her carriage when she was busy or out of town.

There were many different models of horse-drawn vehicle. A coach was heavy, well sprung, and pulled by two or more horses. A coach could be kept for private use, but the word was more often applied to commercial vehicles such as stagecoaches. *Carriages* were usually private and had many names depending on their shape, purpose, and number of wheels. Reference works on horse-drawn transportation usually have several pages picturing the carriages used at various times. Gigs, curricles, Victorias, chaises, phaetons, and cabriolets were all popular carriages during the nineteenth century. A barouche was an open four-wheel two-horse carriage with facing seats. The brougham, a light enclosed carriage pulled by one horse, was popular for middle-class use. A dog-cart was not pulled by dogs; it was an open vehicle with space behind the seat for luggage—or for a sporting man to carry his dogs.

Country families might keep a governess cart or pony carriage for the governess and children. The governess cart was a low vehicle with high sides; a woman could drive it while also keeping an eye on her passengers. The slower gait of a pony or donkey made the cart less likely to tip over. Some single women also kept ponies: they were cheaper to feed and much easier for a woman to harness and handle by herself.

Most people, however, walked to their destination or used public transportation (described in chapter 4). In the country where cabs and buses did not exist, rural carriers made regular trips hauling goods to market and parcels back. They took passengers if they had extra room or if arrangements had been made in advance.

SHOPPING

Food was bought from specialized shops: butcher, baker, greengrocer (who sold fruits and vegetables), confectioner, fishmonger,

A low carriage with high sides called a *govern-ess cart* was often drawn by a pony or donkey; the small animal and the stable design made it especially safe for a woman to drive. This draw-ing illustrated a story in the children's magazine *Chatterbox* in 1906.

cheesemonger, pork butcher, dairy. Even a small village usually had a baker; a butcher and a greengrocer probably made scheduled rounds once or twice a week. The village general shop (perhaps run from someone's front room or as a sideline for the pub) carried a few staples and household supplies.

Grocers, strictly speaking, sold dry and bulk foods: tea, coffee, spices, sugar, oatmeal, crackers, vinegar, molasses, currants, rai-sins. They also carried supplies such as soap and candles. The pork butcher, like the dairy, might sell butter, eggs, and cheese as well as sausages, bacon, hams, and pork. Usually a bakery sold bread and a bakeshop produced meat pies and some other cooked dishes, but (as in the case of the dairy and the pork butcher) their func-tions could overlap. In all shops, goods were unpackaged; the shopkeeper weighed out the required amount, wrapped it in rough paper, and tied the parcel with string.

Many items were still bought from stalls and street traders. Country towns had regular market days when retailers as well as producers set up stalls. Some towns established covered markets that were open six days a week. The old market square would be roofed over and the stalls became semipermanent booths or lock-up shops. In working-class neighborhoods a great deal of selling was done at street markets on Saturday night and Sunday morning, when people had their week's pay and some free time. They bought food for Sunday's dinner and all sorts of new and secondhand merchandise: clothing, household goods, toys, treats.

London's *costermongers* were a special breed of street sellers. They bought from wholesale markets—fruit and vegetables from Covent Garden and fish from Billingsgate—and sold from handbarrows and donkey carts. Costers, working in family clans, were known for their flashy clothing and distinctive slang. They provided a valuable service by bringing fresh food into neighborhoods where working people could buy it and by developing regular routes that served the new suburbs.

Most food bought by middle-class people was delivered to their houses, since it was difficult to carry parcels home without private transportation. The housewife or cook stopped at shops in the morning and left a written order for food, which was delivered later in the day. The baker and milkman stopped daily to see what was wanted. The system generally operated by account books: the order was written, for example, in the butcher's book, which was then left at his shop. He filled in the price and sent the book back with the boy who delivered the order. (The butcher kept a duplicate copy for himself. So did the careful housewife, to prevent fraud on the way or at either end.) Accounts were settled at some regular interval, usually monthly or quarterly.

In the earlier part of the century, most other retail goods were bought from artisans' shops; they were produced on the premises by the craftworker and apprentices, and sold from a counter in the front room by a member of the family. Small shops were a source of great anxiety for timid purchasers. Prices were not marked on the goods. After asking to look at something, it was embarrassing to leave without buying if the price was out of reach. Bargaining, which was common in many countries, was sometimes done at market stalls but was not usual in English shops.

For fashionable clothing, a woman visited a workroom or ware-
house devoted to a single item such as silk fabrics or gloves or
straw hats. She sat in a chair and described what she wanted.
Samples were brought out for her to see; sometimes they were
modeled by an attractive young assistant. After the woman made
her choice the goods were put in her carriage or delivered to her
house. Dresses, coats, shoes, and other such items were made to
measure. Either the customer returned to the workroom for a fitting after the garment had been cut and basted, or someone was
sent out to fit her at home. A very rich lady did not even need to go
into shops to make purchases. Her carriage stopped in front; her
ladies' maid or footman went inside to explain what she wanted;

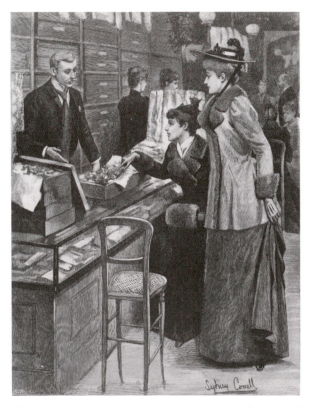

Even in a large new store, customers described
what they were looking for and shop assistants
brought out items for them to see, as shown in this
illustration from *The Girl's Own Paper*, December
9, 1893.

and the shopkeeper or chief assistant brought a selection of goods out to the carriage for her to inspect.

After the 1850s, rail transportation improved the variety of merchandise available in country towns. Shopfronts were added to tradesmen's houses; glass display windows showed the goods. In city centers large outlets that sold a variety of different wares came into being. They were called *bazaars* at first, and later known as department stores. Peter Robinson, Swan and Edgar, Dickins and Jones, and other entrepreneurs put up big new buildings with showrooms on the lower levels, workrooms above, and living quarters for the shop assistants on the upper stories. Fashionable shopping areas such as Regent Street and Oxford Street were jammed with waiting carriages. Most of the monumental nineteenth-century stores that still do business in London grew from draper's shops, which originally sold cloth and textile goods. One exception: Charles Harrod—founder of Harrods department store, which still features a series of magnificent food halls—began as a grocer.

In addition to the range and variety of their merchandise, department stores displayed goods with prices clearly marked. Although there were still assistants behind the counter to take things out and show them (the concept of self-service was not common until after the middle of the twentieth century), shoppers could walk around and look without feeling obliged to buy. Most department stores paid salespeople a salary rather than commissions and instructed them not to put pressure on customers. Department stores kept prices down by doing all business in cash (no losses on bad credit), but they did make deliveries and accepted orders by telegraph. Tea shops, lunch rooms, and lounges where customers could rest as well as using the toilet facilities encouraged shoppers to linger over their purchases. By the 1880s, it was safe and pleasant for unaccompanied middle-class and upper-class women from as far away as Bath or Norwich to come up to London by train for a day's shopping at least once in each season of the year.

CLOTHES

During the Victorian period, men's clothing became less colorful and more businesslike. The basic woman's dress had a fitted bodice and a long full skirt, although there were frequent changes in shape, detail, and trimming. Colored plates in women's magazines and popular prints of people in high society publicized the newest designs; the constant small changes promoted (for the first time) a sense that fashionable women should have new clothes in the latest style for every season. Most people, however, even among the middle class, had only two or three changes of everyday clothing at any one time.

Many good books about historical costuming are available in libraries; in big cities and university towns it's fairly easy to find collections of nineteenth-century fashion magazines. It is important to remember, however, that only a very few people (then as now) wore the elaborate clothes typically featured in magazines. Museum costume collections tend to display wedding dresses and other garments that survived in good condition because they were seldom worn; even the outfits that people put on to have their photograph taken are unlikely to be ordinary everyday wear.

Men's Clothing

From the 1840s onward, the clothes men wore in the city (either for work or for evening) were generally dark and plain. The bright colors, ruffles, and delicate fabrics of the Regency vanished. By 1820, trousers had replaced knee-breeches except for a few ritualized costumes (and footmen's livery). Changes in men's clothing involved relatively minor matters such as the way coats were cut, the tightness of trousers, and the details of collars and lapels. Men working in offices or professions almost always wore a black coat and trousers with a white shirt. Checks and stripes were "unserious"—and considered the mark of a loafer or con-man. Other colors and fabrics were permissible on social occasions. Special clothing for certain sports became common towards the end of the century. Travelers and outdoorsmen wanted practical boots and overcoats; Charles Macintosh and Thomas Burberry began producing the outerwear that turned their names into household words.

According to an etiquette guide published in the 1890s, in the summer a gentleman going to a big London function, to the Ascot races, or to a wedding must wear a suit with frock coat, a light waistcoat, a high silk hat, gray gloves, and a dark gray tie. In winter, the coat and waistcoat were black, and the trousers striped gray. On the river or at the seaside he could wear plain gray flannel trousers with a shorter gray coat, or white ducks. A suit with knickerbockers was appropriate for cycling, golfing, or shooting. Tweeds were worn only in the country, on an estate or in the nearby village. A gentleman's clothing was made for him by a tailor.

Working-class men wore clothing of plain cut and heavier fabric. Ready-made canvas trousers were available, though many working men bought both coats and trousers from used-clothing stalls. Some trades still required traditional garments, especially those that had a practical function (e.g., the smith's leather apron or the sailor's bell-bottom trousers). The farm laborer's linen smock gradually went out of use during the period. Working men generally wore short jackets rather than the longer coats of the middle class. At the end of the period, standard sizing for factory-made garments and shoes improved the look and comfort of the clothes available to people with limited budgets.

Poor people slept in their clothing or underwear. Among other classes, men wore nightshirts. Both men and women usually slept in a nightcap. Remember, bedrooms were unheated; caps helped the body retain its warmth.

Only rarely did men go outside bareheaded. The style of hat—and when and where it was worn—revealed a great deal about a man's class, his status, and even his politics. In very general terms, boys and working men wore cloth caps. Bowlers were for office workers; floppy-brimmed soft felt hats for artists and other bohemians; straw hats for summer and especially for the seaside. The various top hats and silk hats (all of which look the same to modern eyes) had strictly appropriate uses and significant class connotations.

Men's hair was usually just above or below collar length. Only a few men had beards in the early 1800s. Working men shaved once a week, on Saturday night. A man with a mustache was probably either a military man (especially a cavalryman) or a fashionable fop. Full beards became increasingly common after 1850. At first they suggested rugged masculinity—beards were worn by explorers, adventurers, and men who had served in the Crimean War. Later they were extremely widespread, although men in domestic service and some other jobs had to be clean-shaven.

Cigarettes also came home from the Crimea. Early in the nineteenth century, gentlemen used tobacco only in the form of snuff. Working men smoked pipes. After the Napoleonic wars, cigars came into common use; intellectuals and artists took up pipes. Since the smell of cigars and pipes was very unpleasant when it got into heavy curtains or women's long hair, men at home smoked in their private study or went outside to the garden. Working men smoked in pubs or the street, not generally at home. Even at the end of the period, only 17 percent of the tobacco sold was in the form of cigarettes. Elderly countrywomen sometimes enjoyed a pipe, but women who smoked cigarettes usually did it in secret with a woman friend—cigarette smoking by women was definitely "fast" behavior.

Children's Wear

In the first half of the period, children in middle-class and upper-class families wore clothes that were very similar to adult garments. Separate styles for children first appeared in the 1860s and 1870s. Books created some of the fads: *Little Lord Fauntleroy* inspired black velvet suits for boys; many styles of girls' dresses were based on the illustrations for *Alice in Wonderland* or the loose mock-Regency gowns in Kate Greenaway's drawings. Also popular (in imitation of the queen's children and grandchildren) were Scots tartans made up into kilts for boys and dresses for girls. As with elaborate adult garments, outfits of this sort were probably worn more often for family photographs—which were a rare and special event—than in actuality.

There were, however, also new and practical children's clothes from about the 1870s. Instead of trousers boys wore knickerbockers fastened below the knee; although the socks slipped and drooped, the full upper leg and loose knee were good for running and climbing. Boys' sailor suits (usually with shorts rather than long trousers) were also easy to put on and less constraining than a fitted coat. Schoolgirls could wear a dark skirt and middy blouse or a comfortable, loose, pleated dress.

Younger children had long, full pinafores to cover their clothes. They were often made of a sturdy brown or dark blue fabric instead of the impractical white, which one usually sees in pictures. Children, like adults, wore hats or caps outside. Boys were *breeched*—given their first trousers—when they started learning lessons, usually between age three and five. Until that time their clothes were like loose dresses—actually, rather practical for a child in diapers. Young children in poorer families wore the same garment, but among the well-to-do a boy's skirts were less frilly and delicate than his sister's.

A little girl wore her skirts just below the knee, with dark socks or stockings for most of the year and white when dressed up or in the summertime. Her skirts were lengthened somewhat as she grew older. Girls' hair was worn loose while they were younger and pulled into a ribbon at the back of the neck when they approached their teens. Putting her hair up and letting her skirts down to her

An illustration for a story in *The Girl's Own Paper* for October 3, 1885, shows a nurse-maid who has just given the baby a bath and three children standing by the fire-guard that protects them from the flames in the nursery fireplace. The child in the center is a boy who has not yet been put in trousers.

shoe-tops signaled a girl's transition to womanhood. A working-class girl generally made the change when she started her first full-time job, even though she might be only 12 or 13 years old and still physically pre-adolescent. For girls in higher circumstances the change could be made any time between age 15 and 18, depending on her family and their social customs.

Poor and working-class children did not often have clothes that were bought or made for them. Their garments were hand-me-downs or secondhand; they might be cut down from adult cast-offs. Shoes were a particular difficulty. Autobiographies and memoirs recollect going through a winter with shoes two sizes too large, and handing them on to a brother just as they began to fit. Photographs from the period show that the poorest children, in both city and country, played outside and even went to school with bare feet.

Women's Clothing

Despite the annual excitement over new fads and fashionable designs, the general principle of women's dresses did not change a great deal over the Victorian period. The loose high-waisted dresses of the Regency disappeared before 1830. Low-necked daytime clothing, which had been worn for three centuries, was seldom seen after 1840. The basic shape for the rest of the century involved a fitted bodice that came at least to the base of the neck, long sleeves, and a small waist. The skirt, made of the same material as the bodice, was at least moderately full and came down to the shoes.

Within that framework, the general outline of women's clothing altered roughly by decade. At the beginning of the 1840s, skirts had no special padding to hold them away from the body; they were full but more or less natural in shape. Petticoats then grew increasingly heavy and stiff. By the mid-1850s, the fashionable skirt was enormously full and supported by crinolines or steel hoops—which provided a good deal of fun for humor magazines. The crinoline was not popular for long, and many women did not adopt it. (Queen Victoria never wore one.) It was impractical, inconvenient, and immodest (since the swaying hoop revealed a woman's underclothes when she bent over). Hoop skirts also increased the danger that a woman's skirt would brush into the fireplace. Accidental deaths caused when delicate fabrics suddenly burst into flame were fairly common; one household guide recommended that a large table-cover or piano shawl of firmly woven wool gabardine always be kept at hand for quickly enveloping a victim and smothering the fire.

By the late 1860s the crinoline was passé. Women's dresses for the next two decades passed through a series of shapes created by pulling fullness to the back, sometimes with the support of a bustle or some other kind of padding. At the end of the century skirts were long and flowing but not padded; the popular outline was the puff-sleeved bodice and gored skirt seen in illustrations by Charles Dana Gibson.

Fashionable clothing required a great deal of expense and care. Women's dresses were not bought ready-made until the very end of the period, because the closely fitting tops required that bodice, shoulders, and sleeves be individually measured and cut. A woman who was clearly middle-class but not very well-to-do (including, for example, the novelist Elizabeth Gaskell, who was married to a clergyman and had four daughters) might have a dressmaker to do the cutting and fitting but then take over the time-consuming hand stitching of all the seams and hems herself. Poor women generally wore secondhand garments that fitted badly, or ignored styles and made themselves looser bodices in which they could comfortably do physical labor.

Most middle-class women wore two or three woolen dresses in rotation, perhaps replacing the oldest each year and having the others remade. Most dresses were not washable—and there was as yet no satisfactory dry cleaning. Clothes were sponged, brushed, and protected by layers of underwear. To remake a dress for another season, a woman unpicked the seams and gently hand-washed the pieces. She could make a few changes in style and trimming when she sewed it up again. A middle-class woman had a plainer garment to wear while doing chores at home. When a woman *dressed* in the afternoon, it did not mean that she had been wearing her nightclothes all morning, but rather that she changed from her working dress into something better. Servants' clothing was made of cotton fabric with very little in the way of ruffles or trim; it could be washed easily and frequently.

Dressmaking became less time consuming once sewing machines were available. Women's magazines began selling paper patterns in the 1850s, although adult garments were so complicated that cutting and assembling them took more skill than most untrained women had. Later in the century, some shops sold partly made clothing. The skirt and sleeves were already put together; the garment would be fitted before sewing the final seams of the bodice and waist.

In the 1870s, women of the intellectual and artistic middle class took up a style known as *Aesthetic*. Dresses were softly draped and made of the printed *art fabrics* sold by Liberty and Company of 218 Regent Street. Most well-to-do women continued to wear stiff and tightly fitted clothing, but there were acceptable alternatives. Women professionals and office workers in the 1890s happily adopted a new costume: the skirt and blouse. Attractive garments could at last be bought ready-made; with a loosely cut blouse and no waistline seam, fitting was no longer a problem. One dark skirt, carefully brushed, could be worn every day with a change of blouse; the lightweight linen or cotton blouses were easily washed.

Elaborate clothing made of fragile fabrics, which made moving difficult and required a servant's help to dress, was a declaration of upper social status. Etiquette books suggested that when women paid calls or visited friends on foot they should dress plainly so as not to attract attention. The style was called *morning dress* but really means daytime wear, with arms and shoulders fully covered.

Truly fashionable women changed clothes several times a day. Women wealthy enough to pay calls in their private carriage could wear *carriage dress*, which was cut according to daytime fashion but made in brightly colored silk with feathers or lace for trimming. Tea gowns, worn on a country estate when the ladies had afternoon refreshments while the men were still occupied with outdoor sports (or the drinking that followed), were loose and comfortable, though made of delicate fabrics. Dinner dress was somewhat low-cut and usually made of silk or velvet. Ballgowns had short sleeves and were cut still lower.

Other social events had their own costumes. For garden parties, flower shows, and similar summer affairs, young women wore bright or flowered dresses in thin cotton. Older women wore light silks. All wore large hats. Tailor-made serge or tweeds were worn in the country. Lawn tennis called for a flannel dress with a full bodice and a skirt of about ankle length.

Respectable women did not use visible makeup. Fictional works written during the period mention that girls would bite their lips and rub their cheeks to bring out some color for a special appearance. Some women used dangerous chemicals to promote beauty: arsenic in small quantities was said to be good for the complexion, and belladonna drops were said to make the eyes sparkle. Women's magazines advertised invisible (uncolored) face powders for red or shiny skin. There were also preparations of "healing lip balm," which included a mild pink coloring.

Women and girls wore some sort of hat outdoors on every occasion. Fashions in millinery changed often, from high to low, wide-brimmed to narrow, with great variety in color, decoration, and trim. Photographs of theatrical audiences in the 1890s show large hats that would have been truly annoying to people in the seats behind. Although buying a dress was a major purchase, getting a new hat was a relatively inexpensive way to keep up with the season's latest style. Basic hat shapes were sold untrimmed; older girls brought their collections of ribbon and braid and artificial flowers to trimming parties where they traded advice and finished their own hats.

Customs about indoor head covering changed during the period. In the 1840s, almost all women wore a cap in the daytime. Young women in the classes that dressed up in the evening put flowers or ribbons in their hair. Ten years later, young women had stopped wearing caps in the daytime, and their mothers soon followed. Widows wore a distinctive mourning cap for the first year or two after losing their husbands; some continued to wear a smaller headcovering for the rest of their lives. By the 1880s, however, it was usually only elderly women who wore caps in their own homes. Women's caps had largely become occupational badges, seen on people such as servants, waitresses, shopworkers, and nurses.

7

FAMILY AND SOCIAL RITUALS

FAMILY AND PRIVATE LIFE

Family Roles and Relationships

The family—made up of a father, mother, and children living together—was increasingly idealized during the Victorian period. People developed firm ideas about how things ought to be, although not everyone could meet these standards. At the same time, real changes in work and income allowed family relationships to develop more fully. In the working class, growing prosperity allowed more space for shared activities and enabled childhood to last longer. Among aristocrats, extended families had formerly promoted economic and political interests rather than encouraging close affectionate ties. But with Queen Victoria, Prince Albert, and their nine children as models, the upper classes now paid more attention to family celebrations and to establishing a public image of closeness and intimacy.

The middle-class family in its private home was central to the new ideology. Middle-class houses were large enough for family activities yet too small for the separate smoking rooms, morning rooms, and children's wings of aristocratic households. Middle-class women could focus their attention on family and children; they did not need to earn money (as did wives in the working class), nor did they have the social and political obligations of aristocratic women. The model of mother at home, father at work, and family as the center of children's lives—the model taken as "natural" for much of the twentieth century—had its origin in middle-class patterns of life. During the nineteenth century, English middle-class households were less likely to include unrelated persons (except for servants), and grown children lived at home as long as they were single. An unmarried aunt or widowed grandmother might also be in the house.

Ideologically, the middle-class home and family represented the essence of morality, stability, and comfort. The husband had legal and economic control over his wife, children, and servants. The family depended on his income: the wife did not bring in money through labor (as in the working class) or have a private settlement (as among gentry and aristocrats). The children remained subordinate and obedient. Boys, who needed extended schooling to reproduce their parents' style of life, were under their father's authority until they had enough training and experience to make their own way in the world. Middle-class daughters were not expected to "make their own way"—with a very few exceptions, they stayed at home unless or until they married.

Families influenced one's economic prospects as well as one's affections. Many sons took up their father's occupation. As apprenticeship grew less common in skilled trades, fathers and uncles became an important source of boys' training. Kinship connections helped young men find positions in politics, foreign service, business, medicine, and the church. As late as the 1890s, 40 percent of all clergymen were the sons of clergy.

Extended families were still significant. Working-class girls in their early teens might become part of a married sister's household to help with baby care. Middle-class girls were sent to live with cousins in the city as *sister governesses*. They helped teach the younger children and shared the adults' social life, thus gaining an opportunity to meet more marriageable men than would be found in the country or in a small town.

Most marriages took place between people of the same occupation or social set. The only regular exceptions were women domestic servants, who might marry lower-middle-class tradesmen. Victorians married later than most people imagine. For the country as a whole, the mean age at first marriage was 25 for women and 27 or 28 for men. Members of the working class, on average, married a bit younger; but both men and women of the middle class were often older than 30, because a man wanted to be financially established before he took on the support of a family. The marriage age grew increasingly later throughout the century. More than 10 percent of the population as a whole never did marry, and among the professional classes one-third of all women may have remained single.

The average number of children per family was six at midcentury. About one-fifth of all families had 10 or more children. Because of poor nutrition and other dangers, infant deaths were more common in the working class; many of the really large families were found among the middle and upper classes. The situation changed by the end of the century. Families grew smaller, partly because of later marriage but also because reasonably dependable ways to prevent conception were available. The middle class were the first to limit family size, probably because they recognized the expense of educating children so they could equal their parents' economic status. By 1900, the average manual laborer had twice as many children as the typical professional man.

The death rate among adults in their twenties and thirties was relatively high; workplace accidents, childbirth, infections, epidemics, and tuberculosis killed far more people than nowadays. By some estimates, as many children lived in single-parent families in Victorian times as today, although the cause was death rather than divorce or lack of marriage. Whichever parent died, there was hardship. Working women seldom earned enough to support young children; they usually had to go into the workhouse. A father who could not provide child care while working 12 or 14 hours a day might also have to go the Poor Law for help. Children were sent to orphanages or split up among relatives. Among the middle class, an aunt or paid housekeeper would live in a widower's house as a substitute mother; widowed mothers moved in with a relative. Second and third marriages created complicated stepfamilies and half-families. The Victorian "nuclear family" was often, therefore, large and complex, but the rate of birth outside marriage was—in all classes—extremely low.

Within the family, all legal authority rested with the father. Nevertheless, as middle-class advice books recognized, fathers who worked in business and the professions spent long hours away from home. Mothers were made responsible for moral and spiritual guidance, as well as for supervising all of the household's practical affairs. Fathers were typically distant and reserved.

Middle-class married women with three or four servants did not have a great deal to do with themselves all day; nor were they rich enough for the constant visiting, shopping, and entertaining that occupied women higher on the social scale. Single women had an even more problematic role. Although the barrier was weakening by the end of the century, most people considered it socially unacceptable for any middle-class woman to do paid work. In some circles, a sort of moral barrier even prevented unpaid charitable work; it might expose her to things an unmarried woman should not know. A middle-aged single woman was expected to stay with her parents as long as they remained alive. After that, she might make herself useful as housekeeper to an unmarried brother or as unpaid companion and help to a sister or sister-in-law with a large family.

Daily family prayers became a middle-class custom in the 1830s and 1840s. Parents, children, and servants gathered in the dining room just before breakfast. The father read a passage from the Bible and then, while everyone knelt, called the attention of God (and the family) to special concerns about private affairs and ethical behavior.

Family meals, on the other hand, were not the norm. Children ate separately with their nursemaid. The *children's hour* was their regular daily time with parents—usually after children's five o'clock supper and before the adults' dinner. In some families it was a formal event, with children dressed up and on their best behavior. In other cases, the children were already in their nightclothes, and the children's hour was for romping and stories. When adults had dinner in the middle of the day, children were brought to the dining room for dessert. This was supposed to be a great treat, but many people remembered hating it, since they were expected to show their most polished table manners and practice making polite conversation with grownups.

Sunday was the family day. In the middle class, parents and children went to church and afterwards came home to dine together. Sunday tea was also a family event. Tea was taken in the parlor or drawing room, not the dining room. Relatives who lived nearby or unmarried adult sons were often regular teatime visitors on Sundays.

Sunday was also a family holiday for most of the working class. Children were sent to Sunday school, although adults probably did not attend church. The father had a late sleep and some time to relax; the mother cooked. Sunday dinner might be the only meal the whole family could have together. Everyone wore better clothes than during the week. Even men who did rugged manual labor had a *Sunday suit* if they could afford it. In the afternoon, parents and children went out on a walk or other excursion, perhaps meeting with relatives or close friends for a Sunday evening treat.

During the rest of the week, working-class and middle-class adults were busy and (except for middle-class women) much of their time was spent away from home. Even in classes where work and wages were not a consideration, children's lives were largely separate from those of adults, as the next section explains.

For adults of the leisured classes, the day began when a servant brought in hot water for washing and a cup of tea or coffee with something small to eat. Most then spent the next hour or two in their own rooms writing, reading, or attending to private business. Among aristocrats and the substantial gentry, there were usually more than two adults in the house. Houseguests and long visits from relatives were common; single or widowed aunts and sisters were part of the family group. A large midmorning breakfast began the social day.

After breakfast, the men engaged in sports, walked out to look over the estate, and conferred with their agent about business. A country squire spent a few hours serving as justice of the peace when the occasion arose. Women occupied their time with calls, visits, reading, music, and needlework. They went out for a walk or ride as exercise, and perhaps did some social welfare work. A young woman, for example, might stop at the village school to drop off a book, hear a lesson, and keep her eye out for laborers' daughters who seemed likely to make promising domestic servants. After a late-afternoon rest, everyone changed into dinner clothes for an elaborate meal.

Childhood

Where were children in this life? Despite our sentimental belief that Victorians worshipped motherhood and family values, most mothers did not do much child care. In the working class, children looked after themselves and younger children; a seven-year-old might have almost full responsibility for the baby. Parents in better circumstances were supported by nurserymaids, governesses, and boarding schools. The idealized loving mother probably spent only an hour or two with her children each day. Families in India and other distant parts of the Empire sent children home (to England) to foster parents and boarding schools at the age of five or six, and might not see them again until they were teenagers.

Upper-class parents delegated the entire care of children to a nurse (or *nanny*). She and the children had a separate floor or wing of the house. Ideally it had a day nursery, one or more night nurseries for children of different ages, bedrooms for older children and for their governess, and a schoolroom or older children's sitting room. The fully staffed nursery had additional nurserymaids, a schoolroom maid, a laundress, and sometimes a cook. Children were separated from adults to give them a sheltered and structured routine and to train their character. Adults were freed for their own pleasures and responsibilities, and for the London season and foreign travel, which were an expected part of aristocratic life.

The idealized nanny was largely a figure of late-Victorian and Edwardian upper-class households. Most nursemaids and nurse-girls could more properly be described as child-minders or mother's helpers. In fact, several hundred people who listed their occupation as *children's nurse* on the census of 1851 were themselves under nine years of age.

The full-fledged nanny was a professional who had full charge of the children and their upbringing. Mothers recognized their own amateur status and deferred to a nanny's training and experience. For the first month after a child was born, a specialist *monthly nurse* was hired; she only looked after the infant and slept beside the cradle in a room next to the mother's so she could bring the baby in to be breastfed at night.

After the monthly nurse left, the new baby was moved into the nursery. In a substantial home, a nanny had help from a nursery-maid who lit fires, did wash, fetched meals from the kitchen, and cleaned the rooms. The nurserymaid also took the children for an afternoon walk and looked after them when the nanny had her meals. When there were many children, families that could afford it had additional under-nurses to help.

Children spent virtually all of their time with the nanny. Her bed was in the night nursery where they slept. Parents paid little attention to what went on from day to day. Even among the wealthy, nurseries were usually furnished with cast-offs from the rest of the house. There might be a rocking horse and perhaps a swinging chair suspended from the ceiling, but the sofa was old. A high fire-guard protected children from the flames and provided some bars for drying wet garments.

All the children slept in the same room at night. During the day they ate, played, and had early lessons in the day nursery. Their meals were deliberately plain. At age five, children began to spend

INFANT TRAINING

The nurse should keep the child as clean as possible, and particularly she should train it to habits of cleanliness, so that it should feel uncomfortable when otherwise; watching especially that it does not soil itself in eating. At the same time, vanity in its personal appearance is not to be encouraged by overcare in this respect, or by too tight lacing or buttoning of dresses, nor a small foot cultivated by the use of tight shoes.

Isabella Beeton, *The Book of Household Management* (London: S. O. Beeton, 1861).

mornings in the schoolroom with a governess. When they were about eight years old, their lessons occupied more time. Boys were sent to boarding school or began learning Latin from a neighboring clergyman. Girls became primarily responsible to the governess. They might still sleep in the night nursery or share a bedroom with one or two sisters.

Nannies learned their trade by spending a few years as nursery-maid and under-nurse. (Norland Nursing School began to train the most exalted nursery professionals in 1892.) There was some concern about children learning to talk from servants and therefore acquiring a lower-class accent and incorrect grammar. A few families employed a *nursery governess*, who was typically an orphaned or impoverished teenager from a good family. She was expected to play with young children, read to them, and teach them colors and letters and other beginning lessons. In theory she would not do any of the physical labor expected from a nurse. This, however, was more theory than practice; girls who took such posts almost always found they had become true servants rather than having the light and pleasant work they expected.

Despite their absolute authority, nannies used "Miss" or "Master" when speaking of the children or to them: "Now Miss Anne, Master John—no hitting." The austere life of nursery children was intended to teach them self-control, obedience, and discipline. Nanny made sure they treated their parents with respect. At the same time, however, nursery children knew they were socially superior to the people who took care of them. In fact, one reason for sending older boys to boarding school was the worry that servants would spoil them.

Most of the middle class could not afford a full-scale nursery and professional nurse. In families with two or three servants, a nurserymaid or nurse-girl—often a very young teenager—did the physical work of looking after children, washing and mending their clothes, taking them for walks, and sleeping in their room. Their mother spent a few hours every day doing the early teaching and watching the children while the nursemaid did other work. Once they could sit at the table and behave, the children probably ate one or two meals a day with their parents, although they would continue to have an early supper and be put to bed while the adults had dinner.

Children in poorer families helped their mothers from a very early age. Even after schooling became compulsory, girls were kept home to look after babies. They did more work as children than boys; school records from the 1870s show girls from age 9 to 12 spending between 20 and 30 hours a week on housework, errands, and child minding. Social investigators and charitable workers (then as now) concentrated on pathology: cruelty, malnutrition, immorality, dirt. Yet memoirs written by people raised in poor working families emphasize warmth, sharing, cooperation, and the kind of careful discipline and self-sufficiency needed to live comfortably in crowded quarters. Infants and young children were physically close to their caretakers. They were carried everywhere and most of the time. There was usually no cradle or crib; toddlers shared a bed with older children.

In close and friendly working-class neighborhoods, children addressed most adults as "uncle" and "auntie." A girl eight or nine years of age might be sent to live with an elderly person or with a sister or auntie who needed help, and remain there as daughter until she married. Although laws for formal adoption did not exist until the 1920s, informal adoptions of orphans and other needy children were commonplace among the working class.

Despite the difficult conditions of many children's lives, the sentimental idealization of childhood is a striking characteristic of Victorianism. In books by Charles Dickens and in thousands of other novels, poems, magazines, and illustrations, children are depicted as innocent, spontaneous, appealing, and naturally good. It was partly to protect—or create—this innocence that nursery children were separated from the adult world. Many facts of life (economic facts as well as moral and sexual information) for the first time were considered unsuitable for children. Even teenagers were forbidden to read newspapers and sent out of the room when grownups had serious discussions.

Society's focus on the young led writers to create a significant body of children's literature, including many books that are still popular. For the first time there were juvenile magazines and styles of clothing especially for youngsters. A separate culture of childhood began to take shape when schooling removed young people from the family and working world. In everything from toys and games to the creation of juvenile courts and the development of pediatric medicine, childhood was perceived as a distinct and special stage of existence.

Most children's lives did improve during the century. Rising prosperity, compulsory schooling, and restrictions on child labor extended the length of childhood. Idealized expectations for mothering expanded into the working class, where women didn't have nurserymaids to help them raise clean, obedient children who were well prepared to begin school. By the 1890s, mothers in all classes were being given a good deal of advice from experts about feeding, discipline, play, and healthy exercise. To a certain extent, middle-class ideals for children's behavior became more relaxed, while working-class children were more strictly disciplined and trained than in earlier years.

SOCIAL RITUALS

The formalities of Victorian social life may be fascinating because they seem so distant. But it is important to remember that fine points of etiquette mattered only to the leisured classes. People who worked for a living did not pay calls or worry about being presented at court. A vast number of guides to correct behavior were published during the period—a number out of all proportion to the size of the population who actually observed fine manners. The upper classes, for that matter, did not need books; they learned how to behave at home. Etiquette books sold well for two reasons. People who were rising in status (especially those new to the middle class) were anxious about their behavior. They had no need to learn about high-society life, but understanding the standards of behavior made them feel protected against outrageous errors. Second, reading etiquette books is like looking at the pictures in glossy magazines: it provides glimpses of the strange life led by the very rich.

Names and Naming

People in the middle and upper classes were careful to use titles and family names when speaking to or about others in their own class. No one past the age of childhood used first names until invited.

Schoolboys, especially boarding-school boys in their teens, called each other by last name only. (If two brothers were at the same school, they would be known as "Finch" and "Finch minor.") High-status men of the same social class continued to use surnames (or the landed name attached to their titles) among themselves throughout their lives, unless one man was much older than the other. That is, the Earl of June and the Viscount May (whose family name is Samuel Manning) call each other "June" and "May," though to men not of the aristocracy they would be "Lord June" and "Samuel Manning, Lord May."

Older girls and young women addressed each other as "Miss" until they became close friends. Early accounts of life at the women's colleges contain sentences such as "Miss Gouvenay invited me to cocoa tonight and proposed"—which means that she suggested they begin calling each other "Edith" and "Eleanor" instead of "Miss Gouvenay" and "Miss Craik."

Between single men and single women, first names were not used until they were engaged. (In a Victorian novel, when a young female character reads a note, blushes, looks up, and says, "Oh, Alfred!" the reader understands, without being told, that the note has proposed marriage and, by using his first name, she has answered "yes.") Cousins, however, could use each other's first names freely, regardless of age and sex.

The eldest sister in a family with several daughters was called, for example, "Miss Bowen." Younger sisters were called "Miss" with both first name and surname: "Miss Anne Bowen," "Miss Cecilia Bowen," and so forth. The same principle applied to younger sons among the higher ranks of the peerage. The eldest son of the Duke of August has a courtesy title (as, perhaps, the Viscount May), but the younger son is called "Lord Henry August" or, more familiarly, "Lord Henry."

Servants, workers, tradespeople, and others of lower status addressed the adults in a family as "Sir" and "Madam" and, if speaking to others, used a title before their surname. This held true even in the middle class; a cook in the family of an accountant or barrister referred to her employers as "Mr. Brown" and "Mrs. Brown." Children under age 12 or so would be called "Miss Amy" and "Master John." However, another family of similar social status would not refer to their neighbors' children as "Miss" and "Master"—first names were used for children even when the adults called each other "Mr. Anderson" and "Mrs. Bennett."

Paying Calls and Leaving Cards

Paying calls was the social recreation of women who had some leisure; the ritual of cards was a way to regulate acquaintance and send signals about important events. Calls were short visits lasting 15 to 30 minutes. There would be a bit of social chat and a chance to meet another friend who might be calling at the same time. Tea was usually offered to the visitors. In some circles, women had a designated *at home* day when casual acquaintances could call; only intimate friends came on other days.

The usual hour for paying calls was between 3 P.M. and 5 or 6 P.M. (depending on the neighborhood and season). It may be confusing to modern readers to learn that they were known as *morning calls*. The word indicates that callers wore morning dress (i.e., daytime clothing) rather than evening dress.

If a woman was busy (or not in the mood for visiting), it was perfectly acceptable for her servant to tell callers she was "not at home." The phrase simply meant "not receiving visitors today" and implied no insult. The caller, for that matter, need not actually come to the door: calls could be made by a woman who remained in her carriage and sent a servant to the door with her card, especially when the card was to signal that she was prepared to welcome visitors at her own home. For example, cards would be left when a bride was settled in her new home, when a woman after childbirth was up and ready to see friends, and when a family came back to town after being away. When someone died, friends showed their sympathy by writing *with kind inquiries* on their cards. The bereaved woman sent cards returning thanks for the kind inquiries when she was ready to resume a quiet social life.

Etiquette books were full of instructions about the wording of cards and the number to leave; they even explained that turning down a certain corner of the calling card sends particular messages. Overall, calling was a way to maintain and regulate social networks. Paying a call on someone new was a means of seeking further contacts, and returning calls signaled that an acquaintance-ship could continue.

Chaperones

In its strictest form (at about midcentury) the custom of chaperonage dictated that an unmarried young woman of good family could not go anywhere alone. Even in her parents' house, she could not be in any room with a man who was not a close relative unless a married woman or a mature servant was present. The rule held until she was about 30, after which she had greater liberty. A single gentlewoman—no matter how old—could not act as chaperone unless she was a governess. Although governesses were expected to be of good families and were treated as ladies rather than servants, they did not need to be chaperoned and could serve as chaperone for younger women.

On the street and in public, chaperones provided safety. Any woman alone was apt to be harassed by men. Working women learned to protect themselves, but except in villages and very small towns, a middle-class woman was accompanied by a servant whenever she went out. Or so the etiquette books said, but middle-class single women with professions, including artists and journalists, as well as married or single women active in charitable work, walked alone even in crowded urban streets. Late in the century, secondary schoolgirls walked to school without anyone to protect them if they went in a fairly large group. Women and girls who traveled alone by train were escorted by a male friend of the family except on routes where a first-class ladies' carriage was available. Careful families secured an escort for young servants if they had to travel any great distance.

The social chaperone (as opposed to the chaperone who supplied protection on the street) had another role. In addition to making sure that men treated her young charge with respect, the chaperone took her out in society so that she would make adult friends and be introduced to appropriate men. Although arranged marriages were no longer acceptable, choices were regulated by carefully mixing suitable young people. At a dance or reception, a chaperone was needed not to prevent improper behavior but rather to evaluate men's rank and character.

A girl's mother did not usually act as her chaperone. The role was better filled by a young married cousin or family friend. The ideal chaperone was good-natured, sensible, and had a wide social network. Well-connected gentlewomen with limited incomes placed discreet advertisements in ladies' magazines offering to serve as chaperone; pay was not mentioned but it was surely substantial. The very wealthy American heiresses who entered high society in the last 20 years of the century were chaperoned by titled Englishwomen.

By the 1880s, chaperones were not essential at outdoor events such as garden parties but were still required whenever unmarried young people would have opportunities for privacy. Chaperones were also essential at dances, dinners, concerts, theaters, and evening parties. Some independent young women of good family had reached a sort of compromise by the end of the century: they were chaperoned when courtship was clearly in the air (e.g., at a dance) but insisted on the personal freedom of going to plays or concerts with a woman friend.

The Social Season

Society, in the restrictive sense of the word, was composed of fewer than 1,500 families drawn from the aristocracy and substantial gentry. People who were *in society* had country estates. During the social season, they moved to a town house in a fashionable part of London and occupied themselves with shopping, paying calls, going to the opera and to concerts and sporting events, and giving entertainments.

The London season took place in May, June, and July. Because Parliament was in session, peers came up to town for meetings of the House of Lords. By tradition, the season's first important social event was the opening of the May exhibition at the Royal Academy of Arts, when new works by the most respected contemporary painters were shown. Summer evenings were long; the weather was pleasant for garden parties and light dresses. There was horse racing at Ascot. The regatta at Henley took place in July. In Hyde Park, fashionable people walked or rode in the area known as Rotten Row between 11 A.M. and 2 P.M., taking the air and nodding to their friends. The *church parade* after Sunday services was especially well attended.

Society life had its serious side as well. Since many of society's men were highly placed in the government or other central institutions, the social events provided an opportunity for cementing alliances, conducting political business, and promoting the interests of the elite. Large dinners were held on Wednesdays and Saturdays, when Parliament had no evening sessions.

The other central function of the social season was its role in making marriages. Private balls and parties were arranged so that young men and women of suitable backgrounds could meet. (For much of the year they lived separate lives on country estates or in male institutions such as the universities and the army.) Before a girl could be considered eligible for marriage, she *came out* of the schoolroom and was introduced to society.

Formal entrance into fashionable society was marked by presentation at court. Daughters of the aristocracy were automatically eligible. Other girls could be presented if their fathers were important country squires, members of the higher clergy, high-ranking military or naval officers, or substantial physicians and barristers. It also helped if their mothers could arrange the right contacts, since technically a woman had to be presented to the queen by someone who already knew them both. Daughters of wealthy manufacturers and merchants were presented only toward the end of the Victorian period.

Presentations took place at *drawing rooms* held by the queen at St. James's Palace or Buckingham Palace on several afternoons during the social season. The girl being presented was generally about 18 years of age, but could be older. She wore a short-sleeved white dress with a long train; her hair was decorated with a distinctive plume of white feathers. After her name was announced, she curtsied very low, kissed the queen's hand, and then backed out of the room. Girls about to be presented assiduously practiced with their friends, but nevertheless the prospect of walking backward in a low-cut dress with a train gave them nightmares.

The social season ended when Parliament recessed, by tradition for the opening of grouse season on August 12. Families in society might travel in Europe or to warm countries such as Egypt during the late winter and early spring, but the autumn was devoted to country sports. Foxhunting began on the first Monday of November. The more active members of society engaged in a round of reciprocal visits to estates in various parts of the country, often lasting for several days. The ladies walked, talked, and amused one another while the gentlemen were outdoors shooting or hunting. The visit might end with private theatricals or a ball. By the last half of the century, however, only a very few members of society really spent most of their time in the pursuit of pleasure.

RITES OF PASSAGE

Courtship

Among the elite, the social season or two after a girl's presentation was known as the time that she was *on the marriage market*. Her parents and sponsors planned dances and other events to make sure she was introduced to well-connected young men. Marriages were no longer literally arranged by parents to cement territorial or political alliances, as they had been in earlier centuries, but mothers, aunts, and grandmothers put careful thought into throwing together young people who had compatible interests and comparable social standing.

Girls in the middle classes also came out in some fashion before they were eligible for romance. Their entrance into adulthood depended on their parents' circumstances. Sometimes there was a party or a private dance. Others came out at a public event such as a county hunt ball. Girls in more modest circumstances marked the transition by putting up their hair, wearing long skirts, joining the adults for dinner, making calls with their mother, and taking part in their parents' ordinary social life. Middle-class women, like those of the upper classes, usually married men they met within their family's social circle.

Among the respectable middle and upper classes, all courtship was essentially conducted in public: at parties, dances, and teas; during afternoon calls; at picnics and musical evenings; in the presence of chaperones. Private conversations were brief, and usually in the open air—a couple might drop behind the rest of the group while walking to church or skate together when everyone was enjoying the frozen river in wintertime.

There was no dating—young people from respectable families did not go places together except in the company of other people. It was hard to know someone well under these circumstances. Cousins had much more freedom to be together. Since the Church of England did not prohibit such marriages, a good many cousins fell in love. Modern euphemisms sometimes mislead readers of Victorian fiction. In the nineteenth century, *making love* meant "flirting." A *lover* was a suitor or admirer. This was all perfectly respectable; no sexual activity was involved.

Since maintaining an acceptable middle-class life required a substantial investment in housing, furniture, and servants, middle-class men tended not to marry until they were past age 30. Engagements could last several years. It was not ethical for a man to pay serious attentions to a woman unless his financial prospects would allow them to marry at some predictable date. Similarly, it was dangerous for a young woman to let herself fall in love with a man who had not indicated his interest, because she might be committing her heart to a man who would not be able to marry.

The convention that a man asked permission from a woman's father before proposing was required, according to even the most exalted etiquette books, only if a large fortune was involved. Otherwise, in both the elite and middle classes, the man proposed (in person or by letter); after the woman accepted, he approached her father or guardian for a formal interview. The father's duty was to inquire into the suitor's prospects and establish how long it would be before the marriage could take place.

Only after the father had accepted his prospective son-in-law did the couple exchange gifts. Diamonds were not yet popular; engagement rings were set with turquoise, pearls, or other stones. Sometimes a gold ring with an engraved pattern had no stones at all. The woman generally gave the man a ring as well. They exchanged lockets containing a lock of hair; hers was worn around her neck and his hung from his watch-chain. During the engagement, rules of chaperonage were relaxed in the house—though a door was always open, and someone might be in the next room—but the couple never appeared in public without a chaperone.

Young women and men who worked for their living had more independence, although most people in the lower-middle and skilled working classes felt it was crucial to maintain respectability. Men and women met at work, through social events, at chapel, and in organizations such as singing clubs. There was no chaperonage, though private conversations generally took place out-of-doors. *Walking out* was the synonym for "going steady." When the couple were ready to marry, they announced it without getting "permission" from their parents.

In order to observe the proprieties during their engagement, a respectable working-class couple often used a young brother or sister as a sort of chaperone. (Taking that role was called *playing gooseberry*.) The couple might spend all day together in the country and hire a boat for a trip on the river if they took along a child to play gooseberry—and the child's presence probably ensured that even a kiss would be reported to the family at home.

Others among the working class and the poor walked out together freely. Demographers who look at the marriage registers and christening records in village churches have observed that a rather large proportion of first babies were born less than nine months after their parents' weddings. In many rural areas the older tradition of binding betrothal seems to have remained in force among the laboring class. Sexual activity was acceptable as long as a couple intended to marry, and they did marry as soon as a child was on the way.

Marriage

Elaborate weddings were usual only for the elite, although they became more widespread towards the end of the Victorian period. Poor and working-class people saved and sacrificed to provide a proper funeral but made less fuss over marriage. The bride's mother might not attend the ceremony; instead, she stayed home to cook a wedding breakfast for the new couple. The bride and groom, in their ordinary Sunday clothes, went to church early with friends to serve as witnesses. Afterward they went to her home for breakfast. Usually they took a day's holiday from work, but sometimes the

In the painting "Signing the Marriage Register" by James Charles, the bride wears an ordinary dress under a white veil. There are orange blossoms in her hair, and her father has a traditional white favor pinned on his farmworker's smock. Courtesy of The Art Archive/Bradford City Art Gallery/Ellen Tweedy.

husband went off to earn his wages while the bride unpacked and made their new lodgings look homelike.

Many middle-class couples also slipped into church before the morning service on a weekday and had a small family breakfast afterwards. White gowns did not become especially common until the 1870s; most middle-class brides were married in a colored dress. It would be new for the wedding but made in a style that she could use for going to church and making calls during the following year. Pastels were sometimes preferred, but other wedding dresses seen in museums are bronze taffeta, wine velvet, and deep purple silk. Whatever the color of her dress, the bride wore a delicate white veil covering her head and upper body.

The Victorian elite developed certain wedding customs that became traditional. After the prospective bridegroom had spoken to the bride's father, lawyers for both sides went to work drawing up the settlements (described in chapter 5). The best length for an engagement, manuals suggested, was 6 to 12 months. Ordinary church weddings were by banns: the bride's parish clergyman gave notice during the regular morning service for three consecutive Sundays. According to some etiquette books, however, having their names read out in church was not suitable for people of quality. If they planned to be married in the parish church, they could pay for a license to avoid the banns. A special license (which was even more expensive) let them be married in a fashionable church elsewhere instead of in the bride's home parish.

Before 1857, couples who wanted to marry secretly and without delay could elope to Scotland. The traditional site for runaway marriages was Gretna Green, just over the border, where—custom said—the blacksmith acted as witness. A Gretna Green elopement was both romantic and scandalous. There was always a suspicion that the couple needed to keep their marriage date concealed, or that the groom had persuaded the bride to run away before he signed a settlement, so that her entire fortune was in his hands.

Summer was preferred for fashionable weddings. The bride's family had an *at home* on the afternoon before the marriage for friends and acquaintances who were not invited to the ceremony. Afterwards they gave a dinner party attended by the bridegroom and best man. At some time during the evening, the men withdrew to the library to formally sign and witness the marriage settlements.

The bridegroom had only one attendant, traditionally his brother or closest friend. Until the 1890s, men in the wedding party did not usually wear black; they had coats of blue, wine, or purple with trousers of a paler shade. In the 1880s, the frock coat (which is long both front and back) was replaced by a morning coat (cut away in front from the waist).

The bride had up to 12 bridesmaids. She chose their gowns, which were of similar styles but not necessarily identical nor in the same color. Her own dress was a fashionable afternoon dress, not low-cut like an evening gown. A bride who was *in society* was presented to the queen for a second time, after the wedding, as a married woman. Partly for that reason, white became traditional; the wedding gown was worn a second time for her presentation. However, court dress required low necklines and short sleeves. This gave rise to the custom of making wedding gowns with a separate lace underbodice that modestly covers the bride's neck and arms in church.

Despite the importance of mourning, a wedding would be postponed only when someone in the immediate family had died. Brides or attendants in mourning for other relatives wore grey or lavender. In very fashionable weddings, the bridesmaids as well as the bride were dressed in white. Small boys wearing some popular fashion such as Fauntleroy suits or kilts served as trainbearers.

By the 1840s, orange blossoms had become the traditional bridal wreath. Other flowers were provided for male wedding guests to wear as favors. In the country, village girls spread wildflowers in the bride's path. The wedding ring, according to etiquette manuals, should be heavy plain gold, because the bride would never remove it. The groom also gave the bride a gift of fine jewelry, preferably a family heirloom.

A church wedding could not be private, because the law prohibited any marriage from taking place behind closed doors. Strangers as well as guests might sit in the church, and for a fashionable marriage many people crowded into the churchyard to see the wedding party in their finery. After the guests arrived at the church, the

---

AN UP-TO-DATE WEDDING, 1895

A curious departure which was inaugurated last season was the alteration of the place of the bride in the procession. From time immemorial the custom has obtained of the bride leading the way up the church, leaning on her father's arm, her bridesmaids following her, two and two in their proper order. . . . But last season a society bride started the idea of coming last in the procession, following in the wake of all her bridesmaids instead of leading the way as before.

"Hints on Etiquette," *The Woman's Signal,* October 3, 1895.

bridesmaids took up a position at the door. The bridegroom and best man waited at the altar. After the service, the bride and bridegroom went to the vestry, where the clergyman filled in the register, which was signed by the couple and two or three witnesses.

Church weddings had to be performed during the *canonical hours*, which were 8 A.M. until noon (or, after 1880, until 3 P.M.). When the ceremony was in the morning, a wedding breakfast followed. After 1880, the most fashionable hour for weddings was 2:30 P.M. and the reception (at 4 P.M.) was an elaborate afternoon tea. In either case, families in good society held the event at the bride's home, in their own spacious reception and drawing rooms.

After the bride had cut the cake and changed to her traveling clothes, the newly married couple departed for their wedding trip. Their young friends went for a drive or played tennis; the older people had a chance to rest. If there were many out-of-town guests— or if the parents had a lot of friends they wanted to entertain—they gave a ball in the evening. This event was only for family and guests; the bride and groom did not attend.

Death and Mourning

Almost all deaths (except for sudden accidents) took place at home; hospitals only admitted patients who were expected to get well. During the final stages of an illness a family member would remain in the room, day and night. After death, the person's eyes were closed and a large copper penny was put on each eyelid to hold them shut until rigor set in. The body was washed and dressed in a winding sheet (which covered everything except the face) or a shroud. The shroud, a white garment like a nightgown, also covered the hands and feet. In a village or among the poor, these services were performed by an older woman, often the same woman who acted as midwife. Otherwise, an undertaker or one of his employees was called in.

After the death, windows and doors were opened, blinds pulled down, and mirrors were covered. The church bell tolled. These customs, which had ancient ritual origins, served a practical purpose: they announced that death was in the house and protected the family from inappropriate visits. Likewise, mourning clothes made other people aware of a loss and prevented intrusive personal remarks. Friends and relatives were informed of the death in notes written on black-edged paper and sent in black-edged envelopes sealed with black wax.

The dead were laid out at home, in a separate room if possible. A member of the family or a paid watcher sat by the body until it was buried. This custom had two purposes. First, there was great fear that someone in a deep coma might be buried alive; the watcher remained alert of any sign of warmth or breathing. Second, the dread that a body would be snatched and sold to a medical school remained strong—although it almost never happened after 1832, when the Anatomy Act provided a legal way to obtain bodies for dissection.

Funerals usually took place in the morning. Among the gentry and prosperous middle classes, the coach was draped in black velvet and the horses wore black plumes. The coffin was carried by the family's menservants and by the undertaker's men. Male friends or hired mourners called *mutes* walked alongside. Sometimes they carried the heavy black pall that was draped over the coffin. Everyone attending the funeral wore black garments made of wool and crepe. Men wore black gloves; flowing bands of black cloth known as *weepers* were tied around their hats.

The funeral procession of the Duke of Newcastle is just entering the church. Notice the weepers, the flowing black mourning scarves, and the black pall draped over the coffin. Other mourners, riding horseback, can be seen in the background of the drawing published in the *Illustrated London News* on November 5, 1864. Courtesy of The Library Company of Philadelphia.

Among well-to-do people, the family lawyer and the close friends of the deceased gathered in the dining room or library before the procession. The ladies of the house generally did not attend the funeral. The coffin was carried into the church and then to the grave, attended by the clergyman and mourners. After the burial, the head of the family went into the vestry and provided the information the clergyman needed to fill out the register. The family then returned to the house, and the lawyer read the will aloud in their presence.

Working-class people (especially in the country) had walking funerals. Eight friends (often fellow members of a lodge or burial society) acted as bearers; four carried the coffin on their shoulders and four walked beside them as relief. The family walked immediately behind the coffin and the other mourners followed. Everyone wore at least some token of black such as a band around the arm. After the burial there was a substantial meal at home or in the neighborhood pub for close friends and for relatives who had come from a distance. When the deceased left a widow or orphans, money might be collected; in some places it was traditionally used to buy the widow a *copper* so she could support the children by taking in laundry at home.

People in better circumstances often criticized the poor for spending too much on funerals. Working-class people, however, felt that to be buried by the parish was the ultimate disgrace. Many of them paid a penny or two a week for burial insurance or belonged to a friendly society that collected dues for members' funerals. (A number of lodges and fraternal organizations had their origin as burial clubs.) The money provided a coffin and tips for the gravediggers, paid for the meal after the burial, and bought mourning for the immediate family.

Even among the poorest, it was important for immediate relatives to wear black clothing. In more prosperous families the whole household, including the children and servants, would be outfitted in mourning wear. The conventions varied by class and neighborhood and changed somewhat during the course of the century.

For strict mourning, clothing was made from fabric with a dull finish. Thus even among the wealthy, fine silk was not appropriate. The usual materials were bombazine (a mixture of silk and wool) and crepe (the crinkled surface keeps it from reflecting light). Servants and the poor used heavy black cotton. Jewelry worn during mourning was made of jet, hard rubber, and dull-finished pewter. Very close relatives might wear a brooch or watch-fob woven from the dead person's hair.

Full-scale widow's weeds (i.e., mourning garments) in the middle of the century required a crepe dress with a plain collar and broad cuffs made of white muslin, a bombazine cloak, and a crepe bonnet and veil for outdoors. A widow's cap covered most of her hair and had streamers that masked the sides of her face. After a year, she no longer wore the veil, although she could continue to dress in black for as long as she wished. Queen Victoria wore mourning for the last 40 years of her life.

Etiquette books and women's magazines went into enormous detail about the degrees of mourning appropriate at various times, though it is not clear whether people really paid attention to the fine points. Small children in mourning for their father, a columnist instructed the readers of *Sylvia's Home Journal* in 1879, should wear crepe for seven months, black cloth for the next six months, and "slight mourning" (plainly made clothes with no bright colors) for another three months. By the end of the century, the rule among the middle classes was to wear some sort of mourning one year for a member of the immediate family and six months for aunts, uncles, or cousins. When Queen Victoria died, almost everyone in England wore black for three months.

8

EDUCATION

Children in Victorian England were educated in many different ways—or not at all—depending on their sex and on their parents' financial circumstances, social class, religion, and values. Unlike the United States, where common schooling unified communities and shaped national life, in England there was little agreement about what to teach, how to pay for schools, or whom to educate. Disputes about religious instruction and a conviction that every father had the right to determine how to raise his own children delayed the development of compulsory schooling.

Although there are exceptions to any generalization about nineteenth-century English education, a few terms were widely used. Elementary schools provided low-cost instruction for working-class and lower-middle-class children. Depending on their type of organization and funding, elementary schools were called by several names: board school, district school, parish school, village school, voluntary school, national school. Few elementary schools were entirely free until the 1890s; the usual charge was between one and four pence a week.

Children of more prosperous parents received their early teaching and their secondary education (if any) either at home or in schools described as public or private. In either case, the fees were higher than those of elementary schools. Private schools were owned by a single proprietor and provided almost any kind of education. A widow who gave lessons in her dining room during the morning to five or six young children was considered to run a private school. A technical college that taught accounting, surveying, and other vocational skills to youngsters between age 14 and 18 was also considered a private school. Thus the term *private school* gives little clue about the pupils' age or the curriculum.

Public schools were usually more expensive and exclusive than private schools. They were *public* because some of their funds came from an endowment or from selling shares. A public school therefore did not belong to one person; it was run by a corporation or board of governors who hired the school's headmaster or headmistress. Thus public schools (unlike private schools) had a degree of oversight as well as continuity and tradition.

Education not only varied among classes but also helped determine class. Some historians consider that improved education was the reform on which all other Victorian reforms rested: schooling made democratic elections possible and supplied the training to both develop the economy at home and rule an empire abroad.

ELEMENTARY SCHOOLS

At the beginning of the period, education was entirely noncentralized. Elementary schools (where they existed at all) were run by voluntary, charitable, or religious societies. It's hard to evaluate how many people could read and write. Some authorities count the proportion of brides and grooms who signed their name rather than marking an X in the marriage register. Some contemporary surveys asked people to read and explain a short verse from the Bible. The 1841 census reported that 67 percent of males and 51 percent of females were literate. In any case, few people in the working class had more than two or three years of full-time schooling.

Sunday schools provided some education for children (and adults) who worked all week. Their original mission was to give people the ability to read the Bible for themselves. In morning and afternoon sessions the scriptures were used as textbooks for teaching basic literacy. Some Nonconformist Sunday schools developed into vigorous working-class institutions, with classes for people of all ages and an extensive range of singing clubs, sports teams, and social activities. In country parishes, teaching a class in the local Church of England Sunday school was a social duty expected from daughters of the clergy and gentry.

Another source of free education for the poor were the *ragged schools*. Funded through charities and staffed by both paid teachers and middle-class volunteers, ragged schools offered free meals and clothing to lure impoverished children into the classroom. In addition to giving elementary instruction, some ragged schools ran lodgings, nurseries, and employment agencies.

Working-class children who did have full-time education for a few years generally attended the elementary schools built by religious organizations. The National Society for Promoting the Education of the Poor, which drew support primarily from members of the Church of England, operated schools in many country villages. The British and Foreign School Society served other Protestant denominations. (Local elementary schools throughout the century were generally referred to as the *British school* or the *national school*, which sometimes misleads readers into thinking they were comparable to the U.S. public school system.)

These schools were inexpensive but not free. Costs were kept down by teaching a great many children in one room with a single

This picture of a boys' classroom in a London elementary school shows a typically large number of pupils in a single room. Several different lessons are going on at once, taught by a head teacher, an assistant teacher, and a monitor or pupil teacher. It was printed in the *Illustrated London News* supplement for April 2, 1870. Courtesy of The Library Company of Philadelphia.

THE REVISED CODE OF 1862: STANDARDS
OF ACHIEVEMENT

Standard I

Reading: Narrative in monosyllables.

Writing: Form on blackboard or slate, from dictation, letters, capital and small manuscript.

Arithmetic: Form on blackboard or slate, from dictation, figures up to 20; name at sight figures up to 20; add and subtract figures up to 10, orally, from examples on blackboard.

Standard II

Reading: One of the narratives next in order after monosyllables in an elementary reading book used in the school.

Writing: Copy in manuscript character a line of print.

Arithmetic: A sum in simple addition or subtraction, and the multiplication table.

Standard III

Reading: A short paragraph from an elementary reading book used in the school.

Writing: A sentence from the same paragraph, slowly read once, and then dictated in single words.

Arithmetic: A sum in any simple rule as far as short division (inclusive).

Standard IV

Reading: A short paragraph from a more advanced reading book used in the school.

Writing: A sentence slowly dictated once by a few words at a time from the same book, but not from the paragraph read.

Arithmetic: A sum in compound rules (money).

Standard V

Reading: A few lines of poetry from a reading book used in the first class of the school.

Writing: A sentence slowly dictated once, by a few words at a time, from a reading book used in the first class of the school.

Arithmetic: A sum in compound rules (common weights and measures).

Standard VI

Reading: A short ordinary paragraph in a newspaper, or other modern narrative.

Writing: Another short ordinary paragraph in a newspaper, or other modern narrative, slowly dictated once by a few words at a time.

Arithmetic: A sum in practice bills of parcels.

Parliamentary Papers, 1862.

teacher. Monitors chosen from the older children helped with the instruction. The first government funding for education, provided in the 1830s, was in the form of grants for these two societies to help them put up buildings and train teachers.

By 1851, according to the census, there were almost five million children between age 3 and 15. Two million were in school, 600,000 at work, and the rest were neither working nor attending school. (This does not mean they were idle: many would have been help-ing with their parents' work, minding children at home, or being taught by their parents.) Recognizing the importance of a literate and numerate workforce—as well as the value of schools to keep children off the streets and promote discipline—Parliament increas-ingly provided money for existing schools and exerted control over the curriculum.

The government's revised code of education in 1862 established a system known as *payment by results*. Schools that sought funding were visited by a government inspector every autumn. This was a great ordeal for both children and teachers. Children who passed the inspector's examination moved up to a higher standard—and the size of the school's grant (as well as the teacher's salary) depended on the number of children who passed. Very little was taught except reading, writing, and arithmetic. The church societies required that a clergyman come into school regularly for religious instruction, but teachers had almost no motivation to spend time on history, geography, science, or practical subjects.

In smaller villages, the elementary school had one classroom with a single teacher in charge of girls and boys whose age ranged from 3 to 12. She might have help from monitors or a pupil teacher. Daughters of the gentry and clergy made it a duty to visit the vil-lage school and hear children read or recite a lesson. The code also required that girls learn needlework. Because it was hard for them to pay for supplies, lady visitors provided material for girls to make things which could be given to charity. The squire's wife, for example, could give a layette to a poor mother after small girls hemmed diapers, more advanced students made garments, and the star pupil embroidered a dress.

Larger schools had three classrooms: one for boys, one for girls, and one for the youngest children (who were called *infants*). In very large schools each of the three rooms might have movable parti-tions. Not until the 1870s was it usual for each standard to have its own room. In one London school, 868 children were taught by one master (for the boys), two mistresses (one for girls, one for

Two young ladies (wearing hats) are visiting the village school in this illustration by W. J. Hennessy for Charlotte M. Yonge's 1889 novel *Scenes and Characters*. The teacher is at her desk in the upper right-hand corner, a boy is being punished in the left-hand corner, and a monitor looks after the youngest children at the lower right.

infants), and 12 pupil teachers. That works out to 58 children for each adult—and 12 of the so-called adults were age 18 or younger.

Discipline had to be strict under these conditions. When possible, small children had gallery-style seats on long benches with shelves (serving as desks) in front that kept them all in place until the whole row moved. All pupils sat still in their seats, stood when an adult came into the room, and lined up to enter or leave. Girls curtsied to the mistress at the end of the day. Knocking a ruler on the knuckles or caning a child on the palms enforced order. For serious infractions, a pupil's name was written in a punishment book. This might lead not only to a more serious caning but also to a poor reference when an employer asked the school for a dependable worker.

In 1870, W. E. Forster succeeded in convincing Parliament to pass an elementary education act requiring that schools be available in every part of the country. Local school boards were given the power to collect taxes for elementary schools. Many so-called British and national schools then became *board* schools. In 1880, education was made compulsory for all children between age 7 and 10; and in 1891 board schools could stop charging fees. The curriculum expanded; the age for compulsory attendance lengthened; and the schooling of working-class and lower-middle-class children throughout the country became more uniform.

Infants were allowed in school from the age of three. (Some schools took babies at 18 months if an older child would otherwise be kept home to look after them.) If the school was large enough, the smallest children had a room of their own and those between five and seven were put into classes by ability. At age seven, if they had passed the examination for Standard I, they moved on to the boys' school or the girls' school.

As schools grew larger they were divided into classes according to standard; promotion from one class to the next depended on passing the examination, not on age. Additional subjects came into the curriculum, especially for older children. Most buildings were constructed with separate classrooms, entrances, and play-yards for each of the three divisions, which were called *schools*. That is, the infants' school, the girls' school, and the boys' school were all in the same building, but each had separate space. A head teacher was in charge of each of the three schools; assistant teachers supervised individual classes. The classes were still quite large. Assistant teachers had pupil teachers or monitors to help. Each classroom had a portrait of Queen Victoria and a map of the world (with the countries of the British Empire colored red).

School was typically in session from 9:00 A.M. to 12:30 P.M. and from 2:00 P.M. to 4:30 P.M. With some exceptions, children went home in the middle of the day for dinner. Rural children who had a long walk brought food and stayed at school. In some poor neighborhoods, a local charity provided meals. Because part of the school's funding depended on average attendance, stringent efforts were made to make children come to school every day. There was a two-week holiday at Christmas, one week at Easter, and three or four weeks from mid-July to mid-August. The leaving age was raised to 12 years by the end of the century, but exceptions were made for hardship (if the child's earnings were needed) or if the child passed an examination at the level of Standard IV.

Becoming an elementary teacher was one of the more common routes from the working class into the middle class. Intelligent boys and girls were encouraged to stay at school by choosing them to act as monitors. After turning 13 years old they could be hired as pupil teachers, although the pay was barely enough for clothes and spending money; they had to come from families that could afford for them to continue living at home without contributing to the family income.

In addition to helping in the classroom, pupil teachers received evening lessons in secondary-school subjects from the head teacher or attended Saturday classes at a regional pupil-teacher center. When they reached age 18, they could pass an examination (called *the queen's scholarship*) and attend training college to earn their teaching certificate. The length of the college course varied during the century. At the end of the period, some training colleges were associated with universities.

A certified teacher in a village school in the 1840s earned a salary of £30–£40 per year. In addition, she received rent-free accommo-dation in a school house; fuel was provided; and some of the older girls would do her cooking and housework to practice the skills they needed for domestic service. In London board schools in the 1890s, the starting pay for a woman teacher was £85 a year. For men, pay started at £95. There was an annual raise of £5 for men and £3 for women. Experienced head teachers earned a comfort-able income, especially if they had no family to support.

In addition to recruits from the working class, growing numbers of women from middle-class backgrounds entered elementary teach-ing after it became possible to attend training college directly (by passing the entrance exam) instead of serving an apprenticeship as pupil teacher. Compulsory schooling and longer attendance vastly increased the demand for teachers. Men with enough education for teaching had access to other jobs with better prospects. Except in one-room village schools, older boys usually had male teachers, but teaching girls and infants became a women's vocation.

EDUCATING GENTLEMEN

The Public Schools

The elite British boarding schools that educate boys from the upper classes had their origin in old charitable foundations meant for teaching Latin to boys who would enter the priesthood. After the Protestant Reformation, some became local grammar schools but others raised private endowments and took paying boarders to make up for the lost income from the Roman Catholic Church. By Victorian times, there were nine public schools of outstanding stature: Charterhouse, Eton, Harrow, Merchant Taylors', Rugby, St. Paul's, Shrewsbury, Westminster, and Winchester. During the second half of the century, many additional public schools were founded. Of these, Marlborough, Cheltenham, and Wellington achieved reputations almost equal to the old nine.

The public schools were in disrepute in 1800: education was poor, living conditions were worse, and schools were periodically closed down when the teenaged students rioted. Improvement began with reforms carried out during the 1830s and 1840s under the influence of Thomas Arnold, headmaster of Rugby. The value of education, he believed, was not primarily intellectual. Rather, public school training should develop character, religious and moral principles, gentlemanly conduct, and the boy's ability to govern himself and others.

The actual teaching was (in many cases) neither useful nor particularly good. Up to three-fourths of the class time was spent on Greek and Latin. These languages were studied to promote mental discipline; boys read, translated, parsed sentences, and wrote laborious imitations of Latin verse. Rugby in the 1830s had one head

---

PUBLIC SCHOOL BOYS

The following passage is taken from *Tom Brown's Schooldays*, a novel written by Thomas Hughes in 1857; it was based on his experiences at Rugby School at the beginning of the Victorian period.

The lower-fourth form, in which Tom found himself at the beginning of the next half-year, was the largest form in the lower school, and numbered upwards of forty boys. Young gentlemen of all ages from nine to fifteen were to be found there, who expended such part of their energies as was devoted to Latin and Greek upon a book of Livy, the "Bucolics" of Virgil, and the "Hecuba" of Euripides, which were ground out in small daily portions. The driving of this unlucky lower-fourth must have been grievous work to the unfortunate master, for it was the most unhappily constituted of any in the school. Here stuck the great stupid boys, who, for the life of them, could never master the accidence. . . . There were no less than three unhappy fellows in tail coats, with incipient down on their chins, whom the Doctor and the master of the form were always endeavouring to hoist into the upper school, but whose parsing and construing resisted the most well-meant shoves. Then came the mass of the form, boys of eleven and twelve, the most mischievous and reckless age of British youth. . . . The remainder of the form consisted of young prodigies of nine and ten, who were going up the school at the rate of a form a half-year, all boys' hands and wits being against them in their progress.

Thomas Hughes, *Tom Brown's Schooldays* (chapter 8) (Cambridge: Macmillan, 1857).

teacher and nine assistants. The school was divided into nine classes: 1st form, 2nd form, 3rd form, lower remove, 4th form, upper remove, lower 5th form, 5th form, and 6th form. Some boys came to school as young as age seven; others began later after having studied at home with a governess or tutor. The forms (the name refers to the bench on which each class was once seated) grouped students by ability. Everyone had the same subject at the same hour, so boys might be moved to different forms in different subjects. Because all boys had Greek at the same time, every master had to be able to teach Greek—although the man who took the most advanced form in mathematics might have the beginners for Greek.

As the schools grew larger—and they did grow enormously during the century—the flexible grouping was abandoned. New buildings and new classrooms were constructed. When a boy came to school he was examined by the headmaster and placed in an appropriate form; he advanced to the next form, when he was ready, by passing an examination. As enrollment pressure increased, most schools raised the age of entry to 13. Private preparatory schools (called *prep schools*) took younger boys to make them ready for public school entrance. Most prep schools were small; their boarding houses were supervised by a married master and his wife.

In most public schools, younger boys slept in long, open dormitories, and older boys had private rooms, with fires where they could make toast or cook a snack to supplement the relatively austere meals. An older boy would traditionally choose a new boy to run errands and do chores; meanwhile the older boy (at least in theory) provided friendship and guidance for the lonely youngster. The younger boy was called the older boy's *fag*—the word did not then have a sexual meaning.

Public-school boys were essentially self-governing outside the classroom. Thomas Arnold's ideal for education was to create Christian gentlemen who would be leaders in Parliament, the church, the professions, and the military. He developed a system of prefects so that older boys would learn how to govern. Under this system, boarders were divided into houses. Boys between age 17 and 19, from the upper 5th and 6th forms, were appointed prefects. They were responsible for discipline, sports, and supervising the activities of younger boys. A head of each house and a head of school were appointed from the oldest boys. Intellect was not really what mattered. By the time he left school at age 19, a boy who had been a responsible prefect had the management and leadership skills he needed to serve as an army officer or a colonial administrator.

Rough outdoor sports had always been essential for working off energy when hordes of adolescent boys were shut up in boarding school for months at a time. During the nineteenth century, a sporting ethic took hold. Schools built new playing fields and set up conferences to agree on rules so they could organize matches between schools as well as between the houses of one school. Games were seen as essential to forming a healthy body and a manly character; they provided training in teamwork, loyalty, obedience, and command.

Discipline was enforced with corporal punishment. Not only masters but also prefects could administer a caning when boys broke rules or behaved dishonorably. The ordeal of public school education created an idealized and largely unstated moral code widely shared by men at the upper reaches of society. They knew what a gentleman did and how he acted—although they might be hard put to express it in any words intelligible to people who had not shared the public school experience.

Both the old elite and the growing middle class came to believe that public school was essential to their sons' future. Railways made it easier to send boys away and still have them come home for the holidays. Entry examinations for the civil service and the educated professions implicitly favored boys with public-school backgrounds. The older schools added classroom and boarding space so they could take up to eight hundred or a thousand boys. New schools were established. Some of them had a particular character and reputation; Marlborough, for example, was largely attended by sons of the clergy.

Most public school boys did not go on to university but entered directly into some public service—or, in the case of aristocrats and gentry, into their landed life. (One "advantage" of the classical curriculum was that Greek and Latin had no practical value. Gentlemen, in the strictest sense of the word, did not need to earn a living.) Science, history, English literature, and modern foreign languages were added during the 1880s as an *army* or *modern* curriculum. Religion remained central at almost all schools. Chapel attendance was compulsory; many of the masters were university graduates who were Anglican clergymen.

By the end of the century, public schools had produced an easily recognizable type of "old boy" and made a single elite out of the aristocracy and gentry, the upper middle class, and the sons of successful businessmen. Regional differences diminished as the so-called public school accent became the typical speech of the

An advertisement in *Dickens's Directory of London* for 1888 offers school outfits for "youths" (roughly age 12 to 18) who attend public schools or other expensive secondary schools. Note that the jacket and vest which were required wear at Eton can either be bought ready-made or, like all gentlemen's clothing, made to measure.

English upper classes. The ideal of education was its preparation for responsible service. Boys were not pampered, even at Eton.

Other Secondary Schools

Other secondary schools served less elite portions of the middle class. Some local grammar schools that had not become great public schools gave a general academic education to sons of businessmen and farmers. Legal actions in the middle of the century eliminated the old wills that required grammar schools to teach nothing but Latin and Greek. They developed a good modern curriculum with an emphasis on mathematics and science. These were day schools with relatively modest fees; students lived at home or boarded privately with a nearby family. Some, such as Manchester Grammar School, were known for their academic excellence and regularly sent boys on to the universities. Most pupils, however, left at age 16 to go into business, engineering, banking, and local government or to begin apprenticeship as a solicitor or surgeon. New schools with a similar focus were established in larger towns and cities through the efforts of tradesmen and merchants who wanted a sound practical education for their sons.

In addition, private business and technical schools taught vocational subjects to boys in their middle teens, and other private and denominational schools offered education of one sort or another to boys whose parents could pay the fees. Some boarding schools specialized in year-round supervision for troubled or troublesome youngsters.

During the 1850s, Oxford University and Cambridge University developed a series of examinations rather like the standardized achievement tests in the United States today. Boys at age 16 or 18 attended regional testing centers to take the Oxford and Cambridge Local Exams. Often called the *middle class exams*, they were especially useful to boys who had not attended a public school. A passing score in certain parts of the *local* served as qualification to enter engineering schools, military colleges, medical training, and other professional programs. Some city governments and school boards used scores on the locals in evaluating candidates for civil service and teaching jobs. Girls were admitted to the Cambridge locals in 1875 and the Oxford locals in 1880.

By the end of the century, it was evident that secondary education could no longer be restricted to people who could pay high fees. A systematic, state-supported system of teaching secondary subjects to youngsters in their teens was essential to provide wider opportunities and an educated public. The Education Act passed in 1902—the year after the end of Victoria's reign—required local education authorities to provide secondary schools throughout the country.

GIRLS' EDUCATION

Both social customs and practical circumstances meant that girls were less likely than boys to go to school. Girls did not need preparation for public life. A girl who would grow up to be a married woman like her mother could obtain her vocational training at home. Girls in the working classes began their "apprenticeship" very young, by looking after babies and helping their mothers with the laundry or needlework that brought in some of the family's income.

Families in better circumstances saved and sacrificed to give sons an education that would lay the best possible foundation for their adult lives. Daughters were not deliberately neglected, but their schooling seemed less important. In addition, girls were thought to need more social and moral protection than boys. Parents disliked having them away from home or at large schools. Small neighborhood private schools were run by women who gave lessons in their homes. It was more important for a girl to have personal attention than intellectual training. Best of all, when parents could afford it, was private teaching by a governess in the girl's own home.

The Governess

Although the name *governess* could apply to any woman who taught middle-class or upper-class girls, including those who worked in schools, the term most often describes teachers who instructed children in their homes. A daily governess (usually in a city) came in to give lessons in particular subjects or for part of the day. Resident governesses lived with the family. They taught boys until they were old enough for prep school or public school and girls of any age from infancy through the teens.

The most thoroughly educated Victorian women were probably those who had been taught by their parents. A leisured father who was interested in instructing his daughter, a mother who enjoyed intellectual pursuits, and a well-stocked home library provided a solid grounding in the basics and a lifetime habit of independent learning. Educated women continued to pursue new subjects throughout their adulthood. Studying languages was especially widespread. Many women became thoroughly competent translators by spending an hour or two every day with a dictionary, a grammar, and a substantial book written in another language.

Mothers who did not have the time, the education, or the social confidence to serve as a daughter's primary teacher hired a governess. Like the nanny, the governess was seen as a substitute for the child's mother. Her qualifications were not essentially intellectual. She was expected to be a model of appropriate values and behavior. Moreover, it was important that she have the right social status. The ideal governess was a clergyman's orphan, an officer's widow, or some other well-born woman who had been forced (through no fault of her own) to find a means of support.

Far too many women wanted to find work as governesses, which kept the pay very low. The resident governess had a safe place to live and some of the comforts to which a woman of her class was accustomed. In theory, the governess was treated as an equal. She had her own bedroom in the children's wing (if her room was in the attic, she at least slept alone instead of sharing a room as servants did). Whereas the nanny was addressed as "Nurse" or "Nanny," the governess was addressed as "Miss Anderson." Nanny called the children "Miss Edith" and "Master Edward"; to the governess they were "Edith" and "Edward."

Her status was nevertheless ambiguous, because she was neither family nor servant. She ate with the children instead of with the adults. Although she was usually invited to join the family in the drawing room after dinner, she might feel uncomfortable about intruding—yet she also didn't feel at home in the servants' sitting room, especially if some of them resented her education and class standing.

Mothers who interviewed a governess were often more interested in her manner than her teaching ability. They wanted their daughters to acquire some general knowledge—but largely so they would (as women) be able to carry on pleasant social conversations. Posture, speech, manners, taste, and personal presentation were considered more important than geometry or philosophy. In addition to lessons, a governess provided companionship and supervision for girls and adolescents. This role was especially important when mothers were incapacitated or if they had busy social lives.

If a family was high on the social scale, girls might have a series of governesses. A nursery governess gave early lessons to both boys and girls. At age eight or so, boys went to prep school and a more educated governess began teaching the girls English, history, geography, and conversational French. She also helped them learn to draw, play the piano, and sing—these skills (known as *accomplishments*) were important both for social life and as a means of lifelong recreation. From about age 14, a girl might have visiting masters (often political refugees from European countries) to give more advanced lessons in art, music, and languages. Finally, in her later teens, she would be sent to a fashionable boarding school or provided with a finishing governess who polished her dancing, conversation, and social graces.

That pattern was more of an ideal than an actuality. One governess often had (at the same time) a set of pupils ranging from early childhood to middle teens. People in relatively modest circumstances shared a governess; that is, two or three neighbors sent their daughters to have lessons with the governess who lived with one of the families. In addition, governesses were often hired for very short periods and then let go when the family decided to go away for the winter or send a daughter to stay with relatives. Doing without a governess was an obvious economy when money was short; an older sister or aunt would take over the teaching duties.

Anything like an organized sequence of education or coherent curriculum was unlikely under these circumstances. Except for the relatively few girls (including novelist Charlotte Brontë) who attended good schools specifically to improve their qualifications, the quality of teaching rested on what she had learned from her own governess. Autobiographies have amusing passages about the garbled knowledge girls acquired. One governess-taught child wrote down her daily schedule at age eight: piano practice, breakfast, copy books, arithmetic, history, break, geography, poems, dinner, rest, Bible reading, reading aloud from a novel, walk, tea, sewing while listening to someone read aloud. Other governesses depended on catechism-style teachers' manuals. Children memorized a page or two every day and were required to recite the answers to a series of questions in no perceptible order: Which monarch signed the Magna Charta? What are the main products of Brazil? Name a blue flower which has double blossoms. In what year were the Turks turned back at Vienna?

The profession of governess was in decline before the end of the century. By then, good secondary schools for girls were being established as middle-class parents realized that a decent education helped girls as well as boys. Nevertheless, daughters of the aristocracy continued to be taught at home until after World War I. Governesses with good credentials were also hired to go abroad with colonial and military families who wanted their daughters to receive an English education without sending them home to boarding school.

Girls' Schools

When girls from the working classes had any formal education, it was in the elementary schools discussed earlier in this chapter. Because their help was needed at home (and because literacy had no particular value for them), working-class girls early in the period usually had less education than their brothers. During the latter half of the century girls had many more opportunities for jobs that required a solid elementary education: shop work, teaching, nursing, clerical work. Larger communities added *senior elementary* classes in the board school, which were often specifically for girls, since boys of the same class took apprenticeships or had on-the-job training for skilled work.

Girls with families too prosperous for elementary schools but too poor for a governess were taught by their mothers until they reached age 9 or 10 and then were sent to a private day school for a few years. In cities, upper-middle-class families were less likely to have a resident governess than in the countryside; they made use of a combination of home education, daily governesses, and day schools until their daughters were in their teens.

Parents who could afford private schools worried about what their daughters might learn from other children. Like families who used governesses, many thought their daughter's speech, manners, and standards of behavior were more important than academic performance. Larger communities had many small private schools; in any one school all the pupils were of very similar social standing. Typically, a widow or a single woman over age 30 who had a modest inheritance would lease a house in an appropriate neighborhood and let the women in her own social network know that she was taking pupils. Her assistant teachers—if she had any—were often her sisters or daughters.

Personal attention and close supervision were the private school's selling points. Parents believed a school was too big if it had more than 20 pupils. Students were not put into classes by ability, and they might range in age from 4 to 15. The curriculum and teaching methods were much the same as when a governess taught girls at home.

Except when girls were orphaned, they were not usually sent to boarding school before their teens (unlike boys, who might leave home at age seven or eight). As adolescents, however, girls in the middle and upper classes were often sent away to school for two or three years. Girls' boarding schools before the last quarter of the century were similar to the private day schools—homelike establishments run by two or three women who needed to support themselves. Healthy seaside locations were especially popular for city girls, whereas schools in London and the suburbs (which provided access to concerts, galleries, and other cultural events) were chosen by parents who lived in remote rural areas or industrial towns.

A BOARDING SCHOOL FOR YOUNG LADIES

The following is copied from the handwritten prospectus for an expensive London boarding school in the 1830s.

Miss Sawkins will receive at Christmas a limited number of young ladies, on a plan which combines the comforts and advantages of domestic and school education.

Board and Instruction in History, Chronology, Geography, the use of the Globes, English Literature &c 100 Guineas per Ann. Washing not included.

Additional charges—
Entrance: Ten Guineas
Pianoforte: 20 Gs per Ann
Singing: 20
Drawing: 14
Dancing: 12
Italian: 12
French: 8
English Master: 8
Writing & Arithmetic: 6
By professors of the first reputation.
Masters for the Harp, Latin and any other acquirement will attend if desired
    by the friends of the pupil.
The Calisthenic Exercises by Miss Marian Mason 2 Gns per quarter
Particular attention will be given to the health, the regulation of the temper,
    the formation of good habits, and the establishment of moral and religious
    principles.
The accounts to be settled at Midsummer and Christmas.
Each young lady must bring a knife, silver fork, tea & dessert spoon, a pair of
    sheets and six towels.

The young people who are on the point of finishing their education will be allowed to visit their friends, and I shall be happy to chaperone them, & to introduce them in my own circle; but it is necessary to add that the expense of the carriage used for the purpose of visiting must be charged to the pupils.

Young ladies wanting advantages of Town life but no longer desiring instruction, will be taken as Parlour Boarders (escorted sometimes to morning concerts and exhibitions of pictures). Additional charges will be made for hiring and tuning of pianos, and for seats at Church.

Address Miss Sawkins No. 4 York Gate London

Cobbe Papers, Private Collection.

The education offered in private boarding schools depended entirely on the proprietor's interests and abilities. Some provided first-class instruction in foreign languages. Others emphasized culture, social graces, and appearance; girls wore a backboard (with their elbows looped through the handles on its sides) for several hours a day to develop an upright posture, and they studied the tables of precedence in *Burke's Peerage* in the hope that they would need that knowledge to arrange seating for their future dinner guests. They also practiced various forms of internal snobbery. The term *parlour boarder* described girls who paid an extra fee and took their meals with the head teacher's family instead of with the rest of the students.

By the 1850s and 1860s, many middle-class parents understood that girls' education needed reform, and new academic schools were established. The first was North London Collegiate School, with Frances Mary Buss as headmistress. A *collegiate* school—as opposed to a *homelike* school—had enough pupils to divide into separate classes by age and ability. Specialist teachers gave advanced training in various academic subjects. By the 1890s, North London's curriculum covered English literature, English grammar and composition, history, mathematics (through trigonometry), French, German, Latin, Greek, biology, chemistry, physics, political economy, singing, drawing, painting, and gymnastics.

Schools similar to North London were built in most towns of any size (and in other London neighborhoods) during the 1870s and 1880s. Many of them were funded by the Girls' Public Day School Trust—like the boys' schools, they were *public* because the school was run by a board of governors. Because there were no expenses for boarding, fees were relatively low. In addition, day schooling answered some of the objections against sending girls to school: daughters remained emotionally close to their parents; mothers could supervise their friendships and behavior; and girls had a chance during their teens to learn about household and family responsibilities.

These academic day schools for girls were often called *high schools*. Pupils were usually between 12 and 18, though some schools had a preparatory department for younger girls. Although high schools were found only in towns of some size, because they needed enough pupils to form classes for each subject at each level, some country girls lived with relatives or in small private boarding houses so they could attend. Because the fees were relatively low (and scholarships were provided), high schools drew pupils from a wider social spectrum than did boys' public schools. Girls who had studied in a good high school were well prepared to take the Oxford and Cambridge Local Examinations, which in turn qualified them to become teachers in good schools or to enter higher education.

New and more rigorous girls' boarding schools also came into being. Cheltenham Ladies' College and its imitators combined academic education with certain aspects of the former finishing school; they were socially selective in admissions and gave students practice in pouring tea and making conversation. Other new schools, such as Roedean and Wycombe Abbey, set out to imitate boys' public schools. Often located in remote parts of the country, they were organized in houses with competition, self-government, team sports, and school uniforms. Although most girls at the highest reaches of society continued to be educated at home, these schools began to draw the kind of pupil whose brothers were sent to Winchester or Rugby.

THE UNIVERSITIES

Higher education was available in a number of places during Victorian times. There were well-established universities in Durham and Dublin and new universities in Liverpool, Birmingham, Nottingham, and Manchester. University College in London was founded in 1826 to provide university-level teaching for Nonconformists, Jews, and others who could not attend Oxford or Cambridge because they did not belong to the Church of England. In 1836, University College joined several other colleges and medical schools to form the University of London, which gave degrees by examination to people who had studied on their own or at any college in England or abroad. After 1878, women were admitted to University of London degrees in all fields, including medicine. Nevertheless, to Victorians at large, "going to university" meant only one thing: an education at Oxford or Cambridge.

Both the University of Oxford and the University of Cambridge were composed of about 20 separate colleges, some of them dating from the 1200s. Each college had its own buildings, with lecture rooms, dining hall, library, chapel, common rooms, and student lodgings. Most students had an individual set of rooms including a study and a bedroom.

Students were admitted by a college, not by the university. This might involve making a number of separate applications and taking several examinations. More often, however, admission was uncomplicated. Masters at the good public schools sent their best students along the old boy network to their own colleges. Other boys were recommended by clergymen and family friends. In college, as in the public schools, academic excellence was not necessarily the main focus.

A student was assigned to a tutor who was a fellow of the college. Like the other long-established universities of Europe, Oxford and Cambridge had their origin in a period when priests were virtually the only people who could read. Although they were not seminaries in the modern sense, they retained official connections with the Church of England. In the 1850s, up to half of the undergraduates were preparing to become clergymen. Until 1884, college fellows (i.e., teachers; also called *dons*) were not allowed to marry. Fellows and students lived and ate in college as a semimonastic community of scholars.

By tradition, Oxford excelled for classical studies and Cambridge was best for mathematics and science. (Charles Darwin had been a student at Cambridge.) A number of important reforms were made during the century. In the 1850s, undergraduates who were not members of the Church of England were allowed to take degrees. In 1871, all religious barriers were abolished and chapel attendance was no longer compulsory. Open competitive scholarships were established. Scientific laboratories were built and the range of subjects widened. The size of the undergraduate student body doubled, though it was still very small by twenty-first-century standards.

UNIVERSITY ENTRANCE EXAMINATION: SAMPLE QUESTIONS

1. Assume that 6 men can do as much work in an hour as 7 women, and 8 women as much as 11 boys, and that 5 men can do a certain piece of work in 10 hours. How long will it take 1 man, 2 women, and 3 boys together to do the same piece of work? Express the result decimally.
2. Correct or justify the syntax in the following sentences:—
   (a) They were both fond of one another.
   (b) There were no less than five persons concerned.
   (c) Neither he nor we are disengaged.
3. State what you know of the "Declaration of Rights" and the "Habeas Corpus Act."
4. Describe or draw a map of the coast of Ireland from Bantry Bay to Donegal Bay, indicating the principal headlands, bays, and mouths of rivers.

Walter P. Workman, *The Questions Set at the Matriculation Examination of the London University, June 1880* (London: Joseph Hughes, 1880).

The academic year was divided into three terms of about eight weeks each. With the advice of his tutor, a student arranged his own program of reading and independent study. He could attend university lectures given by noted professors—a schedule of the term's lectures was published in advance—but it was not required. Unlike the U.S. system of higher education, Oxford and Cambridge do not have courses, grades, or credits. After about 10 terms in residence (depending on the degree), a student took a written and oral examination that was spread over several days. A degree was earned by passing the examination; the student's three or four years of reading, tutorials, and lectures were for his own preparation in achieving a passing mark. The university gave the examinations and awarded the degrees; colleges provided most of the teaching and formed the center of students' academic and social life.

Individual colleges within the universities had their own reputation. At Oxford, Christ Church produced prime ministers, Balliol educated colonial governors and African princes, and Trinity turned out sporting men. Until 1870, Oxford undergraduates of noble birth wore a peculiar golden tassel or tuft on their caps; the phrase *tuft-hunter* described other college men whose chief occupation was attempting to ingratiate themselves with the nobility. Students and fellows wore academic gowns for tutorials, lectures, meals, and other events both in and out of college. The gown's length distinguished ordinary students from those on scholarship. Fellows and other graduates had hoods and bands that designated their field and degree.

A typical college schedule involved attending chapel in the morning, meeting with a tutor once or twice a week to read an essay or discuss a reading, and a great deal of sport, talk, entertaining, and visiting back and forth in other undergraduates' rooms. The self-discipline and independent effort required to become a scholar under these conditions could produce brilliant innovative thinkers. It also produced a great many graduates who barely squeaked through. Boys from good public schools, in particular, took pride in never seeming to put any effort into their studies. They spent all their time while at college in pleasure, sports, and conversation— and (sometimes) worked very hard at home or on *reading parties* during the long breaks between the eight-week terms in order to prepare for examinations. In common speech, a man *went up* to Oxford or Cambridge when he began his studies and *came down* when he was finished. If he was *sent down*, however, he had failed a preliminary examination or committed a disciplinary offense, and he was not allowed to come back.

Although the examination subjects differed between the universities and changed during the century, specifics were published in the university regulations. At Oxford in the mid-1870s, preparation in classics was more important than any other background. All students had to pass a preliminary examination (usually taken during their first term) in Latin and Greek grammar, Latin prose composition, one Latin author, one Greek author, arithmetic, and either algebra or geometry. The final examination, at the end of their period of study, covered an extensive list of set topics and texts in one of the following fields: classics (Latin and Greek language and literature), mathematics and physics, natural science, jurisprudence and modern history, theology. (Modern languages and English literature were not yet university subjects.) Men intending to take holy orders often (but not necessarily) took their degree in theology. Jurisprudence and modern history covered topics that appeared on entrance exams for the civil service and diplomatic corps.

Students could work for an ordinary pass degree or, by doing extra reading in more parts of a subject, take the examination for an honours degree. Honours degrees were awarded by class (first, second, third); the lists were published in the London *Times* after the examination period ended. Students who tried for honours were given a pass degree if their work was not quite worth third-class honours. A first was of real importance only for men who hoped to win college fellowships and stay on as tutors and (eventually) professors. At Cambridge the final exams were called *tripos* and the man who ranked highest in mathematics was called the *senior wrangler*. Several nineteenth-century senior wranglers were hired by aggressive new universities in North America to become the chairs of mathematics departments.

The content of the curriculum was not yet the primary value of a man's education. The advantage of attending Oxford or Cambridge—the reason boys of the elite classes were increasingly expected to go to university—was to become friends with the other young men who would, in two or three decades, occupy the highest positions in the government, law, the church, and society. Two or three years at university usefully filled the time until a man was 21 and could begin studying for the bar or embark on a career in politics. Especially when he had a title or an independent income, there was no disgrace in deciding to leave without taking a degree.

Women came slowly, partially, and in very small numbers into the old universities during the last third of the century. At Cambridge, a residence established in 1869 in the suburb of Hitchin became Girton College in 1873. A second women's college, Newnham, took its first students in 1875. They were not officially part of the university, but a number of fellows and professors, including political scientist Henry Fawcett, economist Neville Keynes, and logician John Venn, helped out with teaching and political support.

An essay written in 1876 by a woman student gave details of the college schedule. Students rose at 7:00 A.M., had prayers in the lecture room at 8:00, and sat down to breakfast from 8:15 to 9:00. Then they went to their own rooms for reading and study. Lunch was available in the dining room so they could help themselves at any time between noon and 3:00 P.M. After lunch, most students went out for a walk or other exercise. Late in the afternoon there was a lecture by one of the Cambridge dons who volunteered his time to come out to Girton or Newnham. After a 6:00 P.M. dinner, students again studied in their rooms until about 9:00, when they gathered with friends for tea or cocoa made over someone's bedroom fire.

Some professors allowed women students to attend their regular lectures in Cambridge, although most required that a chaperone come along so male undergraduates would not misbehave. Beginning in 1872, examinations were given to women. The university did not award them degrees, but it did provide a certificate saying they had passed the examination for such-and-such a degree. After examination results were read out loud in front of the university at the end of the year, it became the custom to report women's names and the place they would have taken had they been officially ranked: *between nineteenth and twentieth, equal to fifth*, and so forth. In 1890 there was an enormous sensation when the name of Philippa Fawcett—whose father had been professor of political economy and whose mother would shortly become president of the National Union of Women's Suffrage Societies—was announced along with her place in the mathematical tripos: "above the senior wrangler."

Residential halls for women were opened at Oxford in 1879. Lady Margaret Hall was connected with the Church of England; Somerville was nondenominational. After a time Oxford also admitted women to exams (but not degrees). Oxford, furthermore, gave special examinations for women in subjects such as English literature that were not yet university studies for men. A very modest number of women had studied at any of the women's colleges in Oxford or Cambridge by the end of the nineteenth century. It an advanced and unusual thing to do; even professors' daughters sometimes had trouble persuading their fathers they were serious about wanting to undertake university study.

9

HEALTH AND
MEDICINE

GENERAL HEALTH

Life expectancy was much shorter in the nineteenth century than
it is today. In England, rural people lived longer than city dwellers, and members of the upper classes were healthier than workers.
Unlike many aspects of daily life, medical care made no dramatic
advance during the century. Nutrition was poorly understood, and
physicians had very few effective ways to treat illness. Epidemic
diseases swept through crowded cities. Although the bacteria that
caused some of them were identified by the century's end, it would
be another 40 years before cures were found.

Most people depended on traditional remedies, herbal medicine,
homemade prescriptions, and the health advice passed along by
household manuals and elderly women. Even in an aristocrat's
country house, there was apt to be a servant—perhaps a laundress
or one of the kitchen staff—whose medical knowledge was helpful
not only for the other servants but also for members of the family.
She made poultices for injuries and sore muscles, lanced boils, put
herbs in boiling water to soothe coughs and croup. Her observation, experience, traditional herbal knowledge, and authoritative
assurance were as useful as most therapies available to doctors.

Some people suspected that plentiful energy and a hearty appetite were not *ladylike*, as women and older girls were expected to be

delicate. It was widely assumed that members of the upper class could not digest the coarse food working people ate. Furthermore, people in the fortunate classes thought that cold, wet, and exhaustion were far more dangerous for themselves than for their servants. Evidence reveals, however, that men and women who did heavy labor were usually too old to work by the time they reached age 40; their health was depleted from long hours, poor nutrition, and the physical stress of beginning full-time employment before their bodies had matured.

Today, at the beginning of the twenty-first century, females almost everywhere in the world are hardier than males at every age; but in the mid-nineteenth century, the death rate for girls and young women was greater than that for boys and men. The difference did not arise directly from the dangers of childbirth; young girls and childless women also died more frequently than males of the same age. Women's nutrition suffered from the widespread working-class custom of giving the best food to boys and men. In addition, girls and women of all classes spent most of their time indoors, where air was poor and germs spread easily. Their risk of infection was increased by their responsibility for nursing family members who got sick.

Household manuals explained that "bad air" and "bad smells" caused most illnesses. The observation (if not the explanation) was correct: when the air smelled bad because of rotting garbage and inadequate sewers, the as-yet-undiscovered germs that caused many diseases were likely to be present. People who followed the advice to avoid bad air by cleaning drains and choosing a house on high ground promoted their families' health. However, the common practice of sealing up windows to keep night air out of the

---

MOTHERS' RESPONSIBILITIES

Every mother should know the mode of treatment and the use of remedies for simple or other ailments. . . . She should also look after the *drains* of the house, for a fertile source of mischief and sickness lies here. Mention to nineteen women out of twenty that a drain in the house is offensive . . . probably each will reply, "Yes, but I can't help it." By-and-bye her children sicken one after another, her husband gets up with a headache, his temper becomes variable and irritable, and she herself is weighed down with lassitude and weariness.

Eliza Warren, *How I Managed My Children from Infancy to Marriage* (London: Houlston and Wright, 1865).

house was not so good. Close indoor environments promoted the spread of airborne bacteria. Tuberculosis, in particular, was so widespread that almost any medium-sized group of people was likely to include a carrier.

Girls and women in all classes complained of tiredness. Adolescents suffered from "green sickness"—which describes the skin tone seen among white women who are a severely anemic. The tiredness and anemia grew from their lack of iron-rich foods: red meat and eggs were not available to working-class families, and even the wealthy seldom ate fresh vegetables. Beef was considered a masculine food; when dishes were offered at a dinner, upper-class women generally took fish, chicken, or lamb. When there are other sources of iron in the diet, these are healthy choices; but in the nineteenth century, the cultural bias against hearty female appetites damaged girls at puberty and younger married women who were either pregnant or nursing for several years at a stretch.

Although in the past the people in European countries were not as tall as they are today, by Queen Victoria's time men of the well-to-do classes were much the same height as at present. Among most of the population, however, growth was stunted by poor diet. During the Boer War, only two out of every five volunteers were physically fit for military service; of those, more than half the enlisted men were under 5′6″ tall. School health examinations showed that 13-year-old girls from working-class families were three inches shorter and eight pounds lighter than girls from middle-class neighborhoods.

Middle-class and upper-class men not only ate better than the rest of society but also had more outdoor exercise, especially in the latter part of the century after the games mystique had swept through the public schools. For women of the same classes, by the end of the period, competing ideals of delicacy and vigor struggled for acceptance. During the 1880s, reformed girls' schools required all students to participate in hockey, tennis, or gymnastics. In many private schools, however, the earlier model predominated: the proper daily exercise for girls and women was a decorous walk in the open air.

Dress reform, corsets, and tight lacing were also part of the debate over women's health. A corset, strictly speaking, is simply a close-fitting undergarment. Although Victorian corsets were usually boned and sometimes padded to create a fashionable silhouette, they were not necessarily tightly laced. Both physicians and feminist dress-reformers harped on the dangers of tight lacing and repeated horror stories about women whose livers had been cut in two by their attempt to achieve a 16-inch waist. Very small waists, however, were only intermittently in fashion—and when they were, the illusion of a tiny waist could be created by full and padded skirts. Whether any significant number of women actually damaged their health by exaggerated lacing remains in doubt.

Infant mortality (the number of babies who die before reaching their first birthday) is one sensitive measure of a community's physical condition. Even at the end of the Victorian period, infant mortality was about 10 times as high as it is today in industrialized countries. Then, as now, variations in the number of infant deaths reveal important information about poverty, housing, sanitation, access to medical care, and general health. In 2007, the average infant mortality rate in the United States was just under 7 per 1,000—but in some poor inner-city neighborhoods the number was three times as great. In Liverpool in 1899, the rate was 136 per 1,000 in upper-class areas; 274 per 1,000 in working-class areas; and as high as 509 per 1,000 in the most impoverished slums.

It's important not to confuse infant mortality (the death *from all causes* of babies in their first year) with infanticide (the deliberate killing of a baby through abuse or neglect). Late Victorian reformers sometimes blurred the two. Appalled at the extremely high number of infant deaths in poor urban neighborhoods, they wrote impassioned articles claiming that women did not know how to take care of babies because they had gone to work in factories at such a young age, or that their maternal feelings were so blunted that they neglected or drugged their infants. Deliberate (or even careless) killing, however, accounted for only a tiny number of infant deaths. In the nineteenth century as in the twentieth, the babies most likely to die soon after birth were those born prematurely or underweight. Many working-class women were undernourished, continued doing hard physical toil throughout their pregnancy, and had no access to prenatal care. Rickets (a bone disease caused by insufficient vitamin D) narrowed and deformed a woman's pelvis. The lack of meat, eggs, green vegetables, and fruit in the diet made a woman anemic. All these factors contributed to premature delivery and babies who were seriously low in birthweight.

Even in the upper classes, more than 1 baby in 10 died before reaching its first birthday. All children were at risk from recurrent epidemics of influenza, which led to pneumonia, and other infections now controlled by antibiotics. There were no inoculations for diphtheria, scarlet fever, measles, whooping cough, polio, tetanus, or typhoid. Polluted water, unsafe milk, and the lack of refrigeration made diarrhea a continual danger, especially in summertime. Health guides advised mothers never to wean a child in warm weather. Until piped water and public washhouses for doing laundry were available towards the end of the century, it took a great deal of effort just to keep clean.

DISEASES

The leading killer of the nineteenth century was tuberculosis. It was responsible for one-sixth of all deaths in 1838; although somewhat less common by 1900, it was still the most frequent single cause of death then. Tuberculosis—rather than the dangers of childbirth—was the real reason that so many mothers died young: it accounted for half of all deaths in women between age 15 and 35.

Chronic pulmonary tuberculosis was usually called *consumption*. The symptoms are fatigue, weakness, night sweats, loss of appetite, wasting, and coughing. In the nineteenth century, patients survived anywhere from a few months to several years before they died. Opium was used to control the cough. Rest and a healthy diet helped slow the disease; periods of natural remission sometimes led to false hopes of a cure. People who could afford it extended their lives by taking long sea voyages or moving to warm climates. Italy, Egypt, California, and the South Seas were all popular.

Tuberculosis was not so easily recognized when it infected bones and joints. Scrofula, marked by swollen glands and skin ulcers, was another form of the disease. Fast-moving cases of tuberculosis could be confused with typhus. Other names used for tubercular diseases were asthenia, inflammation of the lungs, hectic fever, gastric fever, and decline.

Until the bacillus that causes tuberculosis was discovered in 1882, the disease was thought to be hereditary. It did often strike several members of a family—especially the ones who did the nursing or spent a lot of time in the invalid's room. (The germs are spread through the air, especially by coughing.) Hospitals generally refused to take tubercular patients. People who could not be cared for at home were sent to the workhouse infirmary.

Tuberculosis was so widespread that almost everyone must have been exposed to it. Those who fell ill were most likely to be overworked, poorly nourished, and confined indoors in badly ventilated spaces. Servants, seamstresses, miners, potters, and married women were especially apt to die of tuberculosis. The disease grew less deadly after the end of the century when improved nutrition and better general health made people less susceptible to germs.

Epidemic diseases seemed worse in the Victorian period than they had for several centuries. Crowded urban conditions allowed them to spread quickly—moreover, better diagnosis and record-keeping made people aware of the problem. The first great victory was the conquest of smallpox. The effectiveness of vaccination had already been demonstrated; and after epidemics in 1837–1840 and 1848–1849, Parliament passed a series of acts making vaccination free and (later) compulsory. Although many people continued to resist the frightening prospect of letting a disease be put into their bodies to promote immunity, better publicity and enforcement virtually eliminated the threat of smallpox after a final epidemic in 1870–1873.

The term *fever* applied to many illnesses. Epidemics of typhus and typhoid appeared from time to time. Because it spread in crowded places, typhus went under such names as Irish fever, gaol [jail] fever, ship fever, and putrid fever; it is, in actuality, an infection of the blood carried from person to person by body lice. The symptoms of typhus were often confused with typhoid, an intestinal disease spread by contaminated food or water. (Typhoid caused the death of Prince Albert in 1861.) Influenza and scarlet fever were often fatal, not only because there were no effective treatments but also because of lowered resistance due to poor nutrition. Diphtheria (sometimes called *inflammation of the throat* or *putrid sore throat*) killed between 15 percent and 25 percent of the children who caught it. An especially widespread epidemic struck in 1855–1856.

Cholera aroused terror in 1848–1849, in 1853–1854, and in 1866. The disease first spread from India across Europe to England in 1831. Its cause was unknown; there was no treatment; and about half the people who caught cholera died of it. Death could be very quick (within a few hours) but more often came after several days of stomach pains, vomiting, and diarrhea.

We now know that cholera is spread through food or water contaminated by sewage that contains infected human wastes. Because germs were not yet discovered in early Victorian times, scientifically minded physicians who paid attention to the available evidence thought that cholera and other intestinal problems were caused by *miasmas*, or bad smells. Opposing that common assumption, William Budd and John Snow argued in 1849 that cholera was "a living organism . . . which multiplied in the intestine." In 1854, Snow traced a large number of cholera cases to a single London pump and argued that water carried the disease.

Despite Snow's prestige (he was the anesthetist who administered chloroform to Queen Victoria during the birth of her eighth child in 1853), most doctors rejected his analysis of cholera. But although the miasma theory was wrong, it led to a number of practical improvements. To prevent bad odors, drainage was improved, sewage was treated, manure piles and rotting garbage were removed. Cities smelled better—and, coincidentally, the bacteria found in decomposing garbage and untreated sewage were less likely to contaminate the water supply.

Even when Louis Pasteur published the germ theory of disease in 1861, many sensible people (including scientists) refused to accept it. Why should disease be blamed on organisms that no one could see, when cleaning up smelly refuse heaps had lessened the incidence of illness? In the effort to eliminate odors, people started paying more attention to bathing and washing their clothes—and thus got rid of the fleas and lice that spread other diseases such as typhus. By 1890, however, microscopic research had identified the organisms responsible for tuberculosis, cholera, rabies, typhoid, and diphtheria. Although treatments that would safely kill the bacteria without harming the patient were not yet in sight, the miasma theory of disease was abandoned.

Other ailments grew from living conditions and occupational hazards. Rickets (caused by lack of sunlight and insufficient vitamin D in the diet) stunted the growth and twisted the limbs of working-class children. Well-to-do men's overconsumption of meat, wine, and rich sauces led to painful cases of gout (which swells joints, especially in the toes) and to the apoplexy (stroke) that resulted from high blood pressure. Smokey and polluted air caused the chronically inflamed nose, throat, and sinuses known as catarrh. In wintertime, a day or two of dense fog that trapped the smoke always led to a sharp upward spike in deaths from pneumonia and bronchitis.

Lung diseases were widespread in factories where the air was thick with cotton dust or metal fragments, as well as among coal miners. The phosphorous used to make matches ate away at workers' teeth and jawbones. Mercury and arsenic sickened the workers in many industries. Arsenic, indeed, was used so extensively in color printing, fabrics, carpets, wallpapers, bookbinding, and other everyday products that it may have caused much of the headache and nausea that appear so frequently in Victorian diaries. Lead-based pigments caused *painters' colic*—and lead in the air near pottery factories must have done a great deal of unrecognized damage to babies and children.

MEDICAL TRAINING AND PRACTICE

Medical Workers

Doctors

The training and organization of regular medical practitioners—that is, the people we would call *doctors*—became increasingly professionalized. However, it was still possible, even by the end of the period, for people to see patients and prescribe treatments without having any formal qualifications.

Among the regular practitioners, apothecaries not only sold drugs and compounded prescriptions but also gave medical advice. Surgeons set bones, pulled teeth, and treated wounds and skin diseases. Double qualification in these two fields was common: most ordinary general practitioners until the latter part of the century were apothecary-surgeons.

Medical workers were traditionally trained by learning from someone who was already in practice. Apothecaries served a five-year apprenticeship, which had to include at least six months of hospital work. Surgeons were also apprenticed. Other boys became a doctor's *paying pupil*. They read his books, watched him treat patients, and acted as his assistant. Medical students (whether apprentices or paying pupils) began in their middle teens and had a reputation for rowdiness.

Physicians, who had more prestige than other members of the profession, were the only ones who had university degrees. A medical degree from Oxford of Cambridge required students to read a great deal of Greek and Latin theory but did not provide any clinical experience. Physicians were gentlemen; their wives could be presented at court. The wives of apothecaries or surgeons could not, since those medical men were trained by apprenticeship and did manual labor. Because gentlemen (in theory) did not work for money, a physician's fee was wrapped in paper and quietly put down on a table near his hand. In aristocratic households, the physician might be invited to dinner, but an apothecary-surgeon who was caring for a member of the family would have his meal with the housekeeper.

Edinburgh University, in Scotland, provided excellent clinical training; its doctors were among the world's best. In the early Victorian years, English medical education became more practical and more rigorous. Several London hospitals set up medical schools. In 1838 the University of London began to offer degrees that required students to have formal courses in medical subjects as well as supervised hospital experience.

The Medical Act of 1858 established a General Medical Council to certify medical degrees and establish a register of qualified practitioners. After January 1, 1859, only those persons whose names were on the register could sign death certificates, hold public medical appointments (in military or poor law hospitals, for example), or use the title *Doctor of Medicine* or *General Practitioner.* Others could practice medicine so long as they did not claim to hold a license; there was nothing illegal in being an herbalist or homeopath.

By 1900, most registered practitioners entered training at 18 and had a five-year curriculum of classes and clinical work before passing a licensing examination. The usual degree was *Bachelor of Medicine* and the initials were *M.B.* rather than *M.D.* By the end of the century, however, *Doctor* was the ordinary form of address. (In the middle of the century, a man called *Dr. Arnold* was more likely to be an important clergyman who held the Doctor of Divinity degree.) Surgeons continued to be addressed as *Mr.*

The 1858 Medical Act effectively prevented women from becoming licensed by requiring that medical qualifications be earned in the United Kingdom. But two women managed to get their names on the medical register before the act went into full force: Elizabeth Blackwell, who had a degree from an American school; and Elizabeth Garrett Anderson, who used a temporary loophole in the Apothecaries' Act. For the next 20 years women tried to gain admission to medical schools. Sophia Jex-Blake and four others were admitted to Edinburgh University in 1869 but were then prevented from taking required courses. In 1874, Jex-Blake organized the London School of Medicine for Women. Sympathetic professors from several London medical schools agreed to provide the teaching. In 1878, women were admitted to all degrees—including medicine—at the University of London and small numbers of women began making their way into the profession.

Most doctors practiced from a room in their residence. (The home office was called his *surgery* even if he was not a surgeon.) Doctors saw patients without appointment during specified hours. When someone was injured on the street, a bystander would run to the nearest surgery and get the doctor to come help. Middle-class and upper-class patients were usually seen in their own homes. The doctor or his assistant might spend many hours watching at the bedside while judging the course of a fever or watching the effect of a dangerous drug.

The usual price of a doctor's visit at the end of the century was five shillings, although most doctors charged only two shillings sixpence if they knew the patient was in difficult circumstances. Often they set aside one morning a week to see charity cases. Some working people belonged to lodges that provided medical care (as well as burial insurance) by contracting with a doctor to treat all their members. Trade unions also offered medical care. Teaching hospitals and some other charities had dispensaries (outpatient clinics) that charged a very small fee.

A gentlemanly physician usually received a fee of one guinea per visit, and a consultant (specialist) was paid between three and five guineas. A successful practice among the socially prominent could make a man very rich, but the ordinary general practitioner had an income similar to other middle-class workers. A beginner or a man with no connections looked for an appointment at a poor law hospital, because each union was required to have medical officers available. The salary was only £60 or £70 per year (which was barely above average for a working-class man). Nevertheless, it gave the beginning doctor a steady income while he worked to establish the connections and referrals that would bring him private patients and allow him to give up hospital work.

Midwives

Midwives delivered most babies born during the century. Traditional midwives were trained through informal apprenticeship. They worked for several years with an older midwife not only attending births but also learning about anatomy and herbal pharmacology. The local wisewoman who delivered babies, gave advice about infant care, helped in ordinary illness, and sat beside sick people probably knew more about women's and children's health than most physicians did.

Whether she was attended by an obstetrician or a midwife, a Victorian woman was far safer delivering her baby at home than in a hospital. Puerperal fever (also called *childbed fever*) was easily transmitted in hospitals. Midwives had a much better safety record than doctors, because they typically stayed with one patient through the birth and for several days afterwards. Doctors, who went from patient to patient, were much more likely to carry the infection.

In the early part of the century, charity patients were the only women who gave birth in hospitals. Obstetricians began to replace midwives in the second half of the century, after the licensing act gave them control of most drugs. Chloroform for "painless childbirth" made women who could afford it prefer to have an obstetrician—and puerperal fever became a major killer. The medical evidence that it was an infection spread by doctors' hands was published at least a generation before it was widely accepted. Only in the last 20 years of the period did doctors habitually begin to scrub between patients.

The transition from traditionally trained to medically trained midwives began in the 1860s, when the Nightingale Fund established a training course at King's College Hospital in London. Midwifery was not, however, subsumed under nursing (as it was in the United States). Although there were various dissenting voices (especially from male obstetricians), the Midwives Act of 1902 secured a continued role in England for women trained and licensed to deliver infants and provide well-baby care.

Nurses

Florence Nightingale made nursing into a popular career, but she overemphasized the faults of earlier nurses. The women hired to look after sick people in charitable hospitals or in their homes had no training, but because they stayed constantly with their patients they might be more perceptive than doctors in tracing the course of a disease and understanding the effect of certain treatments. They slept in the ward or just off it so they were on call day or night; they cooked patients' meals and did cleaning as well as nursing care. But the pay (a shilling a day in London, plus room and meals) was relatively good for a working-class woman; pre-Nightingale nurses were not, therefore, the dregs of their class.

The earliest well-trained sick-nurses in England belonged to Protestant orders modeled after the Catholic nursing sisterhoods of Europe. St. John's House, founded in 1848, provided nurses for London teaching hospitals. After the *Times* had stirred up public agitation about the horrible conditions in the military hospital at Scutari, Florence Nightingale (who had studied briefly at a Protestant nursing foundation in Germany) was empowered by the War Office to take a party of nurses out to the Crimea. Her staff consisted of 10 Catholic nuns, 14 Anglican sisters, and 14 hospital nurses.

When the war ended, a grateful public rewarded Nightingale by pouring money into a fund that she used to found a training school at St. Thomas's Hospital. The school she designed and the regimen she established determined the shape of nursing as a profession. Despite its name, St. Thomas's had no religious connections. Probationers, in training for one year, were paid a salary of £10 plus room and board. Each had her own room in a nurses' residence. Free uniforms were provided. They were taught both by doctors and by experienced nurses and worked under supervision on the hospital wards.

When she had completed her probation, a new nurse spent three years in the service of St. Thomas's. She was paid about £20 a year (and board and lodging) and assigned to various duties in the hospital and elsewhere. After that, her name was put on the register. In the early years, when there were very few trained nurses, she could choose among posts as chief nurse, hospital matron, or district nursing director. So-called Nightingale nurses became the founding directors of new training schools established in hospitals throughout the English-speaking world.

By the end of the century, girls' fiction portrayed nursing as a glamorous career and girls' magazines printed many articles about

An illustration from the cover of *The Girl's Own Paper* for June 16, 1894, shows that nursing—especially military nursing—appealed to young women as a romantic and adventurous career.

how to become a trained nurse. Except in a few children's hospitals, women were not accepted as probationers until they reached age 23 or sometimes 25. This generally excluded girls from the classes that had to begin full-time work at 12, except for some who spent the intervening years as nurserymaids. But it also meant that beginning nurses were fairly mature. Often, by the time they began training they had already reached a decision not to marry.

The probationer was expected to have a good general education and some experience with housework and cookery. She was also required to have character references, including a recommendation from her clergyman. Her training, which generally lasted three years, included lectures, laboratory work, and experience on a variety of wards. Both probationers and nurses lived under strict supervision in quarters provided by the hospital. A typical day shift ran from 7:00 A.M. to 9:00 P.M., although the nurse had time off for meals and two additional hours for recreation. Maids did the scrubbing and heavy carrying, but probationers were responsible for bedmaking, bathing patients, carrying bedpans, and maintaining linen supplies.

After finishing her probationary year, the trainee became a staff nurse. In that capacity, she changed dressings, gave medicines, carried out doctors' instructions, and provided most of the skilled care for six or eight patients. Over her, supervising the ward, was a fully trained nurse known as a *sister*. (In a U.S. hospital, she would be called a *head nurse* or *charge nurse*.) A qualified sister at the end of the century earned between £30 and £50 per year; room, meals, and uniform were provided at no cost. Hospital work was laborious, but since well-to-do patients continued to be treated at home for most illnesses, many older nurses turned to private duty. Most towns of any size also had public health agencies and well-baby clinics that employed trained nurses.

Drugs and Other Treatments

No matter who provided the medical care, there were not many ways to interrupt the progress of an illness. (As late as the 1950s, young doctors were told that 90 percent of the practice of medicine lay in keeping patients comfortable while nature took its course.) The heroic medicine practiced by some Victorian physicians— attacking disease by purging, bloodletting, and dosing with dangerous drugs—probably did more harm than good. Practitioners often simply recommended cleanliness, rest, and nourishing food.

Poor law doctors could actually write prescriptions for eggs or meat broth to build the strength of impoverished patients so their bodies could overcome disease.

Before the discovery of antibiotics and other specific chemical therapies, drugs did little to cure diseases. Even today many medicines simply control symptoms; cough syrup, for example, quiets a cough but does nothing to stop the cold or flu that causes it. Nineteenth-century medical practitioners used wine, narcotic drugs, and traditional herbal preparations to promote sleep and to relieve coughs, muscle cramps, nausea, and other troubling symptoms. Opium, which could be bought without a prescription, was dispensed by doctors and also used in patent medicines and homemade mixtures. Laudanum (a liquid solution of opium in alcohol) was a common sleeping medicine, painkiller, and cough suppressant. It also prevented loose bowels. Not until the end of the century did doctors begin warning about the dangers of addiction, although many well-known people who regularly took laudanum at bedtime recognized the need to increase their nightly dose as the years passed.

Since people did not usually see doctors except for serious illness, the primary means of medical care was self-diagnosis and self-dosing. Almanacs, household guides, home medical books, and magazine advice columns all provided *receipts* for mixtures that could be used for a wide variety of symptoms and ailments. The sale of drugs was completely unrestricted until 1868, and even after pharmacists began to be registered there were very few controls on dispensing. Heavily advertised proprietary (so-called patent) medicines were bought over the counter from grocers, chemists, and many other outlets. Products for treating menstrual problems were generally sold by mail. Some of them advertised with coded phrases to suggest they would cause abortion: "invaluable to married women, it removes all obstructions and restores regularity." Most patent medicines contained large amounts of

---

CRAMP AND SPASM

It frequently happens that persons are extremely annoyed by cramp during the night, which may be relieved by the following tincture:—
    Take of Tincture of opium, two drachms,
    Æther, half an ounce.
    Mix them together, and take thirty or forty drops every night at bedtime.

The New Family Receipt Book (London: John Murray, 1837).

alcohol. J. Collis Browne's Chlorodyne, advertised as a remedy for coughs, colds, diphtheria, cholera, epilepsy, rheumatism, cancer, and other ailments, contained morphine, chloral hydrate (once known as "knockout drops"), and cannabis, which is the active ingredient in marijuana and hashish.

Doctors continued to use bleeding as a medical treatment, although less frequently as the century went on. A patient was bled by opening a vein or putting leeches on the skin. In the absence of ice, leeches helped reduce swelling and inflammation. Drawing off blood made intuitive sense for symptoms caused by high blood pressure. It was also used, however, on patients who were weak and fevered, when it surely did more harm than good.

Patients who could afford it were often urged to have a change of air. This might be the best treatment for lung problems caused by urban pollution. In addition, since people had to leave their ordinary work or household routine and spend a few weeks at the seaside or in the mountains, "change of air" was probably as effective

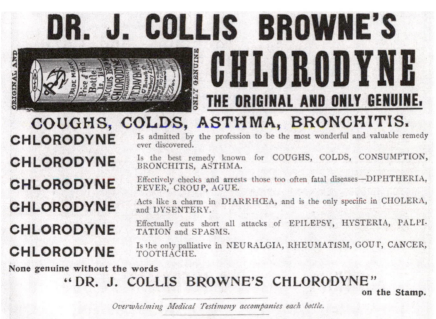

Patent medicines and other so-called cures for diseases of all sorts were widely advertised and sold in many places. Typically, as in the fine print near the bottom of this advertisement for Chlorodyne, "Overwhelming Medical Testimony accompanies each bottle."

as many twentieth-first-century prescriptions for stress-related illnesses. A similar function was served by visiting a spa or having special baths as part of a water cure.

The only field of medical treatment in which the Victorians made great strides—and learned to accomplish cures that were previously impossible—was surgery. At the beginning of the nineteenth century, with no anesthetics and no antibiotics, injuries that tore the skin almost inevitably became infected. A surgeon who was strong and quick could sometimes save a life by amputating a mangled limb and cauterizing the stump, but the death rate from shock, loss of blood, and infection was so high that voluntary operations were almost unthinkable.

Chloroform was successfully used to anesthetize patients in the late 1840s. At first patients were simply knocked out before the operation, but by the late 1850s anesthetists learned how to keep them safely unconscious, giving surgeons time for more delicate and careful work. But as the use of surgery increased, so did the danger of infection. Even before bacteria were discovered, surgeons understood the need for cleanliness and used agents such as chlorine for dressing wounds. Most postoperative complications came not from the doctor's dirty hands and instruments (although that myth remains in circulation) but through epidemics of *hospital fever* caused by staphylococcus and streptococcal bacteria.

Antiseptic surgery was originated by Joseph Lister in the late 1860s. Even though not all surgeons shared his conviction that bacteria were the cause of infection, by the 1890s it was customary for surgeons to scrub their hands and boil their instruments. Both mother and child sometimes survived a Caesarean section, previously used only in heroic attempts to save the infant of a woman who was already dead or dying. Specialists could perform skin grafts, repair orthopedic defects such as clubfoot, remove ovarian cysts, and do appendectomies. Surgeons—who had been very low-ranking members of the medical profession at the beginning of the century—were becoming its most skilled and respected practitioners by 1900.

Hospitals

Hospitals had initially been established to care for the sick poor. By Victorian times, paupers went to the workhouse infirmary, where they were seen by a paid doctor and nursed by other paupers. Later in the century, towns and cities built separate poor law hospitals that provided acute care for destitute people, served as nursing homes for the chronically ill, and had an accident ward for emergency cases.

Outside the workhouse system, most hospitals were charitable institutions supported by landowners, industrialists, and philanthropists for treating the respectable working class. The people who raised money for a hospital had the right to nominate its patients. A sick or injured person got a recommendation (often called a *vote*) from one of the subscribers. A clergyman, an employer, or the squire's family were likely to have votes available. Patients might be charged a small fee for meals and bed linens, although the medical care was free. The charitable foundation paid only a small salary to doctors, but being on the staff of a respected hospital was a good way for a young medical man to build his reputation and acquire private patients.

During the nineteenth century, hospitals (and the patients in them) became increasingly important for training medical practitioners. A few medical schools built teaching hospitals. In many other places, staff doctors had paying pupils who needed hospital experience before their licensing examination. Surgeons in the leading London hospitals could demand indenture fees as high as £1,000 for taking an apprentice.

Middle-class and upper-class people were treated at home. Family and servants did most of the nursing. Until the final years of the century, even surgery was done at home whenever possible. Keeping a hospital ward visibly clean was an important duty of the nursing staff, but until bacteria were understood there were no heavy-duty germicides in use.

Special *fever hospitals* were set up in temporary quarters during an epidemic. (Several early nursing administrators were middle-class women who gained experience as volunteers supervising a local fever hospital during one of the cholera epidemics.) As interest in medical research grew, some specialized hospitals were established. Philanthropist Angela Burdett-Coutts built the Brompton Cancer Hospital in the 1850s. Children's hospitals became an especially popular charity.

In addition, the treatment of mental illness grew more humane. Specialists created diagnostic labels to describe conditions that can be recognized under other names in current psychiatric literature: *melancholia* (severe depression), *monomania* (obsessive-compulsive disorders), *mania* (schizophrenia). The term *partial insanity* was used for hysteria, hypochondria, and other neurotic states. Legislation

The drawing of a ward in the Hampstead Smallpox Hospital shows that by 1871 hospitals for contagious diseases were well ventilated. Courtesy of The Granger Collection, New York.

and public opinion slowly came to recognize insanity as a medical condition rather than a moral disorder. New mental hospitals had pleasant surroundings and opportunities for outdoor exercise. A good private asylum kept people from harming themselves and others through careful separation and constant supervision instead of putting patients in straightjackets or keeping them chained to the wall. For some conditions such as depression (which often ends in spontaneous remission) the new treatment seemed to provide a high rate of cure, since it kept patients healthy until they felt better.

PUBLIC HEALTH

The most significant Victorian medical achievement lay not in individual treatments or the discovery of cures but through legislating effective measures for public health. By 1837, it seemed evident that urban people were sickly. Popular images contrasted the tall, sturdy countryman to the stooped and feeble city dweller. Diseases of all sorts swept out of crowded slum neighborhoods into the dwellings of the well-to do. After the New Poor Law went into operation, the physical condition of the rural poor also attracted notice. Edwin Chadwick's *Report on the Sanitary Condition of the Labouring Population,* published in 1842, was the first comprehensive investigation of the people's health.

Chadwick's work was supplemented by accurate statistics that could be developed once civil registration of births and deaths became compulsory in 1837. By the middle 1840s, reputable numbers could demonstrate that poor drainage, inadequate water supplies, and overcrowded housing were related to increased rates of serious illness and early death. Edwin Chadwick also argued persuasively that poor health was the primary cause of poverty.

As a consequence of these investigations, the Public Health Act of 1848 created agencies that began many new programs. Over the next 30 years sewers were built, pure water was supplied, slaughterhouses were moved away from city centers. Overcrowded city churchyards were closed to burials; new cemeteries were located away from heavily populated areas. The tax on soap was abolished. Standards of purity were applied to food products. Building codes required ventilation and reduced overcrowding. Factory inspectors began to study occupational diseases. Towns were required to provide regular garbage collection. School health examinations were

---

PUBLIC HEALTH REPORT OF 1842: CONCLUSIONS

That the various forms of epidemic, endemic, and other disease caused, or aggravated, or propagated chiefly amongst the labouring classes by atmospheric impurities produced by decomposing animal and vegetable substances, by damp and filth, and close and overcrowded dwellings prevail amongst the population in every part of the kingdom, whether dwelling in separate houses, in rural villages, in small towns, in the larger towns—as they have been found to prevail in the lowest districts of the metropolis.

That such disease, wherever its attacks are frequent, is always found in connexion with the physical circumstances above specified, and that where those circumstances are removed by drainage, proper cleansing, better ventilation, and other means of diminishing atmospheric impurity, the frequency and intensity of such disease is abated; and where the removal of the noxious agencies appears to be complete, such disease almost entirely disappears.

Edwin Chadwick, *The Report on the Sanitary Condition of the Labouring Population* (London: HMSO, 1842).

begun. Public baths and laundries supplied space and hot water for people to wash themselves and their clothes.

The diseases that had been spread by contaminated food and water significantly diminished. Cholera ceased to be a problem after the epidemic of 1866–1867. Summer diarrhea killed fewer children and elderly people. Even viral and bacterial diseases, such as scarlet fever and tuberculosis, grew less deadly when overcrowding and malnutrition were no longer the ordinary condition of life among the poor. Although public health investigations at the end of the century still found much to criticize, people on the average lived longer and were in better physical condition than they had been in 1837.

10

LEISURE AND PLEASURE: HOLIDAYS, SPORTS, AND RECREATION

This chapter merely samples the many ways Victorians spent their free time. Books, magazines, games, crafts, hobbies, and music occupied family evenings at home. Traditional celebrations lingered in the countryside; public entertainments multiplied in town. As working hours got shorter and new holidays were created, most people had more free time. Museums, clubs, and youth organizations encouraged constructive recreation. Railways brought families to the seashore. Sports were organized, commercialized, and professionalized. The leisure patterns of a mass society took shape.

HOLIDAYS

Traditional Celebrations

Preindustrial workers lived by the rhythms of an agricultural year. Some traditional rural customs vanished during the nineteenth century, but others were transformed: their disruptive pagan elements became more modest. Whereas the older May Day rituals built up to dancing in the fields and a night of sexual liberty, the Victorians "tamed" the holiday and made it into a children's festival, with young girls in white dresses decorating a Maypole in front of the church. Guy Fawkes bonfires (on November 5) and

Christmas mumming (in which elaborately disguised men and boys performed plays featuring sword fights or mock battles) also survived, but in less rowdy forms that previously.

Many formerly popular country sports came to an end because Victorian reformers perceived their cruelty. Badger-baiting (setting terriers on a penned badger), bull-baiting, and cock-fighting were outlawed. A form of football once played on Shrove Tuesday pitted whole villages against each other with few rules and no tactics: the game was a mob shoving bout that often led to a riot. Squires and clergymen turned their energy to arranging village sports competitions with organized teams and rules that would keep things from getting out of hand.

In Lancashire and some other areas, traditional wakes involved feasting and games on a summertime saints' day. Whitsun (the seventh Sunday after Easter) was often a two-day festival. By 1800, although some parish fêtes survived, the wakes became a short summer holiday. Mills closed down; machines were cleaned and repaired while mill hands went off in groups to the seashore. Working-class Londoners enjoyed a late summer excursion by taking the whole family into Kent and camping out in the fields while everyone earned money by picking hops.

The local public house *(pub)* was the center of most workingmen's recreation. During the nineteenth century, the cramped drinking space in an individual householder's front room was increasingly replaced by grand new premises. In addition to the public bar (which served as living room and meeting room for men from the neighborhood), there might be a separate room for billiards and darts, a reading room with newspapers, and a parlour where women and children could get refreshments.

In 1841, the only holidays for banking and government workers were Christmas Day and Good Friday. Later, the Bank Holiday Act of 1871 added the day after Christmas, the last Monday in May, and the first Monday in August. Other employers soon followed suit. The two summer Mondays—not linked to any religious or patriotic celebration—made long weekends for outdoor fun. Clubs and Sunday schools hired wagonettes for group excursions; families made quick railway trips to the seashore. Mothering Sunday (the fourth Sunday in Lent) had by custom been a day when young servants were given extra time to go home for a visit. Boarding schools picked up the idea and created a spring break for that week, although Mothering Sunday did not become commercialized as Mother's Day until the twentieth century.

Christmas

The most significant change in holidays was the Victorian transformation of Christmas. Since the seventeenth century, Christmas
had been a simple religious holiday for most respectable people,
although old traditions such as the Yule log and mummers' plays
survived in some places. Families who exchanged gifts at any time
during the winter season did it New Year's Day.

Prince Albert brought the German custom of decorating a Christmas tree to the family celebrations at Windsor. Christmas cards
grew popular after the penny post was established in 1840. By
the 1860s, the middle-class English Christmas had taken shape.
From late November, luxury goods filled shop windows and book-
sellers displayed piles of Christmas books and holiday annuals,
which were a kind of gift book with poems, stories, and handsome
illustrations. Grocers heaped their shelves with fruits, nuts, and
sweets. Soon the geese and turkeys hung in the chilly air outside
the butcher shops. Working people saved for their holiday meal by
putting a few pence every week into a Christmas club at a pub or
local market; if they had no oven, the goose would be cooked at the
baker's shop.

The Christmas pudding had to be made several days in advance.
Mrs. Beeton's recipe calls for raisins, currants, mixed peel, bread-
crumbs, suet, eggs, and brandy. A silver threepenny piece and sometimes other charms were hidden in the pudding. Every member of
the family took a turn at stirring the batter. Then it was pressed into
a buttered mold, tied into a cloth, boiled for six hours, and hung up
in the kitchen to age.

Christmas Eve was for carols and family gatherings. After the children went to bed, their presents were arranged by the tree and their
stockings were filled with nuts, an orange, chocolates, and a small
gift or two. On Christmas Day, after children had their stockings,
many families went to church and did some act of charity—taking
food to a poor family or distributing gifts in a children's hospital.

The traditional Christmas dinner was roast goose, with potatoes,
applesauce, and other side dishes. (Turkey was more expensive.) At
each person's place was an English Christmas *cracker*—a cardboard
tube covered in crepe paper or tissue paper tied at the ends. When
the ends were pulled, the cracker opened with a pop and spilled
out candies, small favors, and a paper hat. As climax to the meal,
brandy was poured over the pudding and lighted; the flaming pudding was carried to the table. After it was served (with sweet custard

or hard sauce) the hidden charms engaged everyone's attention. Who would get the ring and marry during the year? Who would find the silver piece and become rich, or the button and remain a bachelor?

The day after Christmas was known as Boxing Day because coins or boxes of castoff clothing were traditionally distributed to the poor. In Victorian times, it became a servants' holiday. Domestic servants who lived nearby went home for a visit; their employers ate leftovers and recovered from Christmas dinner. Other families organized a treat or party; in some large houses there was a servants' ball. City dwellers gave tips to the lamplighter and postman and delivery boys; in the country, landowners sent game to their tenants and sponsored a treat for the parish Sunday school.

Another new Christmas tradition involved a family visit to the pantomimes that began their annual run on Boxing Day. In its Victorian form, the pantomime was a musical revue with elaborate production numbers. Its plot was loosely based on a fairy tale or other familiar story such as "Dick Whittington" or "Aladdin." The *principal boy* was played by an attractive actress (in tights and a tunic that showed off her legs) and the role of *dame* (the stepmother or wicked witch) was always played by a man, usually a well-known comedian. By the century's end, the pantomime had become a principal source of income for theaters and a magical family outing enjoyed by people of virtually every social class.

Seaside Excursions

As rail travel simplified access to coastal resorts, summertime trips to the seashore became popular. Middle-class London workers went to southern coastal towns such as Ramsgate, Deal, Bexhill, Shoreham, Hastings, Worthing, and especially Brighton. The family took lodgings in a boardinghouse that provided room and meals. During the week, mother and children enjoyed walks along the shore, donkey rides, bathing, band concerts, and puppet shows. Father appeared on weekends and for the one or two weeks of his vacation from work.

A bathing machine was a small wooden shelter on wheels that was pulled out beyond the surf by a horse or donkey until the water was almost up to the floor. The machine provided a place to undress, a sort of private dock from which to swim, and a safe place for nonswimmers to dip into the water. In the *Punch* cartoon, the

As seen in this *Punch* cartoon, bathing machines provided privacy for changing clothes and a platform for entering the water.

woman wearing a bonnet and dress, who is dunking an unhappy baby into the cold sea water, is the bathing machine's operator.

Seaside towns in Lancashire and Yorkshire specialized in day or weekend visits by factory hands. Blackpool was the most popular workers' resort. Piers that extended out into the sea were constructed starting in the 1850s; they provided not only a place for pleasure boats to land but also a promenade and space for amusements: games, rides, fortunetellers, kiosks for food and drink, shops selling inexpensive souvenirs and slightly risqué postcards.

SPORTS AND OUTDOOR GAMES

The Victorians made a distinction between sports (which were serious, manly, competitive) and games (which were playful activities shared with women and children). Both were extremely popular. Croquet, which appeared in the middle 1850s, could be played on suburban lawns or country estates by people of vastly mixed ages and abilities. Other outdoor pastimes, including skating, archery, and lawn tennis, gave young women and young men opportunities to exercise, socialize, and flirt. Bicycling, at the end of the period, was both a popular recreation and an affordable and liberating means of transportation.

Although some sports (e.g., sailing and foxhunting) were only for the wealthy, men educated at public schools had been taught that sports were essential to health and discipline. Because these men realized that regulated competition could promote public order, they sponsored amateur clubs, village teams, factory tournaments, and religious organizations that provided training and competition for boys and men from the working class. Central bodies standardized playing fields and published rules. In the second half of the century, the shortened working week combined with inexpensive rail transportation to permit the development of professional spectator sports.

Upper-Class Country Sports

For the upper classes, riding was more often a pleasure than a means of going somewhere. Invalids and older people took *carriage exercise* daily for fresh air. Ladies rode sidesaddle. (A sidesaddle is designed so the rider hooks her right leg around a prong at its front.) With a well-made saddle, a practiced rider was secure enough to race across country, jumping fences and streams as she went. Riding habits had a tailored jacket and long skirt, with no bustles or crinolines or elaborate trimmings.

Hunting meant foxhunting, a sporting and social ritual through which aristocracy, gentry, clergy, professional men, and substantial farmers developed local bonds. The season began in November and ended when frozen ground became dangerous for horses. Hunts were informally organized into *countries* so that each had its own territory. The hunt maintained a pack of hounds, generally through subscriptions paid by its members, although some wealthy men kept their own packs. It is actually the dogs that do the hunting: hounds chase and kill the fox; riders follow on horseback to watch. The excitement is in the chase. The fox and hounds pick the route; the riders rush headlong after them across fields, through patches of brush, over walls and fences, across streams.

Hunting required weekday leisure in winter and enough money to keep good horses. As rail service improved, some wealthy city men spent weekends in hunt country, but the core of the tradition rested with aristocrats and squires. From the 1860s onward, increasing numbers of women rode to the hounds. Farmers who hunted usually wore green rather than gentlemen's scarlet. Hunt clubs sponsored an elaborate social life of breakfasts, dinners, balls, and races. Foxhunting traditions were seen as the glue that bonded county society and reaffirmed the value of horsemanship as a sign of manliness and leadership. Polo, which Englishmen in India learned to play during the 1850s, remained a sport for the very rich, since it required keeping several horses and transporting them to matches.

Shooting was strictly regulated by the game laws and therefore was limited to landowners and their guests. Shooting parties were arranged for early autumn. Servants acting as drivers flushed the birds and drove them toward the gentlemen with guns. The day's success was measured by the number of birds killed, which could run into hundreds and even thousands. The excess would be sold in expensive London shops, because even a large houseparty could not eat hundreds of pheasants and partridges before they went bad.

Organized Games and Sports

Sports at English public schools and universities developed the manly code of character: team spirit, loyalty, a so-called stiff upper lip unmoved by triumph, defeat, or pain. Men who took part in matches between Oxford and Cambridge earned a *blue* (the equivalent of a letter in U.S. school sports). Originally a ribbon, it was dark blue at Oxford and light blue at Cambridge. The Oxford-Cambridge boat race, a competition between eight-man crews, took place in late March or early April. The Henley Regatta, during the first week in July, was first held in 1839. In addition to being a major outdoor event of the London social season, Henley was an occasion for serious competition between club, school, and university crews.

Most of the sports that became central to twentieth-century international competition were codified and professionalized in England during the 1800s. The game that the rest of the world calls football (known as *soccer* in the United States) was standardized between 1840 and 1860. Men from various public schools created a set of uniform rules in 1848 so they could play against each other (or play on the same college or army team) without constant disagreements. Local football clubs not connected with any school were formed, and before long some of them had paid players.

The first fully professional teams developed in the 1860s. The Football Association, founded in 1863, initially regulated competition for both amateurs and professionals. As the work week grew shorter and railways made it easier for large crowds to attend games, the professional clubs built their own grounds and charged admission. With the formation of the Football League in 1885, the structure of football as a professional spectator sport attained virtually its modern form.

Rugby football grew out of a disagreement over the Football Association's rules. Men from some public schools (including Rugby) where the ball could be handled as well as kicked refused to accept the newly codified form of the game. They also did not like it when working-class professionals were allowed to join the gentlemanly amateur clubs where grown-up schoolboys continued to play games. Thus although Rugby is far more violent than soccer, it remained throughout most of the nineteenth century essentially an amateur sport for aristocrats and the gentry.

VITAI LAMPADA (HENRY NEWBOLT)

Newbolt's 1898 poem crystallizes the belief that English manliness and imperial success were built on the playing fields of the great public schools. The title may be translated as "Torches of Life"—familiarity with Latin is another hallmark of a gentleman's public-school training.

There's a breathless hush in the Close tonight—
Ten to make and the match to win—
A bumping pitch and a blinding light,
An hour to play and the last man in.
And it's not for the sake of a ribboned coat,
Or the selfish hope of a season's fame,
But his Captain's hand on his shoulder smote—
"Play Up! play up! and play the game!"

The sand of the desert is sodden red—
Red with the wreck of a square that broke;
The Gatling's jammed and the Colonel dead,
And the Regiment blind with dust and smoke.
The river of death has brimmed his banks,
And England's far and Honour's a name,
But the voice of a schoolboy rallies the ranks:
"Play Up! play up! and play the game!"

This is the word that year by year,
While in her place the School is set,
Every one of her sons must hear,
And none that hears it dare forget.
This they all with a joyful mind
Bear through life like a torch in flame,
And falling fling to the host behind—
"Play Up! play up! and play the game!"

Cricket was played in public schools, at universities, and by village and country-house teams formed when young men home for the summer recruited local boys to join them for games. (Cricket requires 11 players on each side.) County clubs emerged in the 1860s. They were made up of *gentlemen* and *players*; that is, they combined local amateurs with a few working-class men hired for their athletic skill. The pay was originally intended simply to make up the wages a man lost when he stayed away from work for a match which could last several days.

Cricket is played on a roughly oval ground that can vary in size. The game's most important field, Lord's (in London), is 180 yards long and 140 yards wide. (Nineteenth-century matches also took place on military parade grounds, village greens, local pastures, and other open spaces.) Two wickets are placed 22 yards apart along the center line of the oval. Each wicket is made of three stakes (or stumps) 28 inches high, which are stuck into the ground with two wooden sticks (called *bails*) balanced in grooves along the top. One team of 11 players is spread around the field, while one batsman from the other team takes up a position in front of each wicket. The ball is bowled alternately a certain number of times (it varies with the level of play) from a position behind one wicket towards the batsman who defends the other wicket.

The object for the bowler (i.e., pitcher) is to dislodge the bail from its position on top of the wicket. When he does so, the batter is out. The object for the batter is (1) to protect the wicket and (2) to hit the ball hard enough so he can score a run by reaching the other wicket before the ball is fielded and thrown back into play. (When one batter hits the ball, both must run; they change positions at the wickets.) As many as six runs can be scored on one hit. There are many subtleties in fielding and scoring; in essence, one innings lasts until 10 batsmen have been put out, and the game is won by the side with the highest total number of runs.

The county championship in cricket (which is still being held) was regularized in 1873, and the test matches between England and Australia (which serve as cricket's world championship) began in the 1880s. Some school matches—especially the one between Eton and Harrow—were also crucial dates in the athletic year. Cricket takes a long time to play; matches may be spread over several days. Except at the highest levels of professional competition, spectators are as much engaged by the summer sunshine, the conversation, and the refreshment tent as they are by the action.

A picture advertising the book *Outdoor Games and Recreations for Boys,* which was published in the 1890s, shows a boy jumping over a hurdle and a cricket player standing in front of the wicket in batting position.

Tennis, once an indoor game for royalty, was revived by the Victorians as a family pastime for people with large enough lawns. The net was higher than it is now and the racquets more like those used for badminton. Both serves and volleys were done in a gentle underhand. As the game grew popular, people with no lawns banded together to build suburban tennis clubs. Good players came to appreciate the smoother, standardized club courts. The All-England Lawn Tennis and Croquet Club, founded in 1869, became the governing body of tennis and began organizing championship tournaments at its grounds in Wimbledon in 1877.

England's Amateur Athletic Association was founded in 1880 to organize university and club championships in athletics (usually called *track and field* in the United States). Athletic contests were strongly promoted by public schools and the military; because many events required little space and no equipment, they were also popular at factory outings and country fairs. Some elementary schools had an annual sports day with footraces and jumping contests.

In addition to sponsoring meets, the Amateur Athletic Association standardized events, kept records, and played a leading role in organizing the first modern Olympic competition in 1896. Records from that event show the difference made by training, equipment, and improved general health during the past hundred years. The 100-meter dash that opened the 1896 Olympics was won in a time of 12.5 seconds. The marathon was completed in 2 hours 58 minutes, and the winning high jump was 5 feet 11 1/4 inches. By the mid-1990s, a good marathon time was 2 hours 12 minutes, and high-school boys could do a 7-foot high jump and a 10.8-second 100-meter dash.

Horse racing, unlike most sports, was already well established before the nineteenth century began, but official regulation was consolidated when the Jockey Club became the governing body for British racing in the 1860s. Races were held more often because horses could be moved by rail instead of walking from course to course. In the 1870s, race courses were enclosed and stands built.

Special bank holiday fares toward the end of the century brought enormous crowds to racetracks. Like certain other traditional pastimes, racing was patronized chiefly by aristocrats and working men; few among the middle classes and very few respectable women went to the races. The four-day meeting at Ascot in June, however, was a central feature of the social season, attended by upper-class women and men wearing their most elegant summer clothes.

The Derby, a race for three-year-old horses, is run at Epsom Downs in Surrey in late May or early June. Derby Day was an unofficial public holiday in the nineteenth century. Even Parliament suspended business. There was as much activity outside the race course as on it; many people came primarily for the sideshows, food, and general excitement. The Grand National Steeplechase (a race for hunters, with a variety of hurdles, ditches, and other jumps) was first run at Aintree near Liverpool in 1839.

Racetrack and offtrack betting were commercialized in the Victorian period. (Individuals have presumably always made private bets with friends.) When professional bookmakers opened city offices, many people who seldom went to the track made regular bets and followed the racing papers. Telegraph connections enabled major bookmakers to post results almost instantly. Like racing itself, betting on the races was not a respectable thing for women or middle-class men to do.

Boxing also united men of the aristocracy and lower classes while excluding almost everyone else. The brutal bare-knuckle sport—which gave spectators a chance to lay bets on a battle that lasted until one of the fighters could not stand up—was modernized with rules endorsed by the Marquess of Queensberry in 1867. Boxers were required to wear padded gloves; matches ended if one fighter could not rise unaided after a count of 10. The Amateur Boxing Association was founded in 1880. Weight classes were set up towards the end of the century; the first heavyweight championship fight, in 1892, matched James L. Corbett and John L. Sullivan.

Athletic Pastimes for Women

Healthy outdoor activities were never completely out of fashion among well-to-do women. Country ladies with horses rode daily; a groom went along if they used public roads. Long walks before breakfast or after lunch were customary. At midcentury, mixed-sex pastimes such as croquet, archery, tennis, and ice skating grew popular. Suburban tennis clubs and subscription skating rinks allowed middle-class women to participate. In these protected spaces, young women and young men could safely share public activities without scandal.

Other women's sports developed along with the reforms in girls' education. As they adapted boys' public schooling to educate girls, teachers recognized that games developed healthy bodies, provided outlets for adolescent energy, and promoted teamwork and sportsmanship. Rules were somewhat modified; girls played cricket, for example, with a softer ball. By the end of the century, field hockey was the most popular sport for girls' inter-school and intercollegiate competition, although matches were also held in lacrosse, golf, archery, fencing, tennis, and netball (an outdoor form of basketball).

Some women (like men) joined local clubs to continue playing sports they had learned at school. There were even a few short-lived professional organizations such as the Original English Lady Cricketers (formed by a male promoter in 1890). However, most women's athletics outside of school took the form of individual sports that required time, space, and equipment—and were therefore primarily for the well-to-do. The earliest women's sport added to the Olympics—for the second modern games in, 1900—was golf.

Swimming was somewhat more accessible. Seaside swimming (usually called *bathing*) primarily involved wading and playing in the water. Men and boys who actually swam in the ocean (and in rivers or lakes) generally did it in the nude; the deep pools and other spots suitable for swimming were therefore (informally) off-limits to women. When washing and bathing facilities were built in the interests of public health, they often included a *plunge bath* or swimming pool. Private clubs also built pools. In response to pressure by women activists, both public and private facilities established special hours when men were excluded, and magazines for girls and women started promoting regular year-round swimming for health.

Gymnastics was another common exercise in schools and clubs. The term covered many varieties of disciplined body movement.

Girls exercising under the watchful eye of their teacher (to the right) use several varieties of equipment and wear typical girls' *gymnasium costumes* for the 1890s.

Drill included exercises with hoops and Indian clubs, as well as routines of the sort now included in aerobic dance. Illustrations of school gymnasiums show girls swinging on ropes, climbing poles, vaulting over horses, walking on balance beams, skipping rope, and doing other exercises individually or in groups.

Women's greatest athletic passion was aroused in the 1890s, by the bicycle. The word was first used in 1868 for high-wheel *penny-farthing* cycles. Some expensive three-wheel and four-wheel foot-powered machines were used by women (and older men) in the 1870s and 1880s; doctors recommend them as gentle exercise for patients who could not ride horseback. The breakthrough came with

A poster advertising Rover bicycles suggests the wonderful new freedoms made possible during the 1890s with the introduction of inexpensive safety bicycles. Courtesy of The Art Archive/Musee d'Art et d'Industrie Saint-Etienne/Gianni Dagli Orti.

the equal-sized wheels and chain drive of safety bicycles, invented in 1885 and improved a few years later with pneumatic tires.

Bicycling blossomed as an enormous fad in the mid-1890s. Bicycle clubs sprang up. Working-girls' newspapers advertised factory-refurbished second-hand cycles for £1, which could be paid in installments. Illustrated articles in better periodicals followed the adventures of women students who spent two-week holidays touring Cornwall or Norfolk by wheel. In addition to providing healthy recreation, bicycles became workaday transportation for schoolteachers, nurses, and shop workers and brought a heady new independence to many young women.

PUBLIC AND GROUP PLEASURES

Music

Making as well as hearing music was more a part of Victorian daily life than of modern-day life. Schoolchildren of all classes were

Young women practice on the piano and violin in a relatively modest middle-class parlor, as illustrated in *The Girl's Own Paper,* July 17, 1886.

trained to sing. Traditional folksongs and country dances still flourished in rural areas. Hymns were important to most religious services; many churches had several different choirs as well as hearty congregational singing.

Playing the piano was an essential accomplishment for young ladies—and many middle-class and upper-class women who were forced to practice for an hour a day through childhood developed an abiding pleasure in playing. Inexpensive upright pianos were available for middle-class homes. There was a healthy commercial trade in sheet music, and magazines printed reviews to let readers know what music was available and how difficult it was to play. Music was a part of most social gatherings. Wealthy people hired professionals or issued special invitations to talented amateurs; middle-class and working-class people were expected to bring sheet music along when they went to a party. Workers who could not afford a cottage piano included someone with a fiddle.

Organized musical groups were sponsored by employers, trade unions, churches, and Nonconformist chapels. Most towns had at least one brass band; in some places every factory had one. Bands held competitions at which they played dance tunes, military marches, and special arrangements of flashy orchestral pieces. Oratorio societies also flourished. Choral singing was especially popular among the working class. There were vast festivals at which dozens of choirs competed. Finally, as a triumphant conclusion, thousands of singers joined in a performance of Handel's "Hallelujah Chorus."

Most social dancing early in the period was in the form of folkdances, reels, and other figures through which couples moved while barely touching hands. The waltz, introduced at the beginning of the nineteenth century, was somewhat disreputable because the partners held each other. Its reputation soared, however, when Queen Victoria and Prince Albert—who were not yet married—danced a waltz together at the coronation ball.

In the upper classes, young children of both sexes had dancing lessons. After the boys went to school, girls continued their instruction. Either a teacher came to the house once or twice a week, or a servant walked the girls to a dancing class attended by others in the same social circle. Dancing was considered not only an essential skill but also a way to acquire graceful movements and an upright posture.

Adult women and men danced at private balls and at dancing parties in middle-class houses: the furniture was pushed back, the carpet rolled up, and a professional pianist or an accommodating friend was engaged to provide the music. Semiprivate balls were sponsored by hunt clubs, military regiments, and organizations whose members paid subscriptions to support a monthly or quarterly dance. Promenade concerts at pavilions in seaside towns provided summer visitors a respectable opportunity for dancing. The tea dance, introduced in 1845, was an afternoon event with a small band of strings and piano. Working people danced to fiddle music in barns and in the open air, as well as at taverns.

When the gentry and upper classes had houseparties, they often engaged in private theatricals, charades (acting out a word), and *tableaux vivants,* in which people dressed up to represent a painting or a famous historical moment. The fun was in the preparation, the dressing up, and the joke of having (for example) a young man with a luxuriant moustache put on a gown and veil to portray a seductive woman.

Shows and Theaters

The paid entertainments available in cities varied greatly in respectability and popularity. Pleasure gardens such as Vauxhall and Cremorne, in London, were past their heyday but still drew visitors at midcentury. After paying an admission fee, people strolled through carefully planted outdoor vistas and listened to bands and singers. Light (and expensive) meals were available—and probably provided most of the owners' profit.

Organ grinders (with a monkey to pass the cup), jugglers, and other performers attracted crowds in working-class neighborhoods and at the seashore. They also moved through better parts of town playing loud music to draw children and young servants outdoors. The traditional English "Punch and Judy," a small puppet show (often operated by one person) that mocked authority figures and featured a lot of slapstick brutality between husband and wife, was primarily a working-class entertainment, although other children and adults allowed themselves to enjoy it on amusement piers or in parks during the summertime.

Shows that were most acceptable in the middle of the century had an educational pretext. People paid admission to see models of battlefields and panoramic paintings with lights and moving panels that gave the sensation of being part of a shipwreck or fire. Some dioramas of exotic places had living people on exhibit as if they were animals in a zoo: Ojibways in a Native American scene,

Mexicans on Aztec ruin, Bushmen in the African veldt. Private menageries drew large crowds; the London Zoological Gardens had opened in Regent's Park in 1828. Madame Tussaud established a permanent London site in Baker Street in 1835 after showing her waxwork models of famous people for several years in the provinces.

The most popular commercial entertainment in the late nineteenth century was the music hall. Most of the audience were men from the working and lower middle classes. Music halls (like vaudeville in the United States) featured a mix of singers, dancers, acrobats, animal trainers, and comic acts. The entertainment originated in pubs that provided a few acts to lure in customers and made their profit from selling drinks. By the 1880s, special halls had been built. One distinctive music-hall genre was the comic song performed with broad gestures and winks that suggested a series of double meanings. Women dressed as men and parodied the seductive style of young bucks; male comics appeared as bawdy old women. By the 1890s, an evening at a music hall usually closed with rousing finale of patriotic songs.

For people in the upper class, the opera was a feature of London's social season. Other theatrical performances grew more popular and respectable during the Victorian period. Early in the century, aristocratic young men had populated the expensive seats, but many among the middle class still found the theater disreputable. Promoters tried to draw in customers by putting on long mixed programs: a farce, a drastically condensed Shakespearean play, and a melodramatic extravaganza that required elaborate machinery to depict a naval battle, a runaway stagecoach, or some other thrilling display on the stage.

During the first year of Victoria's reign, Charles Macready began winning middle-class audiences back to the theater with carefully staged (and more nearly complete) Shakespearean dramas. Several generations of accomplished actors (including Charles Kean, Ellen Tree, Fanny Kemble, Henry Irving, Mrs. Patrick Campbell, and Ellen Terry) built reputations as admired public figures. In the 1860s, Marie Wilton and her husband introduced the box set and detailed staging for domestic dramas that became increasingly more realistic, and a new genre of English comedy also developed. Richard D'Oyly Carte built the Savoy Theatre (the first to use electric lighting) in 1881 for the operettas of W. S. Gilbert and Arthur Sullivan. In addition to London performances, provincial and touring companies drew healthy audiences in all parts of the country.

Because of its emphasis on educational recreation, the Victorian period was particularly notable for building museums and galleries. The Victoria and Albert Museum in South Kensington established working collections that were intended to help designers improve the artistic quality of handcrafted and manufactured goods. The National Gallery's fine art went on display in its building on Trafalgar Square in 1838. The British Museum in Bloomsbury (founded in the eighteenth century) was overwhelmed with visitors on holidays: between forty and fifty thousand people on Boxing Day in 1853, for example. Other cities established their own museums, and some important private art collections were bequeathed to the nation.

Most of these institutions had limited public access, with free general admission on only a few days each year. The rest of the time, uncrowded galleries were available to registered students, wealthy contributors, and members of sponsoring organizations. Class-based questions about vandalism, rowdiness, safety, and "disrespect" were regularly debated. Sunday opening was particularly troublesome. One faction felt strongly that secular institutions should be closed on the Lord's Day. Another argued that working people wanted and needed access to the elevating recreation provided by viewing fine art and historical artifacts, and that Sunday was the only day they were able to come. By the end of the century, free admissions and Sunday museum openings were fairly widespread.

PRIVATE AND FAMILY PASTIMES

Children's Play

Working-class children played with whatever was available at little or no expense: homemade dolls, simple noisemakers, outdoor running and chasing and hiding games. Older girls taught little children "London Bridge" and "Here We Go Round the Mulberry Bush." Purchased toys such as a top or a rubber ball were special treats brought home from a fair or put into a Christmas stocking.

The toys of children in more comfortable circumstances were also fairly simple at the beginning of the period: balls, marbles, tops, wooden soldiers, hand puppets. Often the only toy allowed on Sundays was a Noah's Ark with some wooden animals. A hobby horse was a wooden horse-head on a stick; a child straddled the stick and galloped around pretending to be horse or rider (or both). More elaborate nurseries might have a rocking horse and a toy castle.

Inexpensive paint boxes were available. Surviving evidence shows that some children applied watercolors to the black-and-white woodcuts in their books and magazines.

An extensive trade in commercial toys developed during the century. Several factors helped it grow: new printing technologies; mass production of metal toys; an expanding middle class, which supported a longer childhood, more money to spend, and more attention to children's pleasures. Elaborately dressed baby dolls and fashion dolls with real hair and a trunk full of clothes crowned toyshop windows at Christmas, but attractive and inexpensive dolls' heads were also for sale. Girls' magazines ran holiday contests for readers who made and dressed dolls for the local children's home.

Iron or stamped-tin toys included working boats and railways as well as simpler machines, cap-pistols, swords, and helmets. There were elaborate dollhouses with metal kitchenware. Tin tea sets were more practical than china (although some china doll dishes also survive). Magic lanterns with slides projected pictures on the wall. Toy theaters had scenery and paper characters for acting out familiar stories. Jigsaw puzzles and high-quality wooden toys were imported from Germany. Wagons, tricycles, and other wheeled vehicles became more common toward the end of the century.

Most memoirs about nineteenth-century childhood were written by people who grew up in fairly comfortable families. They record a great deal of imaginative play: acting, storytelling, secret rituals, pretend adventures searching for the hidden treasures of Africa in the back garden. Boys and girls of varying ages played in large groups, especially during summer holidays and when families of cousins got together. Books and almanacs gave instructions for cats' cradle, dominoes, musical chairs, noughts and crosses (called *tic-tac-toe* in the United States), blind-man's buff, stoop ball, and draughts (checkers).

Hobbies and Crafts

Girls were told that their hands should never be idle. When not doing something else, women felt they should be busy at needlework. Those who had servants to sew and mend the family clothing occupied their time with embroidery, tatting, crochet, fancy knitting, and other needle crafts. Many contemporary hobbyists treasure the storehouse of stitches, patterns, and ideas found in Victorian needlework manuals and women's magazines.

Two styles of embroidery were especially popular: Berlin work and white-on-white embroidery. Berlin work made use of bright strands of wool for counted-thread designs. Although it resembles the work now called *needlepoint* or *petit point*, high-quality Berlin work used a wide variety of stitches in addition to cross-stitch and filling stitch. Most Berlin work was purely decorative. Scenic pictures were framed to hang on the wall or used as fire screens. Bell-pulls, eyeglass cases, dresser tidies, cushions, protective shoe-cases, watch-fobs, and similar items were made for Christmas gifts.

White-on-white embroidery, which could be combined with cut-work and sometimes with fine beading, was used to decorate baby clothing and household linens. Many women who could afford to have a dressmaker nevertheless made (and embroidered) their own underclothing and their babies' best dresses. William Morris and his daughter May Morris revived interest in traditional English crewel. For the devout, church needlework was a satisfying occupation. Published instruction manuals helped women of the congregation produce kneelers, vestments, banners, frontals, and altar linen.

Knitting was largely practical: stockings, mittens, caps, shawls, and soft jackets for babies or invalids. (The jersey, or sweater, was a garment worn primarily by sailors, fishers, and some other working people.) Virtually every girl learned to knit, and most women had a knitting project to pick up when the light was poor or the conversation too interesting to pay attention to anything more demanding. Tatting and crochet were used to make fancy edgings for household linens, petticoats, and other garments. Elaborate crochet patterns for lace collars, table covers, bedspreads, and other projects were printed both in *Englishwoman's Domestic Magazine* and in working-class women's papers.

Many other crafts and hobbies were recommended to adults and young people as useful and worthwhile means of filling leisure time. Shellwork, beadwork, upholstery, drawing and painting, calligraphy and manuscript illumination, woodcarving, mosaic work, painting on glass and china, and making wax flowers are only a few examples. People made decorations for mantles and dressing tables, stenciled walls and furniture, painted silk for fans and screens, tinted photographs, did leatherwork.

Family magazines read by the working class and the middle class were full of *parlour pastimes* for evenings at home: chess, backgammon, songs for family singing, hints for acting charades, optical illusions, scientific tricks, demonstrations to do with simple equipment, puzzles, and word games. The most popular Victorian card game was whist, which is an early form of bridge.

DOUBLETS

This game was first described in the magazine *Vanity Fair* in 1879. It was invented by Lewis Carroll, author of *Alice's Adventures in Wonderland*. Under his real name, Charles Lutwidge Dodgson, he taught mathematics at Oxford's Christ Church College.

Change one word into the other, altering only one letter at a time. All the steps between must be actual words, as:

Drive PIG into STY—
  PIG
  pit
  sit
  sat
  say
  STY

The following may be done:

Raise FOUR to FIVE
Dip PEN into INK
Make WHEAT into BREAD
Touch CHIN with NOSE
Change TEARS into SMILE
Get COAL from MINE
Make FLOUR into BREAD
Make EEL into PIE
Evolve MAN from APE
Prove PITY to be GOOD
Cover EYE with LID

Photography was a popular new hobby at the century's end. Early cameras required a lot of equipment. Many of the first amateur photographers were upper-class women, who had ample money, time, and darkroom space. People had their photograph taken only on important occasions. Cheap box cameras, introduced in 1888, were an instant sensation. They made photography possible for working people and even for children.

Collecting was done by people of all classes. Victorian collections found in antique stores today include albums of stamps, autographs, picture post cards, favorite quotations (neatly copied and dated), and souvenirs of special occasions. Working-class girls filled scrapbooks with designs made from the colored advertising cards that merchants handed out for free.

Natural history was very popular. Amateur naturalists combined hobby and science; they collected fossils, seaweeds, mosses, ferns, fungi, butterflies, and other insects—and they also did the basic descriptive and classification work on many species. Bird watchers began keeping local records. Once microscopes became widely available, *specimen clubs* spent Saturday afternoons making local excursions and examining the samples they brought back. Rustic hobbies gave city and suburban people a reason to make trips into the country and a way to bring nature home. Even a small room could have an aquarium or terrarium. Those with more space had greenhouses, ferneries, exotic houseplants, and caged birds.

Girls pressed flowers for both scientific and sentimental reasons. They made little bouquets as party favors. Popular handbooks explained the so-called language of flowers—the meaning of each bloom or combination in a bouquet. The meanings, however, varied in different books, just as the interpretation of dreams varied between the dream books that were also popular.

Household pets became common only after 1800. Before that, watchdogs and other working dogs lived outside; pet animals were an upper-class indulgence. By the Victorian period, however, the English were already notorious for their sentimental love of dogs. Some historians believe that newly urbanized people yearned for the animals who had shared their lives in the country, whereas others credit the growth in surplus money to feed pets and the leisure to walk and play with them. During the second half of the century, the Kennel Club established standards for the different breeds and began holding dog shows. Exhibitors at some shows included coal miners and other working-class men who traditionally bred dogs as a hobby.

Somewhat later, exotic cats such as Siamese and Persians became popular. (Most houses also kept a working cat to patrol the kitchen for mice. One is clearly visible in the publicity photograph of an extremely scientific and sanitary professional cooking school that advertised in women's magazines.) Other popular pets included rabbits, guinea pigs, squirrels, dormice, white mice, doves, and exotic birds.

Popular Reading

The Victorians virtually invented mass literature. High-speed presses, cheap wood-pulp paper, machines for typesetting, new means of reproducing illustrations, railways to send printed material quickly all over the country, and the steadily growing number of people who were literate enough to read for pleasure encouraged the publication of newspapers, magazines, and novels at every price and for every taste. Hundreds of women and men made a good living as professional writers; some grew very rich. Furthermore, reading for pleasure was not only an individual and private occupation but a communal activity shared with family and friends.

New novels were expensive. In volume form they were read primarily by people of the middle and upper classes who belonged to private subscription libraries. In order to increase their profit on rental fees, libraries wanted novels to be published in three volumes. (Imagine, for comparison, that video stores had enough control of the market to insist that films be put onto three separate DVDs so customers had to buy or rent all three to see the entire movie.)

To circumvent the libraries and increase their own share of the profits, novelists and publishers found other ways of putting stories into readers' hands. Serialization proved the most successful. Some novels were sold in monthly parts. To use the work of Charles Dickens as an example, *David Copperfield* was published in 20 parts, issued at a rate of one per month beginning in May 1849. (The last two parts were sold as a double number in November 1850.) Each part was made up of 32 pages, with illustrations, in a paper wrapper, and sold for one shilling. The price for the whole novel was about two-thirds the cost of a three-volume hardback, and the expense was spread out; it would be a easier for people of moderate means to spend a shilling a month than to buy three 10s. 6d. volumes at one time.

Serial publication had another important effect. In many parts of society, reading aloud was the customary employment for an evening at home. While most of the family occupied their hands with knitting or jigsaw puzzles and father relaxed in a comfortable chair, one person sat next to the only good lamp and read from a serialized novel or some other publication that would be interesting to both youngsters and adults. Novelists made people eager to buy the next month's installment by introducing surprising new twists or ending on a note of suspense. When everyone in the family (and most of their friends) was reading the same novel, and when they had to wait almost two years for all the complications to be resolved, people naturally talked about the book and speculated about what would happen next. They knew the characters well and cared about them. Their pleasure in popular novels combined the experience of reading with the public interest now aroused by a favorite television series.

In addition to serialization in separate monthly parts, novels were divided into installments for publication in magazines. To return to the Dickens examples, *Oliver Twist* came out in the monthly issues of *Bentley's Miscellany* between February 1837 and March 1839. Later, once his name became recognized everywhere, Dickens published his own weekly magazines to print his new novels as well as poetry, stories, and essays by other writers. The issue of *All the Year Round* for Saturday, December 1, 1860, sold for twopence and contained 24 pages of two-column print. In addition to the first two chapters of *Great Expectations* it included an article on dining in Rome, an essay-editorial on a current social problem (in this case, the need to provide financial assistance for parish clergy who are faced with illness or family disasters), a history of everyday life five hundred years earlier, a love poem, a humorous sketch about Cornishmen, and an installment of another novel, Charles Lever's *A Day's Ride.*

While Charles Dickens was the most successful of the novelists whose reputations have survived into the twenty-first century, many other writers were widely popular. Working-class readers bought their fiction in even cheaper form, in magazines or separate serialized parts sold at a penny per week and printed in 16 pages of very small type on paper about the size and quality of a modern big-city telephone directory. G.W.M. Reynolds, like Dickens, edited his own magazines—and may have sold up to 10 times as many copies of serialized titles such as *Wagner, the Wehr-Wolf; The Mysteries of London; The Bronze Statue, or The Virgin's Kiss;* and *The Seamstress, or, The White Slaves of England.* Although workers had less time for family reading than people of the middle and upper classes, there are accounts of public readings in pubs and of mill girls clubbing together to buy a serial paper that one of them would read aloud during the dinner break.

As literature became popular entertainment, novelists found it possible to direct their work to a one section the reading public. Charlotte Yonge created family stories with overtones of religious activism; Dinah Mulock Craik wrote about women's tribulations; G.P.R. James wrote historical adventures; Robert Smith Surtees depicted sporting men; Sheridan Le Fanu and Marie Corelli specialized in the occult; G. A. Henty poured out tales of military heroism that were read by men and girls as well as by boys; and Margaret Oliphant (along with many other women writers) crafted romantic and domestic chronicles. In addition, most of the Victorian authors whose books are still read (George Eliot, Elizabeth Gaskell, Charlotte Brontë, W. M. Thackeray, Anthony Trollope, Thomas Hardy, Rudyard Kipling) were highly successful in their own time in addition to winning lasting critical reputations.

One of the twentieth century's most popular forms of light reading had its roots in the 1860s, when a large number of competing
shilling monthly magazines were established. Publishers encouraged readers to rush out and buy the next issue by concentrating
on what were called *sensation novels*—stories featuring secrets, sur-
prises, suspense, exaggerated emotions, dramatic chases and train
wrecks, and an overriding mystery whose solution was withheld
until the last installment. Writers such as Wilkie Collins, Ellen Price
Wood, and Mary Elizabeth Braddon, who specialized in sensation
fiction, created many of the conventions that became useful when
a young doctor named Arthur Conan Doyle was looking for a way
to make some money while he waited for his medical practice to
attract patients. The Sherlock Holmes stories began appearing in
The Strand magazine in 1891.

Magazines of many sorts developed loyal readers. The penny
weeklies *Family Herald* and *Bow Bells* published advice, household
hints, and romantic novelettes read by working women and workingmen's wives. (*Bow Bells* also had fashion pictures or sheet music
on its back cover.) *London Journal* mixed sensational serials about
gypsies, vampires, and crime in high places with practical advice

With the subtitle "A Fam-
ily Journal of Instruction and
Recreation," *The Leisure Hour*
(shown here in an issue dated
July 6, 1867) was one of several
very popular penny weekly
journals that contained fiction,
accounts of history, travel and
nature, and paragraphs of miscellaneous information.

on health and emigration. *Eliza Cook's Journal* printed short fiction and serious articles (including reports of American women's rights conventions) for older single women. Comic and satiric magazines such as *Punch* and *Fun* had pictures, satires, parodies, political cartoons, and caricatures. *Ally Sloper's Half-Holiday*, which began in 1884, was an eight-page illustrated joke book that can be seen as forerunner of the comics. It has been estimated that at least 10,000 different newspapers and magazines were published (at least for a few issues) during the Victorian period.

Women's magazines early in the century had been largely for the upper classes, featuring Paris fashions, intellectual pastimes, and court news. In 1852, Samuel Beeton's *Englishwoman's Domestic Magazine* established a new formula: fiction, recipes, patterns for sewing and needlework, advice about gardening and health, and essays on political issues of interest to women (e.g., new public health measures, or laws to improve child welfare). In the 1890s, a new generation of women's magazines added more and more advertising and began to feature articles that helped promote the advertisers' products. These more commercial magazines also printed *personality* news that is useful to modern-day scholars who study the interviews with women musicians, actors, artists, and authors of the era.

At the beginning of the period, few people read a daily newspaper. The London *Times*—which had been published since the eighteenth century—reported parliamentary and other significant news and was essential reading for influential men. But newspapers were expensive; women often had no chance to see them. Men tended to read the paper at their office or club. The novelist Elizabeth Gaskell shared a subscription with several neighbors; they bought one copy between them and passed it around.

As production costs dropped—and even more dramatically, after the stamp duty was repealed in 1855—newspapers became much cheaper and more widely read. The weekly *Illustrated London News* pioneered pictorial journalism by commissioning artists to cover breaking news (as well as predictable public occasions) and transferring the drawings quickly to woodblocks for mass reproduction. Penny and then halfpenny papers made it possible for members of the working class to become newspaper readers. Reading the tabloid-style coverage in the weekly *News of the World* became a customary recreation for a working man's Sunday.

Children's literature of all sorts flowered, owing both to changed conceptions of childhood and new production methods for illustrated books. The period of about 50 years following 1860 is often called the golden age of English children's literature. Earlier books for children were chiefly meant for intellectual or moral instruction, though the lesson might be sweetened with entertaining characters and illustrations. Fairy tales had an unsavory reputation. They appeared in crudely printed, cheap books; they were violent; and they didn't teach good lessons.

Beginning in the 1840s, well-designed illustrated fairy tales began to appear, and folklore collectors gave them an aura of respectability. The new fairy tales of Hans Christian Andersen were translated. English writers began to produce entertaining fantasy literature that did not always have a simple or explicit moral. The illustrators whose work is still admired did their best work in the 1860s and 1870s, after colored pictures could be printed at a reasonable price. Walter Crane, Randolph Caldecott, and Kate Greenaway developed the interplay of text with illustrations that has become the hallmark of good books for young children; they also created wonderful art.

After midcentury, writers for older children produced increasingly realistic stories about ordinary children and their doings, as well as adventure tales, school stories, historical novels, and other genres of popular writing. The books usually provided a model for good behavior, or the characters learned an important lesson about growing up—but they had a great deal of fun and excitement along the way, and their admirable behavior could be good independent heroism instead of good obedience to their elders.

Magazines for little children and for older boys and girls provided a weekly or monthly budget of fiction, illustrations, puzzles, and games for a penny or sixpence. Even cheaper papers for working-class adolescents were published toward the end of the century: for a halfpenny a week boys got jokes and blood-and-thunder serials and girls got horoscopes, advice columns, and contests in addition to fictional adventure and romance.

Although new books for adults remained expensive, children's publications advertise new and reprinted titles in every price range from one or two pence to six shillings and more. Some of the classic English children's books written during the Victorian period are *Alice's Adventures in Wonderland* (1865), *Black Beauty* (1846), *Treasure Island* (published as a book in 1883, but serialized in the magazine *Young Folks* in 1881–1882), *Kim* (1901) and *The Jungle Books* (1894, 1895), *The Water Babies* (1863), *The Little Lame Prince* (1875), *Tom Brown's School Days* (1857), and the Andrew Lang editions of fairy tales from around the world collected in the 1890s as *The Blue Fairy Book, The Green Fairy Book,* and so on.

11

FAITH AND WORKS: RELIGION AND REFORM

RELIGIOUS FAITH

In popular imagination, Victorians were regular and complacent churchgoers. Although this statement does describe some Victorians, nineteenth-century religious life was more likely to be filled with energy, turmoil, and struggles against doubt. A national count on Sunday, March 30, 1851, showed that 60 percent of the people who were physically able to do so attended church services.

The vast majority of England's residents professed some variety of Protestant Christianity. The Church of England—called also the *Anglican communion*, and closely related to the Episcopalian church in the United States—was the established church. The sovereign was its head; Parliament had final authority in matters of doctrine; all property owners paid a tax to keep up the parish church. In the villages and small towns where traditional ways of life were strongest, the Church of England served both gentry and laborers. Church attendance was much higher in the countryside than in industrial areas.

Protestants of other denominations—primarily Methodists, Baptists, Presbyterians, Congregationalists, Unitarians, and Quakers— were known as *Dissenters* or *Nonconformists*. (In literal terms, this means they did not assent to the Thirty-Nine Articles of Faith that formalized England's separation from the Church of Rome in 1562.)

Nonconformity was strongest in towns and cities, and especially among the rising technical and business classes. Of the people who attended services on that March 30, 1851, fully 49 percent were Nonconformists, 47 percent were Anglican, and 4 percent were Roman Catholic.

Roman Catholics were divided: a small number of long-time Catholics among the aristocracy and a quite different body of desperately poor Irish immigrants. Most English people were deeply suspicious of Catholicism, which they called *Popery*. Jews and other non-Christians were free to worship as they wished, but their civil rights were limited.

When the nineteenth century began, a man was required to assent to the Thirty-Nine Articles of Faith in order to sit in Parliament, enter a university, or become a military officer. Only Anglican clergymen could conduct marriages or bury the dead. It was already the custom, however, for Parliament to pass an annual Act of Forgiveness that allowed Dissenters to take their seats. In the 10 years before Victoria took the throne, Roman Catholics were also admitted to Parliament and most other civil disabilities that affected Christians were eliminated. During the second half of the century, Jews and then nonbelievers attained full legal equality.

Although many urban laborers had no interest in religion (and despised the employers who paraded Christian beliefs while paying starvation wages), dissenting chapels were at the center of life for many skilled workers and clerks. Their children learned to read in the Sunday school; their recreation was provided by the chapel's choirs, mission societies, study groups, and excursions; and the working men who served as preachers and deacons were men of power and authority.

By the century's end, church attendance had grown smaller. In London in 1902, only 20 percent of the population went regularly to services. Most people, however, still turned to the church for weddings and funerals. Churchgoing remained important in the countryside and in manufacturing districts where Nonconformist congregations were strong.

Much of the energy in Victorian religion came from the doubts and conflicts that arose during the century. Religious faith mattered, and it was no longer purely automatic. Evangelicals among both Anglicans and Nonconformists emphasized the experience of conversion. Believers were zealous in both faith and works; a spirit of reform fired their mission to improve everyone's life. Internal conflicts swept through the Church of England. Geology and archaeology raised questions about literal truth of the Old and New Testaments. The resulting turmoil called forth new ways of interpreting religious doctrines.

THE CHURCH OF ENGLAND

Church of England parishes are grouped into dioceses; each diocese has a cathedral and is headed by a bishop. The dioceses (there were 37 by the end of the century) are organized into two archdioceses. The Archbishop of Canterbury is administrative head of the entire church; the Archbishop of York heads the smaller archdiocese. Both archbishops and 20 of the bishops were full voting members of the House of Lords.

Cathedral clergy were separate from parish clergy. The dean of a cathedral heads a chapter of canons, who are clergymen attached to the cathedral. These terms are sometimes confusing. For example, the dean of Winchester and the bishop of Winchester are not the same person. In Victorian times, the dean was in charge of cathedral services and the cathedral itself, but the bishop—whose throne was in the cathedral—had jurisdiction over all clergy in the diocese. The bishop performed ordinations and confirmations and celebrated other important services. Cathedral clergy had less work than ordinary parish clergy; they lived in pleasant houses and shared the active social life of a cathedral town.

To be ordained as a priest, a man had to be 23 years old and be approved by his bishop. The great majority of Anglican clergymen were graduates of Oxford or Cambridge, although some were trained elsewhere. The candidate's degree could be in classics or some other subject that had little to do with religion; the bishop appointed a chaplain to give him an examination before performing the ordination.

The Church of England was supported through a complicated system of tithes on the produce of certain landed estates. Each parish had its own income, so some clergymen had higher salaries and more money to spend on church affairs than others. Patronage and connections determined who got the best posts. As the importance of agriculture diminished, parishes depended more on their congregations for financial support. The church also raised money for new churches in suburban and industrial towns.

Three factions within the Church of England had differing approaches to theological and social questions. First, the evangelical party (often called *low church*) stressed personal piety, conversion, individual Bible reading, and the serious Christian life. To evangelicals, Christianity demanded personal morality, social reform, and philanthropic work. Evangelicals put less emphasis on church services than on private reading of the scriptures. This meant (among other things) that evangelicals aggressively promoted literacy and Sunday schools.

By the mid-Victorian period, middle-class evangelicals had a reputation as anti-intellectual and emotionally restrained. They disapproved of dancing, card playing, novels, levity, and the theater. On the other hand, they devoted vast amounts of time and money to charity. Noted Victorians who came from evangelical families include George Eliot, the Brontës, Elizabeth Barrett, Prime Minister Gladstone, and the tireless social reformer Lord Shaftesbury. About a third of the Anglican clergy were evangelicals at midcentury, though the number began to diminish after 1870.

Second, the *high church* or Anglo-Catholic faction emphasized tradition, the sacraments, and priestly authority. The high church revival began with the Oxford Movement of the 1830s. Clergymen who were also members of the university wrote a series of *Tracts for the Times* intended to reform the church and increase its appeal to serious young men who would enter its service. The first tract, by John Henry Newman, reaffirmed that the priest's authority was derived from his ordination by a bishop, and that by that act each clergyman took up his place in a direct line that could be traced back to the apostles. Newman's position ultimately led him to convert to Roman Catholicism in 1845.

Clergy influenced by the Oxford Movement (who were sometimes called *tractarians*) dominated the Church of England by 1853. In high church parishes, Sunday services grew more solemn, altars were decorated, vestments richly embroidered, buildings restored to their Gothic splendor. New parish organizations emphasized religious ritual and service to the church. For the first time since the Protestant Reformation, daily services of morning and evening prayer returned to some churches.

While evangelicals stressed individual conversion and high churchmen emphasized the sacraments, the third faction, usually called *broad church*, had no single center of belief. Broad churchmen wanted to keep the Church of England open enough to appeal to anyone who accepted basic Christian beliefs. Since they tended to be fairly liberal, committed to social reform, and interested in intellectual and scientific inquiry, the broad church party had the easiest time adapting to change. By the early twentieth century, internal factionalism had diminished; broad church precepts were accepted by most Anglicans.

Protestant Nonconformity

English Christians who did not assent to the Thirty-Nine Articles of the Church of England were socially and theologically diverse. Those sometimes referred to as *old dissent* had roots leading back to the Protestant Reformation. They included Congregationalists, Presbyterians, Baptists, and Quakers. *New dissent* arose during the eighteenth century; its most influential groups were the Methodists (split off from the Church of England under John Wesley) and the Unitarians. As is typical when evangelical Bible-centered individualism is strong, there were also many smaller groups and single independent congregations.

Nonconformist congregations usually selected their own clergy and governed their own affairs, although Methodists were centrally organized under bishops. Most nineteenth-century Nonconformists shared with Anglican evangelicals an emphasis on biblical authority and individual relationships with God. Some dissenting clergy were trained in seminaries or theological schools. Others were self-educated. Autobiographies of successful inventors and businessmen often praise their Nonconformist upbringing for teaching them how to work hard and have faith in their own ability. Nonconformist merchants and tradesmen led many town and borough councils.

In national politics, Nonconformists usually supported the Liberal party whereas Conservatives were drawn from the established church. But although nonconforming Protestants had legal equality after 1828, social acceptance was a different matter. Nonconformity was generally seen as an indication of lesser social status. Unitarians and Quakers were somewhat anomalous; they might be well-educated, but did not usually identify with the interests of the gentry and aristocracy. Most Methodists came from the business and manufacturing middle class and the skilled working class. Baptists and members of sects such as the Primitive Methodists or the Plymouth Brethren were usually of lower social standing. When Nonconformist industrialists grew rich, they often started their move into a higher class by having their children baptized in the Church of England.

In the language of the period, Nonconformists worshipped in a *chapel* while Anglicans attended a *church*. A *preacher* was usually

"TRUST IN GOD AND DO THE RIGHT,"
BY NORMAN MACLEOD

Macleod was a Presbyterian minister in Scotland (where Presbyterians were the established church) but his *Good Words* magazine was popular with evangelicals of all denominations. In addition to its manly earnestness, this poem is a fine example of the evangelical emphasis on individual conscience.

Courage, brother! do not stumble
Though thy path is dark as night;
There's a star to guide the humble—
Trust in God and do the right.

Let the road be long and dreary,
And its ending out of sight;
Foot it bravely—strong or weary—
Trust in God and do the right.

Perish policy and cunning,
Perish all that fears the light;
Whether losing, whether winning,
Trust in God and do the right.

Trust no party, church, or faction,
Trust no leader in the fight;
But in every word and action
Trust in God and do the right.

Trust no forms of guilty passion—
Fiends can look like angels bright;
Trust no custom, school, or fashion—
Trust in God and do the right.

Some will hate thee, some will love thee;
Some will flatter, some will slight;
Cease from man and look above thee—
Trust in God and do the right.

Firmest rule, and safest guiding,
Inward peace and inward light;
Star upon our path abiding—
Trust in God and do the right.

Nonconformist; a *priest, vicar,* or *rector* was probably Anglican. Anglican churches were usually named for saints; Dissenting chapels often took names drawn from the Bible or from particular articles of faith (Zion, Beulah, True Word of God).

Other Faiths

By the second half of the century, there were three distinct (and often incompatible) groups among England's Roman Catholics. The first was made up of the large number of Irish immigrants who came to England after the midcentury potato famine. The second included long-time Catholics from the north of England (who had never accepted the Protestant Reformation), who tended to be upper-class. The third group, new converts, were mostly intellectuals and people who found aesthetic pleasure in the Roman ritual. John Henry Newman and other Anglican clergyman who were unmarried when they converted brought a new scholarly energy into England's Roman Catholic priesthood.

In 1850, for the first time since the Protestant Reformation, a Roman Catholic hierarchy was established: one archbishop, 12 bishops, and a formal organization of parishes. Anti-Catholic protesters called this a "papal aggression" and urged the government to halt the spread of "foreign influence." The popular conception of Roman Catholicism remained contradictory: a Catholic was either an ignorant, superstitious Irishman or an effete and overeducated aesthete.

The Jewish population was extremely small in 1837. Jews could not enter Oxford, Cambridge, the army, or Parliament. They had partial but limited access to the legal profession. Removal of these disabilities began in 1858, when Lionel de Rothschild was seated in Parliament without taking his oath "by the true faith of a Christian." In 1890 the last bar to full civil rights was lifted. (Conservative politician Benjamin Disraeli, one of the two great prime ministers of the period, was born in a Jewish family, but his parents had their children baptized into the Church of England in 1817.)

Meanwhile, the Jewish population grew significantly as refugees from Eastern European pogroms flowed into Liverpool, Manchester, and London's East End starting in the 1870s. As with the Roman Catholic population, internal conflicts almost inevitably surfaced. The old Anglo-Jewish leaders were Orthodox and dominated by a few elite families called *the cousinhood*. The new immigrants brought a Yiddish press, a greater range of religious practices, and vigorous support for Zionism (the movement to establish a homeland for Jews in Palestine).

Among the many other religious influences, two that are Victorian in origin need to be mentioned. The Salvation Army was organized by Catherine and William Booth in 1878 as a mission to the poor. Salvation Army bands played in slum neighborhoods to collect crowds. Besides holding religious services, the Salvation Army established shelters, treatment centers, and other social services. Unlike many Victorian charities, it ministered to every needy person, not just to the so-called deserving poor. Women and men did both preaching and welfare work. Women were promoted up through the Salvation Army's military ranks, and married women were expected to have a public role in addition to their domestic duties.

Whereas Salvation Army leaders were largely drawn from the working classes, spiritualism attracted a wide range of people. Spiritualism as the Victorians understood it involved holding a séance during which a medium entered a trance and transmitted messages from the spirit world. The practice, which arose in North America, came to England in midcentury. For some people, spiritualism affirmed Christian belief by proving that human souls survived after death. Others—especially women—found in spiritualism a new, non-Christian, faith. It gave them personal ways to be in touch with a higher power without coming under the authority of clergymen or patriarchal dogma.

Faith and Doubt

When the Victorian age began, most professing Christians in England accepted the Bible as literally true and free from error. This belief was strained by geological evidence and by the linguistic criticism, done largely in Germany, that traced changes in key texts. Other scholars, at the same time, were comparing biblical events with historical records and making archaeological investigations of life in ancient Egypt and Palestine.

Most thoughtful Victorians who lived through the middle years of the century experienced a crisis of faith. New ways of thinking emerged: the seven days of creation could be seen as seven eras; and the events in the life of Jesus as recorded in the Gospels might be understood not as literal historical facts but as parables expressing philosophical truths about the relations between humanity and the divine.

Although science plays a role in most discussions of faith and doubt, the striking aspect of the struggles recorded in Victorian letters and diaries is that the first questions were so often moral. Doubt arose not because of scientific evidence but because of evangelical religion's emphasis on progress and reform. Was it really possible to accept the idea of hell, everlasting punishment, and a jealous deity who demanded obedience? The struggles to reconcile conflicting beliefs gave religion its active presence in many lives—and often, when faith failed, the struggle to live well by works of reform grew even stronger.

RELIGION IN EVERYDAY LIFE

Church of England Parish Life

In the Church of England, the parish clergyman's post was known as a *living*. The right to appoint a clergyman to the living depended on how the parish was organized; it might belong to a bishop, a cathedral chapter, a college, or an individual landowner. Thus contacts and influence were important. Leading clergymen were usually relatives (or schoolmates) of aristocrats or substantial squires. Oxford and Cambridge fellows might wait many years for a vacancy in a parish controlled by their college so they could resign their fellowship and get married. Livings might also be bought when the person with a right to appoint the clergyman needed money.

A clergyman's income depended on parish resources, and it could be quite substantial or barely adequate. He was called either *rector* or *vicar*, depending on how the parish was funded. There was no difference in status or authority between these two titles. A *curate*, however, was a clergyman without his own living. Sometimes he was a *perpetual curate* who had full charge of a parish that had no resident priest (this was the case for the Reverend Patrick Brontë, father of Charlotte, Emily, and Anne). Other curates (particularly young ones) were hired by a clergyman to help do the work in a large parish. Since their pay was fairly low, young curates were generally single—and traditionally a source of great interest to unmarried women in the parish. Like college fellows, a curate might endure long years of waiting for a living that would enable him to support a wife.

Other parish officials included the churchwarden, the parish clerk, the sexton, the verger, and the pew-opener. The post of churchwarden was honorary and unpaid. He was elected by the congregation and usually came from its upper social classes. The parish clerk kept records and might read the scriptures and lead responses during the service. He had to be literate, but because the salary was insignificant the post was often held by a schoolmaster or a small tradesman. The sexton and verger came from the laboring classes: the sexton rang the bells and dug graves, and the verger looked after the inside of the church. The pew-opener was usually an elderly woman who collected tips by escorting important parishioners and wedding guests to their seats.

Church attendance was highest in rural villages with a resident squire and a traditional way of life. The clergyman conducted Sunday services, oversaw the village school, and performed marriages, baptisms, and funerals. In a small village or a slum parish, the clergyman might well be the only person with a university education. Residents turned to him for information of all sorts. He was often a magistrate. If the income provided by the living was narrow, he might take a local gentleman's son as pupil or have a few boarders in his house to prepare them for entry to public schools.

A parish clergyman was expected to be married. His wife was on calling terms with the gentry and middle-class women of the parish, and she enlisted their help in visiting poor and working-class parishioners. In urban parishes, district visiting was increasingly organized as the century went on; women had a roster of assigned days and duties. A visitor came into the cottage or lodging, asked questions, offered advice, read a prayer or passage from the Bible, and (if the parishioner was literate) left behind a printed tract or a moral story for the children. Elderly people may actually have enjoyed the company, but for most people the visit was tolerable only because it offered access to social welfare services. The clergyman's wife or the district visitors arranged for wine or nourishing food when someone was ill, supplied blankets in winter, provided clothing for newborns and for girls about to go out to service. They could line up votes to get parishioners admitted to hospitals, orphan homes, almshouses, and other privately run charitable institutions that were far more acceptable than the workhouse.

Sunday morning services in the parish church were usually at 10 A.M. A second service was held in midafternoon in villages or early evening in town. There were sermons at both services, but communion only in the morning. Marriages, funerals, and christenings usually took place before the morning service; only after midcentury were they performed on weekdays. The families of the squire and clergyman sat at the front of the church. Sometimes they had high-sided box pews with doors that were furnished with comfortable cushions and a charcoal brazier for cold days. Other substantial families paid rental to have their own pews toward the front of the church. Free seats for poor people were at the back.

These worshippers are probably Sunday School children and their teachers using seats in the choir stalls for some part of the service, since most Church of England choirs did not include women or girls. The illustration appeared in *The Pearl of Days* in December 1881.

At the beginning of the century, many clergymen had been fairly lax—showing up to read a sermon once or twice on Sunday, but devoting most of their time to country sports, scientific or literary hobbies, and other gentlemanly pleasures. Later, evangelicalism invigorated the clergy and the Oxford Movement gave them a sense of calling. Aside from paying more attention to their religious duties, energetic parish clergymen hired architects to restore their churches, added daily morning and evening prayers, installed organs, encouraged the choir to become more nearly professional, and set up new charitable and social organizations such as Mothers' Unions, clubs for boys and girls, penny savings banks, and altar guilds. An annual church fête and a Sunday school treat kept volunteers busy for weeks in advance.

Most children were christened at about one month of age, with three godparents (two of the same sex as the child). Even parents who did not go to church had babies christened—the government began officially registering births only in 1837, and people were used to having parish records to prove when and where they were born. Confirmation, at age 14 or 15, was less common. Adolescents who were serious about religion attended classes, after which the bishop of the diocese formally received them as members of the church. Girls wore white dresses and boys had black suits for the ceremony.

Sunday Observance

It's impossible to make broad generalizations about Nonconformist practices, but for many evangelical denominations among the urban working and middle classes, religion was very serious. Midweek prayer meetings, choir practice, and Bible study groups augmented two or three long services on Sunday. Some congregations had organs, orchestras, and a variety of choirs; others were suspicious of any music except the human voice. Large and successful chapels had well-paid clergy, but in smaller congregations the preacher might be a self-educated man who worked at some other job to support himself. The need to recruit members, organize finances, and build their own chapel absorbed much energy in newer congregations.

Sabbatarianism—strict observance of Sunday as the Lord's day—was practiced for most of the Victorian period by many families ranging from high-church Anglicans to members of small Nonconformist sects. People who rigorously kept Sunday as the Lord's day prohibited not only work but also all secular occupations. The entire family went to church both morning and afternoon. In the Church of England, well-to-do girls taught a class in the Sunday school. Their duty was to provide a social model as well as instructing young children, while at the same time they learned to understand and sympathize with the lower classes. In Nonconformist congregations, earnest young men taught Sunday classes to both children and adults.

Sabbatarians did no weekday chores on Sunday. When not at church or chapel, they sat quietly and read the Bible, a book of sermons, or a religious work such as *The Pilgrim's Progress.* There were also special magazines for Sunday reading. Although some of them printed nothing but Bible lessons and moral exhortations, Norman

The picture from the December 1883 issue of a publication sponsored by the Working Men's Lord's Day Rest Association shows an idealized Sunday afternoon, with the family gathered around the fire to share an improving book.

Macleod's *Good Words* (established in 1860) had illustrations by good artists; fiction from writers such as Charles Kingsley, Dinah Craik, George MacDonald, and Margaret Oliphant; and serious articles on contemporary social issues written by authorities in the field. A second magazine, *Good Words for the Young,* printed similar material for children.

Some families did not allow children to paint, run around, or play with their usual toys on Sunday. A Noah's Ark with its menagerie of wooden animals might be permitted. One child raised in a strict Baptist family remembered playing Missionary Lotto, a trivia game with questions about the name of the first Hindu convert and the number of mission hospitals in Madagascar. Sabbatarians pressed for laws that would close pubs, theaters, museums, and retail shops on Sunday. Although they were not entirely successful—pubs and trains were not shut down, and most museums had Sunday hours by the end of the century—the calm (and boredom) of an English Sunday was remarked on by foreign visitors well into the twentieth century.

THE SPIRIT OF REFORM

Evangelical religion—in both its Anglican and Nonconformist forms—propelled many Victorian social reforms. Evangelicals performed works of charity both as a moral obligation and as a means of bringing other people to Christ. They believed they could regenerate society by stamping out sin, and they tried to further that goal by getting rid of conditions that led people into despair, drunkenness, and crime. A new spirit of humanitarianism swept through religious thought: no longer focused on heavenly rewards, evangelicals spread their faith through works that improved life on earth.

Nineteenth-century humanitarian evangelicals abolished the slave trade, ended flogging in the army and navy, got rid of public hanging, strove to convert criminal justice from "punishment" to "reform," established schools, cleared slums, built decent housing for workers, abolished blood sports and protected animals from cruelty, worked steadily toward raising the age at which children could work full-time, founded refuges and orphanages, built schools for the mentally and physically disabled, and rethought the treatment of insanity. Realizing that private charity and district visiting—important as they were—could not cope with wide-scale social problems, they established a stunning variety of organizations to raise money, found institutions, and lobby for social legislation.

Organized charity grew partly because the scope of some problems was overwhelming. In a village, for example, an orphaned child might be taken in by a relative or neighbor (especially if some women in the parish supplied clothing and paid the weekly penny so the child could go to school), but when an epidemic swept through a factory town it left dozens of orphans. At least three separate women's organizations raised money to build orphans' homes after cholera struck in 1866.

Local groups established and funded a vast range of projects: animal shelters, public drinking fountains for horses, libraries, training schools, soup kitchens, farms for recovering alcoholics, isolation hospitals, seaside holiday homes for working girls, reformatories, residential homes for the blind. In other cases, there was a London

CHARITY AND REFORM SOCIETIES

A short list selected from among the hundreds of organized charities and societies working for reform suggests their range:

Aborigines' Protection Society
After-Care Association for Persons Discharged from Asylums for the Insane
Anti-Gambling League
Anti-Vivisection Society
Association for the Sale of Work by Ladies of Limited Means
Bible Flower Mission
British and Foreign Anti-Slavery Society
Cabmen's Shelter Fund
Children's Aid Society
Church Pastoral-Aid Society
Destitute Sailors' Asylum
Distressed Gentlefolks Aid Society
Fresh Air Fund
Governesses' Benevolent Institution
Guild of the Brave Poor Things [aid for disabled children]
Invalid Asylum for Respectable Females
Jews' Free School
Ladies' Society for the Education and Employment of the Female Poor
Metropolitan Association for Befriending Young Servants
Mission to Discharged Prisoners
Mission to the Gipsies [sic]
Pure Literature Society
Retreat for Persons Afflicted with Disorders of the Mind
St Andrew's Home and Club for Working Boys
School for the Indigent Blind
Society for Promoting the Employment of Women
Society for the Prevention of Cruelty to Animals
Society for Suppression of the Opium Trade
Society of Friends of Foreigners in Distress
Travellers' Aid Society
Vegetarian Union
Women's Universal Alliance of Peace
Young Men's Christian Association

headquarters and provincial branch societies. Upper-class patrons (often male) sat on a board of governors, but middle-class women did the day-to-day work. Charity bazaars were social events as well as a means to raise money. Girls and women contributed handicrafts, staffed the booths—and urged their male friends to pay a high price for the bouquets and pictures and embroidered slippers they had for sale.

Many organizations moved beyond their original narrow focus to take up wider causes. Tract and Bible societies at first distributed religious exhortations and gave scriptures to the poor. Subsequently some tried to improve the quality of popular reading by printing cheap editions of good books. The Religious Tract Society eventually published *The Girl's Own Paper* and *The Boy's Own Paper,* weekly magazines with good fiction, helpful articles, and very little religious content. Moral reform societies began with night refuges to get unprotected girls off the streets. By the end of the century they were allied with antipornography campaigns, temperance societies, and organizations such as the White Cross League, which enlisted boys and young men who promised to remain morally pure and to chivalrously protect girls and women of all classes.

Men and women of all denominations supported missionary work at home and abroad. The *mission basket* circulated among women of a congregation; the household that had it for a month sold its handicrafts to visitors and friends and made new knick-knacks to add when the basket was passed on. Mission societies paid for the medical training of women doctors who promised to serve a certain number of years in parts of India or Turkey where women could not be seen by male physicians. Mission sermons gave fieldworkers a chance to describe their adventures and raise more contributions.

Charitable work in England increasingly became a career for middle-class and upper-class women. It made use of traditional womanly skills and provided both an occupation and an emotional outlet for women whose household work was done by servants. Furthermore, the ethic of service made it acceptable to work outside the home. As Sarah Ellis wrote in one of her bestselling advice manuals, "a lady may do almost anything from motives of charity or zeal." Pocket guides for district visitors listed page after page of homes for disabled children, sailors' orphans, destitute needle-women, female servants, aged gentlewomen, soldiers' families, and friendless girls. Each sponsoring organization explained how to get help for people who needed it.

Through their charitable work, women acquired new skills: organization, administration, fundraising, accounting, writing, public speaking, counseling. They led prayer services, elected officers, and discovered that some social problems could be attacked only through legislation. The Charitable Organization Society was formed in 1869 as a network to connect religious and private charities. In addition

Two well-dressed ladies, either district visitors or members of a charitable society, visit
a poor widow and her ailing son in their cottage. The illustration is from *The Pearl of Days*
for February 1888.

to developing professional standards for casework, the unified society vastly enlarged charitable workers' lobbying power. Women
learned through personal experience about social conditions that
men of their own class ignored. They began to wonder why women
should not also be voters. By the end of the century, it was estimated
that half a million women worked as regular organized volunteers
and some twenty thousand supported themselves as paid workers
for charitable organizations.

Working men as well as middle-class women transformed charitable activities into organizations that formed pressure groups,
supported candidates, and promoted fundamental social reforms.
Friendly societies, organized at first through a chapel or a local pub,
collected a small weekly subscription to support members who were
sick and to pay for a funeral when they died. Some developed into

large fraternal organizations with medical and insurance benefits and their own committees for charitable outreach. Lodges such as the Foresters and the Oddfellows began as local friendly societies. Others, restricted to members of a certain trade, were eventually transformed into labor unions.

The temperance movement drew much of its strength from Nonconformists of the skilled working class and lower middle class. Networks of local societies served as lodges for people who did not organize their social life around a pub. Some temperance associations allowed wine or beer in moderation with meals; others demanded total abstinence *(teetotalism)*. In addition to requiring personal pledges from their own members, temperance societies worked for laws to control when and where alcoholic beverages were sold. However, the English temperance movement did not pursue total prohibition to the same extent as in the United States.

Most churches and chapels had temperance societies. Gospel Temperance used the blue ribbon as badge of the teetotaler. The British Women's Temperance Association made the white ribbon its symbol. The Band of Hope (founded in 1847) was an interdenominational temperance society for children. Over three million boys and girls were members. The Band of Hope sponsored sports teams, bands, picnics, trips to the seaside, lectures, meetings, and appearances by clean and sober athletes and other successful adults. Serving in large measure as a nineteenth-century forerunner of the Boy Scouts and Girl Guides, the Band of Hope provided training, discipline, and contacts for upwardly mobile working-class children as they moved into skilled or white-collar occupations.

12

VICTORIAN MORALITY

The phrase *Victorian morality* is often used with contempt. It has come to imply prudery, hypocrisy, sexual repression, and rigid social control. This chapter explores some widespread moral ideals in order to understand their value—and their failings. Remember, however, that *widespread* does not mean *universal*. All stereotypes simplify the real world, and most people's values are too complex to express in easy maxims.

THE CIVIC VIRTUES

Self-Help

The climate of mental and moral improvement was a distinctive feature of the age. Victorians believed in progress, and they believed people could change their lives and rise in the world through self-help. Although Samuel Smiles did not invent the concept, he wrote bestselling books that spread its precepts. *Self-Help* was published in 1859; other Smiles titles include *Character* (1871), *Thrift* (1875), and *Duty* (1887).

Formerly, biographies of great men to emulate had concentrated on political, military, and religious leaders. Smiles, by contrast, drew examples in *Self-Help* from the lives of inventors, business-men, and industrialists. He gave special praise to the self-taught

SELF-HELP

A man perfects himself by work more than by reading.

It is the diligent hand and head alone that maketh rich—in self-culture, growth in wisdom, and in business.

So far from poverty being a misfortune, it may, by vigorous self-help, be converted even into a blessing, rousing a man to . . . struggle with the world.

It is the close observation of little things which is the secret of success in business, in art, in science, and in every pursuit in life.

Necessity, oftener than facility, has been the mother of invention, and the most prolific school of all has been the school of difficulty.

An hour wasted daily on trifles or in indolence would, if devoted to self-improvement, make an ignorant man wise in a few years, and employed in good works would make his life fruitful, and death a harvest of worthy deeds.

The experience gathered from books, though often valuable, is but of the nature of *learning*: whereas the experience gained from actual life is of the nature of *wisdom*.

We must ourselves *be* and *do*, and not rest satisfied merely with reading and meditating over what other men have been and done.

Necessity may be a hard schoolmistress, but she is generally found the best.

The battle of life is, in most cases, fought uphill; and to win without a struggle were perhaps to win it without honour.

Samuel Smiles, *Self-Help: The Art of Achievement Illustrated by Accounts of the Lives of Great Men* (London, 1859).

worker-engineers whose mechanical devices revolutionized transportation and factory production. People who emphasized self-help were skeptical about genius or natural ability; success, they believed, came instead from practical experience and perseverance. Necessity, difficulty, and even poverty were welcomed as spurs to achievement.

Self-help provided a powerful counterweight to the rankings of social class. Humble origins were an asset rather than something to conceal. A businessman or industrialist who reached the top even though he began to work as a child and had to study late into the night after laboring all day was more admirable than the successful man who began with greater advantages. The sense of pride in rising from rude beginnings was (in English society) fairly new; it helped make Dinah Mulock Craik's 1856 novel *John Halifax, Gentleman* (a very readable rags-to-riches story) into one of the century's bestselling books.

Self-help in action led to a massive adult education movement with study groups run by workers themselves as well as workingmen's colleges where university graduates taught classes. However, some advocates of self-help distrusted formal learning and praised only the useful knowledge gained through experience. In any event, success required moral discipline and ethical behavior as well as hard work; there was no admiration for people who got ahead by cutting corners or deluding others.

Work

The values associated with evangelical religion helped promote the growth of business and the advance of middle-class men. Although hard work, frugality, and self-denial were apt to bring economic rewards, most evangelicals believed it was wrong for a man to devote his life to work simply because he wanted to get rich. Hard work was a moral good in itself; if wealth followed, it was a fitting recognition of the man's virtue.

The cult of work was highly useful to business. Offices posted signs such as "You are Requested to Speak of Business Only." Because there was no job security or unemployment compensation, workers at all levels were afraid of being let go. People endured terrible working conditions in order to make themselves irreplaceable—and they were comforted by feeling that steady hard work was morally excellent. By the 1860s, English skilled laborers were respected around the world for their expertise and their dedication to work.

The moral virtue of work extended beyond the world of paid employment. Working-class and middle-class people bolstered their sense of worth by feeling contempt for the idle rich. The

---

DUTY AND SELF-CONTROL

Certain self-evident duties are imposed upon every rational being. One of the first of these is the duty of being usefully employed a large portion of our time. It is probable that nearly all young people have a certain dislike for work, and self-control must come in to help them do the work that belongs to them to do. It may help you in acquiring this self-control to reflect often what a really great thing it is to be able to compel yourself to do from a sense of duty what you are naturally disinclined to do; also what an unworthy and, indeed, contemptible thing it is not to be able to make yourself do what you know you ought to do.

Helen Ekin Starrett, *Letters to a Daughter* (Edinburgh: Oliphant, Anderson, and Ferrier, 1887).

leisured life became less common among the gentry and aristocracy. Women at home felt guilty if they were idle. Some families
thought that reading books was a kind of laziness; even studying
should be postponed until evening when the day's work was done.
The feeling that every person should be usefully employed did a
great deal to promote charity, philanthropy, social welfare work,
and public service by women and men whose income came from
other sources.

Respectability

Respectability was another Victorian watchword. It was used as a
primary social distinction, often more important than the class line.
Especially among the poor and the lower middle class, being respectable was a way to maintain self-respect and public reputation.

Respectable has no absolute definition. For some Nonconformists,
dancing, playing cards, and going to the theater were not respectable. Young people who valued their reputation for respectability
did not eat on the street, wear flashy clothing, use loud voices, or in
any way call attention to themselves. A respectable family had tidy
clothes, a clean house, and good manners; its members were chaste,
sober, and honest. A well-to-do man who was clearly not respectable—who did not pay his debts, or openly kept a mistress—would
not be invited into the homes of most men in his class.

Respectability was closely associated with the concept of independence, which required people to look after themselves and bear
troubles without complaint. Because uncomplaining independence
was a virtue, people felt shamed if they had to ask for charity or
accept poor relief.

Independence required working at a job that provided an adequate income. Self-denial and thrift were needed to stay out of
debt. Respectable people in the lower middle class and skilled
working class had a horror of purchasing anything on credit or
using the pawnshop to raise money, even in an emergency. Working-class children were advised to avoid the *tally-man* (who sold
clothing and household goods on the installment plan) and to
save money by using clothing clubs, friendly societies, and the
post-office savings bank. An 1876 domestic economy book for elementary-school girls exhorted: "If you can't pay for it, do without.
People who buy for cash get better prices than those who need
credit." If someone is sick and out of work, the book said, a good
woman will have friends to depend on; she will not beg, but she

will accept help without losing her self-respect because she has given help to others when she can.

The importance of self-sufficiency was perhaps strongest in the lower middle class. A common maxim was "keep yourself to yourself." There was a strong inhibition against telling anyone about personal problems or family difficulties. Neighbors kept their distance; people seldom invited anyone except relatives into their houses. It was important never to go outside without being properly dressed. In the lower middle class, men as well as women had very little social life. They seldom went into a pub, though not necessarily because of temperance; they might drink bottled beer with meals. Free time on Saturday afternoon was spent taking children to the park. There was a strong emphasis on bringing children up well and protecting them from corrupting influences. Mothers did more childcare than in other classes; the only servant was usually a girl-of-all-work for the cleaning and heavy chores.

Independence and thrift were also important to the rest of the middle class. There was some suspicion, however, of people who accumulated wealth for their children to inherit. Unearned money might tempt them into idleness. The goal, rather, was to live comfortably and to educate sons so they would also be able to earn a good living. Most middle-class men who could afford it bought life insurance to protect their widows, but there was a growing sense by the end of the period that it was better to train a daughter so she could support herself if necessary. Careful fathers earlier in the century had made burdensome sacrifices to accumulate investments that would provide a moderate income for daughters who did not marry.

Earnest and *serious* were other terms of approval. Levity, frivolity, and vanity were frowned upon. Earnestness did not exclude pleasure, but it did suggest that people needed recreation for health and restoration, not as self-indulgence. Hygiene was cast in moral terms. Diseases were caused by drink or overindulgence; they could be prevented by moderation, baths, exercise, and making sure the garbage was collected and the house and street were kept clean.

Most of the lesser virtues associated with respectability circled back, once again, to characteristics that promoted business efficiency and economic success: punctuality, early rising, orderliness, concern for little things, self-denial, self-control, initiative, constructive use of leisure, prudent marriage. These traits were widely promoted in lectures, books, sermons, magazines, and workingmen's self-help societies. A handbook for clerks published in 1878 advises them to cultivate patience, courtesy, and deference; to be quiet and unassuming in their clothing; and to take care that their speech is clear and correct. Thus, in the ideology of the period, both working-class and middle-class men could move up in the world and become independent and respectable citizens.

MEN AND WOMEN

Ideal Womanhood

More nonsense has probably been written about the feminine ideal than any other aspect of Victorian life. Readers should always remember that moralists don't usually waste their time on a topic unless there are alternative viewpoints. When everyone in a society agrees, the subject is simply not mentioned (e.g., advice columnists do not say, "Never serve dog food to human guests.") Many Victorian essays about women's delicacy and fragility, for example, were written by men who wanted to prevent girls from playing sports, studying Latin and mathematics, or planning to practice medicine when they grew up.

In addition, most stereotyped depictions of woman's role are class-bound; they apply only to a narrow segment of society. This is particularly true of the notion that respectable women could not do any paid work. The strongest complaints about women's frivolity and idleness were voiced by people such as Florence Nightingale, who was definitely not idle and was one of the century's most admired women. Economist Harriet Martineau said she was thankful that her father lost his money so she was "forced" to earn her own living. "A Paris Atelier," an 1866 essay by Dinah Mulock Craik in *Good Words*, turned the stereotype on its head. "Working women in all ranks," she wrote, "from our Queen downwards, are, and ought to be, objects of respect to the entire community."

The most conventional image of the perfect Victorian woman is found in the title of a long poem written by Coventry Patmore: *The Angel in the House*. The pure woman's life was supposed to be entirely centered on the home. She preserved the higher moral values, guarded her husband's conscience, guided her children's training, and helped regenerate society through her daily display of Christianity in action. If she successfully made the home a place of perfect peace, her husband and sons would not want to leave it for an evening's (morally suspect) entertainment elsewhere.

Yet the stereotype contains irreconcilable contradictions. Although the ideal (middle-class) woman was legally subordinate,

---

WOMEN'S DOMESTIC DUTIES: WHAT GIRLS WERE TAUGHT

Domestic Economy is the science which teaches the right management of the family home.

The rightful home manager is a woman. On her the family depend for food, clothing, cleanliness, and comfort necessary to health; and for the good nursing necessary in sickness. This science, which belongs specially to the education of girls, is of more importance than all the other arts and sciences put together. From well-managed homes go forth happy, healthy, wise, and good men and women, to fill every position in the world.

If a country were made up of such homes, it would be a nation healthy and happy, noble and good, wise and prosperous. The influence and power of girls are, therefore, enormous. *They* have more to do with success or failure, happiness or misery. learning or ignorance, than kings, statesmen, philosophers, philanthropists, and clergymen.

Domestic Economy: A Class-Book for Girls (London: T. Nelson and Sons, 1876).

economically dependent, and always obedient to her husband, she was somehow supposed to rule the home. The ideology of separate spheres made her entirely responsible for its comfort, beauty, and morality.

Marriage was seen as woman's natural and expected role: it satisfied her instinctual needs, preserved the species, provided appropriate duties, and protected her from the shocks and dangers of the rude, competitive world. In the privacy of the home, her finer instincts—sensitivity, self-sacrifice, innate purity—could have free play. Women had to be kept safe at home; their perfect compliance, obedience, innocence, and refinement would make them too easy to victimize in the competitive public world. This conservative ideal was encapsulated (partly for ironic purposes) in Alfred Tennyson's 1847 poem *The Princess*:

> Man for the field and woman for the hearth;
> Man for the sword, and for the needle she;
> Man with the head, and woman with the heart;
> Man to command, and woman to obey;
> All else confusion.

As long as marriage held so central a place in the conception of ideal womanhood, it was not unnatural that women were trained to please men, help children, and suppress their own wants. But given the state of matrimonial law, the decision to marry defined a

THE SEPARATE SPHERES OF WOMAN AND MAN

The man's power is active, progressive, defensive. He is eminently the doer, the creator, the discoverer, the defender. His intellect is for speculation and invention; his energy for adventure, for war, and for conquest whenever war is just, whenever conquest necessary. But the woman's power is for rule, not for battle,—and her intellect is not for invention or creation, but for sweet ordering, arrangement, and decision. . . . Her great function is Praise: she enters into no contest, but infallibly adjudges the crown of contest. By her office, and place, she is protected from all danger and temptation. The man, in his rough work in the open world, must encounter all peril and trial:—to him, therefore, must be the failure, the offence, the inevitable error. . . . But he guards the woman from all this; within his house, as ruled by her, unless she herself has sought it, need enter no danger, no temptation, no cause of error or offence. This is the true nature of home—it is the place of Peace; the shelter, not only from all injury, but from all terror, doubt, and division.

John Ruskin, "Of Queen's Gardens," in *Sesame and Lilies* (London: Smith, Elder & Co., 1865).

woman's entire future. Marriage established her rank, role, duties, social status, place of residence, economic circumstances, and way of life. It determined her comfort, her physical safety, her children's health, and ultimately—perhaps—even her spiritual well-being. And owing to the code of chaperonage, she had to make her decision with very few opportunities to gain firsthand information about her prospective partner.

Advice manuals insisted that good men were chivalrous although they clearly made women responsible for defending their own sexual morality. Public standards for male behavior were, however, growing more strict. During the eighteenth century and through the Regency, upper-class men (including those in the royal family) made no secret of their mistresses and illegitimate children. By the 1840s, respectable men kept quiet about their premarital or extramarital affairs. Journalists and clergymen publicized urban vice— not because there was more of it, but because they were beginning to see prostitution as a problem rather than a natural feature of life.

Stricter moral standards in the middle classes influenced both the upper classes and the respectable working class. By the end of the period, revelations about extramarital sexuality would cause a man to lose his seat in Parliament. Guides for young women discreetly advised readers to inquire about a prospective husband's personal habits as well as his family's medical history. Alcoholism or

---

REFORMING A HUSBAND

Do not delude yourself that, when you have married him, you will be able to reform a lover who has been an evil liver. He will be older than you, and his habits more confirmed. The probability is, that even if he did leave off his bad propensities for a time to please you, they would be returned to again. Rather make up your mind, that as you find him, so, if you take him, you will have to keep him. This especially applies to a man who drinks to excess or habitually nips. If you marry a man whom you know beforehand to be an inveterate smoker, it will be scarcely fair to complain later of his reeking of smoke!

Lady Bellairs, *Gossips with Girls and Maidens, Betrothed and Free* (London: Blackwood, 1887).

---

tuberculosis among his relatives was a danger. (Both were thought to be inherited.) Careful readers were made aware that gonorrhea blinded infants passing through the birth canal, that syphilis led to congenital malformations—and that even though a man might be free of symptoms, there was no cure for either disease.

Some discussions of ideal womanhood insist that a respectable girl should be completely ignorant about sex and sexuality until initiated by her husband on the wedding night. However, unvoiced assumptions about masculine behavior created real dangers for any girl who was that naïve. Because chaperones were essential to protect innocent girls from assault, it seems evident that men assumed any woman walking alone on the streets was sexually available. *Prudery*—that is, not talking about sexuality or sexual topics—was meant to protect people. Explicit novels, sensuous pictures, and exciting dances were repressed because they might awaken sexual desire in young women and young men who were not yet mature enough to take on its responsibilities.

Although marriage was inevitably presented as woman's natural destiny, the intense and frequent repetitions of the message should make us suspect that it was not universally accepted. There were more women in their twenties and thirties than men to marry them (largely because of male emigration and colonial service), but not all single women were unhappy old maids. In the working classes, women in well-paid trades were more apt to remain single than those whose earnings were too low to provide adequate support. Among the middle and upper classes, too, it was quite possible for women to earn decent incomes and live contented independent lives.

At the end of the century, a counter-ideal of the *New Woman* burst into prominence. *Punch* caricatured her as a muscular bicyclist with bloomers and untidy hair who lorded over men. Like *feminist*, the term was claimed with pride even though cartoonists used it for an insult. The idealized New Woman was single, well educated, and worked at a white-collar or professional job. She lived alone or shared a flat with friends; enjoyed robust good health; traveled by bicycle or public transport; and went wherever she pleased without a chaperone. She was as firmly based in class-bound perceptions as the midcentury Angel in the House—but fewer than 40 years separate one from the other.

The Gentleman

The *gentleman* was a masculine equivalent of the ideal woman. The term's meaning changed during the period. In earlier times, the gentry were clearly defined as a class: they were landowners, and the feudal origins of landed tenure created a warrior caste governed by manly ideals of chivalry, bravery, and loyalty.

By the nineteenth century, people generally understood that a man from the landed classes was a gentleman by birth. In addition, Church of England clergy, barristers, members of Parliament, and military officers were gentlemen because of their profession. Because patronage and personal contacts were needed to enter the professions, a man's gentlemanly standing was, in part, guaranteed by his sponsors.

However, birth was not the whole story. A man of good family would have a better opportunity to acquire the manners and education that marked his gentlemanly status. Nevertheless, even an aristocrat would no longer be considered a gentleman if his public behavior was outrageously coarse or if he was dishonorable in his dealings with members of his own class. Gentlemanly conduct was an obligation—but not necessarily a natural inheritance—for men of a certain social rank.

The idea that being a gentleman did not depend wholly on birth but also required certain values, standards, and modes of behavior helped to make society in England less rigidly stratified than in some European countries. It combined the aristocracy and middle classes into a single ruling elite and, at least to a limited degree, opened the way to class mobility.

By 1862, a writer in *Cornhill Magazine* reported that there was "a constantly increasing disposition to insist more upon the moral and less upon the social element of the word" *gentleman*. Birth mattered

THE DEFINITION OF A GENTLEMAN

Hence it is that it is almost a definition of a gentleman to say he is one who never inflicts pain. . . . He has his eyes on all his company; he is tender towards the bashful, gentle towards the distant, and merciful towards the absurd; he can recollect to whom he is speaking, he guards against unseasonable allusions, or topics which may irritate; he is seldom prominent in conversation, and never wearisome. He makes light of favours while he does them, and seems to be receiving when he is conferring. He never speaks of himself except when compelled, never defends himself by a mere retort, he has no ears for slander or gossip . . . He is never mean or little in his disputes, never takes unfair advantage, never mistakes personalities or sharp sayings for arguments, or insinuates evil which he dare not say out. From a long-sighted prudence, he observes the maxim of the ancient sage, that we should ever conduct ourselves towards our enemy as if he were one day to be our friend. He has too much good sense to be affronted at insults, he is too well employed to remember injuries, and too indolent to bear malice. He is patient, forbearing, and resigned, on philosophical principles; he submits to pain, because it is inevitable, to bereavement, because it is irreparable, and to death, because it is his destiny.

John Henry Newman, *The Idea of a University* (London: Basil Montague Pickering, 1873).

less and less. People used *gentlemanly* to describe a man's ethics and behavior, regardless of his class or profession.

However, polished bearing and carefully correct dress did not make a man a gentleman. *Foppishness* and exaggeratedly genteel manners were despised. At the core of the high Victorian definition of the gentleman was the concept of disinterestedness. A gentleman was intellectually and morally independent. He should care about something other than money. He would do the right thing without thinking about what it might cost him financially. As a landowner, a member of Parliament, a civil servant, or a rural magistrate, he put the good of the community above any personal self-interest.

Owning a landed estate with a steady income made it possible to live a gentlemanly life of disinterested public service. However, a man could be a gentleman even though he worked for his money. Gentlemanly disinterestedness provided a basis for professional ethics. A clergyman should make no selfish use of information he discovered through his pastoral duties. A doctor should not prescribe useless and expensive drugs made by a company he owned. Teachers should not offer to tutor some students for extra money and then base examinations on material covered only in the private sessions.

It was for ethical reasons that the question of whether a business-man could be a gentleman loomed so large—not because working for a living lowered a man's rank, but because business transactions seemed to be motivated primarily for self-interest. The business of business was to make money; the presumed goal in gentlemanly professions was to earn enough to support one's family while per-forming an honorable public service.

By the last quarter of the century, the definition shifted once more. In the minds of many people, any boy who had gone to a public school was a gentleman unless his personal behavior was clearly dishonorable. Public-school boys learned to accept hardship without complaining and to take their place in a hierarchical soci-ety. Older boys supervised and disciplined the younger boys; they learned to give orders in a way that would not arouse resentment and to internalize a sense of responsibility. Public schools created English gentlemen to enter Parliament, become military officers, rule the Empire—and (by the end of the century) to enter business in a gentlemanly fashion.

Gentlemanly behavior was governed by a strict unwritten code of what was "done" and "not done." It was clearly "not done" to cheat at cards or question the honesty of another gentleman. A gentleman was courteous, considerate, and socially at ease. He behaved honorably toward all women. He paid his gambling debts and kept his word—a verbal promise was more important than a handshake, and a written contract seemed faintly disreputable, as if it suggested that a gentleman's word could not be trusted.

A gentleman had to accept and exercise leadership. He lived up to his own standards; as a businessman or a professional man he was honorable, dependable, and ethical. He did what was required without supervision—he didn't become a clock-watcher, but nei-ther did he work excessively long hours just to make more money. Public school boys trained one another in the emotional reserve that came to be called the *stiff upper lip*. A gentleman exhibited stoic self-control. He did not call attention to his own cleverness, or visibly work harder than others, or show too much enthusiasm. He had been schooled in loyalty, team spirit, courage, and fair play; and he was motivated by an enormous fear of giving way or visibly failing to live up to his standards and responsibilities.

13

ENGLAND AND EMPIRE

The period from 1875 to 1915 has been called the *Age of Empire*. The countries that were well-developed economic and military powers carved up the rest of the world into colonial territories. The word *imperialism* was coined in the late 1870s to describe what was happening. The chief empire-building nations were France, Germany, Italy, the Netherlands, Belgium, the United States, Japan—and Great Britain, the most successful of them all. By the time of the 1897 Diamond Jubilee celebrating the 60th year of Queen Victoria's rule, her Empire contained one-quarter of the world's population.

Many of England's people felt a sense of unrivaled national importance. Explorers and soldiers were honored in newspapers, songs, and stories. Boys' magazines, in particular, played endless variations on the theme of conquest and adventure.

England's overseas possessions supplied raw materials for industry and put new foods and fashions into domestic consumption. They also promoted economic mobility. Emigration to Canada, Australia, New Zealand, and South Africa widened the prospects for working men and women. Educated men from the new middle classes flocked overseas, where even a modest clerk in a merchant firm or government office had a status and standard of living that would be unimaginable at home.

"LAND OF HOPE AND GLORY"

The words are by Arthur Benson; they were set to music by Edward Elgar in 1902. Try singing the four-line chorus to the tune familiar as the "Graduation March" or "Pomp and Circumstance."

> Dear Land of Hope, thy hope is crowned,
>   God make thee mightier yet!
> On Sov'ran brows, beloved, renowned,
>   Once more thy crown is set.
> Thine equal laws, by Freedom gained,
>   Have ruled thee well and long;
> By Freedom gained, by Truth maintained,
>   Thine Empire shall be strong.
>
> Thy fame is ancient as the days,
>   As Ocean large and wide;
> A pride that dares, and heeds not praise,
>   A stern and silent pride;
> Not that false joy that dreams content
>   With what our sires have won
>
> The blood a hero sire hath spent
>   Still nerves a hero son.
>
> Land of Hope and Glory, Mother of the Free,
> How shall we extol thee, who are born of thee?
> Wider still and wider shall thy bounds be set;
> God, who made thee mighty, make thee mightier yet.

EXPLORERS AND MISSIONARIES

The mythology of popular imperialism drew on the heroism of explorers and missionaries. Religious societies financed expeditions to China, to the Muslim nations, and especially to Africa. Explorers drew maps, learned languages, conducted scientific observations, and recorded new species of plants and animals. In 1853, Richard Burton, disguised in Arab clothes, became the first non-Muslim to enter the holy city of Mecca. David Livingstone crossed Africa in 1856. John Hanning Speke traced the Nile upriver to the body of water he named Lake Victoria. Henry Morton Stanley explored the Congo and mapped Lake Tanganyika.

The motives of these men were mixed. David Livingstone was sponsored by the London Missionary Society. His duty, as he saw it, was to "go forward to the dark interior" of Africa to spread Christianity, collect information that would be used to suppress the slave trade, and make maps for the Royal Geographical Society.

Livingstone was also a medical man. His published reports portrayed Africans as helpless childlike pagans who needed both Christianity and modern science to rescue them from Islamic slave-traders and improve their health. Evangelical missionaries held to their belief that all people should read the scriptures. They spent years learning a local language, giving it a written form, translating the Bible, and establishing schools. Medical missionaries staffed hundreds of clinics and trained local residents in scientific ways of nursing and healing.

Yet though the motives of missionary-explorers were often honorable, they promoted imperial expansion and caused the deterioration of indigenous societies. Queen Victoria expressed a widely shared attitude when she said that England's duty was "to protect the poor natives and advance civilization." In the eighteenth century, the English had respected Chinese and Indian culture. Victorian missionaries, on the other hand, began to publicize foot-binding, infanticide, slavery or bond-servitude, and suttee (the ritual that led Indian widows to burn themselves to death on their husbands' funeral pyres).

In addition, England's advanced technology encouraged a sense of self-evident superiority over "primitive" people. The British believed that their government and legal system (as well as their science and religion) were the best in the world. Schoolbooks in history and geography said it was good to "bring civilization" to "savages" who welcomed the blessings of peace, security, and justice.

Concepts of race changed as well during the Age of Empire. The English had for a long time believed they were better than the Irish and the French, but they were motivated largely by anti-Catholicism and similar prejudices. They used terms such as the *Irish race* and the *French race* without any real sense of physical difference. Early Victorians who served in India assumed that the Indian people's "failings" and "backwardness" came from cultural traditions rather than "racial" inferiority.

From the 1860s onward, however, anthropological and biological studies began to divide humanity into various categories depending on skin color, hair form, facial characteristics, and so forth. There was a growing sense that "race" was biologically determined: that there were fundamental physical and intellectual differences based on genetic inheritance, and that the "Anglo-Saxon race" had evolved furthest from the primitive, animal roots of humankind. English racism in the late nineteenth century could lead to a parental feeling of responsibility for the health, education, and supervision of others—yet it was a clear and abiding racism that grew from a deep-seated assumption of superiority.

MILITARY LIFE

During the Age of Empire, the British navy controlled most of the earth's oceans. To protect England's access to overseas markets, the navy made maps and charts (some of which are still used) and kept sea routes open for free trade. Between 1810 and 1870 about 50 of its ships were on constant patrol to suppress the slave trade. The army fought two wars (in the Crimea and in South Africa), but its major role was in small engagements and frontier actions that expanded the Empire, protected its borders, and put down attempts by colonized people to reclaim their own territory.

Officers and men of the army and navy spent much of their working life outside England. Conditions for enlisted soldiers and sailors improved enough so that military life was no longer only a last resort for men who could find no other work. Officers in both services were expected to be gentlemen and accustomed to leadership. Military careers were especially popular with younger sons of the aristocracy and landed gentry.

The Army

Until the system of purchase was ended in 1872, a man who wanted to enter the army as an officer usually had to buy his commission. He (or his family) deposited the purchase money with an agent, who then searched for an appropriate regiment that had an opening. A commission would be for sale if the officer who held it was promoted or wanted to *sell out* (which simply meant to "leave the army"; no disgrace was involved). Meanwhile, the young man also found contacts who could recommend him to the regiment's other officers. To buy a commission, then, a man needed enough money to pay the asking price and the proper social status to fit in.

The purchase system was defended because it helped ensure that officers would come from a class high enough to be respected by soldiers who made up the rank and file. The price of a commission varied with the regiment's prestige. The most desirable were guards regiments, also known as *household troops* because they protected the monarch. Because the guards were usually stationed in

London, men who were waiting to inherit a peerage and younger sons of the aristocracy paid £1,200 or more to be a lieutenant in the Life Guards or Horse Guards, which were cavalry regiments. The Scots Guards, Grenadier Guards, and Coldstream Guards (infantry units) were only slightly less prestigious.

Guards officers had elegant uniforms and light duties that were mostly ceremonial. Especially during the London season, they could spend their evenings at grand balls and other social events. When the guards officer was a younger son, most people suspected he was looking for a wealthy bride and would sell out once he found her.

The cavalry was especially glamorous, because aristocratic men traditionally fought on horseback. Cavalry officers were known for their dash and daring—and for their wealth. An officer in a high-prestige regiment not only had to buy his commission but also needed a private income or an allowance from his father. His military pay was not nearly enough to cover the cost of good horses, fine wine, and a busy social life.

Commissions in other regiments—which usually rotated between overseas duty and short stays in a garrison or barracks somewhere in England—were cheaper. They ran from about £400 (in the infantry) up to £800 for a cavalry posting. Promotions were also bought: when there was an opening available, an officer purchased the next higher rank and sold the one he was leaving. In order to buy a promotion, a man sometimes *exchanged* into another regiment. Many regiments, however, had strong traditional loyalties and did not welcome officers who bought in from elsewhere.

There were exceptions to the purchase system. In wartime, when commanders were needed, officers were promoted on merit. Since there were no major conflicts for most of the Victorian period, a serious and ambitious career officer probably choose a regiment stationed in some dangerous and unhealthy part of the Empire. In that way he would earn more rapid (and cheaper) promotions.

Artillery and engineer commissions were not for sale. They went to career officers with special training from the Royal Military Academy at Woolwich. The Indian Army was also a separate matter. Its officers were British (usually from Scotland or England) and its soldiers were recruited in India from peoples with a warrior tradition: Sikhs, Gurkhas, Dogras, Mahrattas. A middle-class man with the right contacts could get a commission in the Indian Army without paying for it. Most of the officers were professionals who lived on their military pay—and their social prestige was correspondingly low.

The army was organized by regiments. A regiment, commanded formally by a colonel (whose duties were honorary) and actually by a lieutenant colonel who was nevertheless called *colonel*, had anywhere from 8 to 20 or more companies (depending on the date and station). Each company had between 60 and 120 men, and was commanded by a captain, who was assisted by two to four junior officers. These were usually lieutenants, although in early years the lowest-ranking commissioned officers were *ensigns* in the infantry and *cornets* in the cavalry. (In the 1870s, both names were replaced by *second lieutenant*.) The headquarters company, which supported the commander and the regiment as a whole, had additional officers for administrative, medical, and other services.

After the purchase system ended, most lieutenants came into the army directly from one of the public schools—but they still needed influence to get the best assignments. The social gap between officers and enlisted men remained enormous. Promotion from the ranks into the officer corps was extremely rare, although a few long-service sergeants were allowed to finish their careers as commissioned riding masters or quartermasters in order to boost their pensions. The *gentleman ranker* who enlisted to escape romantic or financial woes was far more common in popular fiction than in actuality.

The common soldier's lot was hard. Until 1847, a man enlisted for life (or until medically discharged). Various other schemes were then explored while the army tried to balance its need for experienced regiments overseas with its hope that shorter enlistments would bring better recruits. In the middle of the century the basic period of enlistment was 21 years. By 1870 it was 12 years, with the option of serving 6 years on active duty and 6 in the reserve. Another means of developing long-service professionals was the enlistment of boy-soldiers. They were signed on at 14 (or sometimes younger) and initially did *boy-service* as buglers, telegraphers, couriers, and hospital apprentices before formally joining the regiment at 17.

The basic pay for a private was one shilling a day, but deductions were made for food, washing, hair cutting, and some items of uniform. Even with lodging supplied, a soldier's earnings were less than a farm laborer's except for one thing: he had secure year-round employment. Soldiers were recruited from rural areas where agricultural work was in short supply, from the impoverished Irish, and through semivoluntary enlistments: young men brought before a magistrate for minor offenses such as fighting who were given a choice between gaol and the army, and other men who found it useful to disappear into the ranks to escape debts or disgrace.

Most people looked down on soldiers. It was widely assumed that they were drunks, criminals, or men too unskilled for any other work. In the 1850s, less than half of all enlisted men could sign their name. At home or abroad, soldiers slept in barracks and had little privacy or free time. They were kept busy with drill and chores to limit their opportunity for drinking and fighting. Discipline was harsh. Flogging was the punishment even for minor offenses until 1881. Regiments were away from home for years on end, often in unhealthy tropical climates. Mothers mourned when their sons *took the shilling* or *went for a soldier*.

On the other hand, there were cadres of long-service professional soldiers for whom the army was a family tradition and a way of life. Rankers could increase their pay by earning good-conduct badges and marksmanship medals, by taking up extra duty as an officer's servant, or by learning skills such as telegraphy or surveying.

A limited number of enlisted men were allowed to marry *on the strength*, which entitled them to a room in married quarters. The number varied between three percent and seven percent. Their wives had a recognized status and earned money by doing the regiment's laundry and sewing. Marriage *off the roll*, when a man did not have permission, was not punished, but the wife had no quarters or allowance, and her transportation was not provided when the regiment moved.

All noncommissioned officers at the rank of sergeant or higher could be married. Until the army medical corps was formed in the 1870s, sergeants' wives did most of the nursing. Schooling was provided for the children of noncommissioned officers and soldiers who married on the strength. Sergeants' daughters often became pupil teachers, married noncommissioned officers, and continued to serve as army schoolmistresses. Children educated by the army, in turn, became the most professional of its recruits. Census records from the end of the century show that a large proportion of noncommissioned officers had been born at military stations somewhere in the Empire.

At any given moment, about half of the army was at home and the other half abroad. In 1897, there were 52 infantry battalions in India, 23 in Ireland, 7 in Malta, 6 in South Africa, 3 at Gibraltar, 3 in Egypt, 2 at Mauritius, and 1 each in Canada, the West Indies, Singapore, Bermuda, Ceylon, and Hong Kong. Engineers were everywhere, doing surveying and stringing telegraph wires. Officers had extra-regimental assignments training local military forces, providing medical services for foreign rulers, accompanying explorers and diplomats, and drifting around the world gathering intelligence.

The Navy

Commissions in the navy were obtained through contacts and influence, though naval officers did not buy them outright. The navy was more apt to be a real career, and often a family trade; since ships could be away from England for years at a time the naval service did not have much appeal for men who wanted to spend a few seasons doing something glamorous before they settled down.

Navy life began very young. After his family secured an appointment, a boy joined a training ship when he was 12 or 13. He then served at sea as a midshipman, doing whatever officers told him to do. After six years, if he passed an examination, he could be commissioned when an opening was available. Because the senior officers who appointed new lieutenants tended to favor their own sons and nephews, naval officers came from a limited number of families.

Promotion was strictly by seniority. There was, however, no system of retirement; even very old captains tended to hang on to their command. The *half pay* system functioned as a sort of reserve. The size of the navy was periodically reduced—at the end of the Napoleonic wars, after the Crimean war, and at other times when policies shifted. Because the most senior men did not have to retire, younger captains (who had commanded a ship when a larger naval force was needed) were relieved of their duties and put on half pay. They could be called back to active service if an older captain died or if the number of ships was once more increased.

As in the army, the gap between officers and men was seldom crossed. Early in the period, seamen were hired for a single voyage and discharged when it was over. (Impressment—involuntary "enlistment" of sailors in a port or even from a ship at sea—was technically still available, but it was not actually used in Victorian times.) Unlike the army's common soldiers, the navy's ordinary seamen were almost all English (rather than Irish); going to sea was a customary way of life for boys and men from coastal towns.

The terms of naval service were reformed in the 1850s. Seamen were enlisted for 10 years; if they served 20 years they became

THE BALTIC FLEET LEAVING SPITHEAD

When the Baltic fleet left Spithead during the Crimean War, it was a news-worthy event. This drawing for the *Illustrated London News* of April 14, 1855, shows wooden warships under full sail—but the navy's future lies in the vessels that are moving without sails. Look closely to see the smokestacks for their steam engines. Courtesy of The Library Company of Philadelphia.

eligible for a pension. As in the army, the pay, food, punishment, and general living conditions remained fairly terrible. Sailors on merchant ships, however, were treated just as badly, and they didn't have the security or pension that naval service provided. As a consequence, the navy could depend on enlisting a reasonably competent class of seamen.

Naval technology was utterly transformed between the beginning and the end of the Victorian period. The point of transition is visible in the *Illustrated London News* picture of ships leaving for the Baltic in 1855. Most of the fleet are great wooden two-deckers and three-deckers crowded with sail, but two iron-hulled steamships can also be seen. The Crimean War of 1854–1856 signaled the end for wooden warships: the entire Turkish fleet went up in flames after Russian incendiary shells began a chain of explosions. By the end of the century, England's main line of defense lay in sleek steel-hulled battleships and cruisers. In addition to their speed and firepower, the new ships required fewer crew (no sails to set) and had a great deal more interior space.

The new technology brought a new midrange of engineers and petty officers into the navy and raised the professional standards for training commissioned officers. At the end of the century, cadets still entered the service at age 12 (after an examination and an interview), but spent two years at Osborne (which served as the navy's secondary school) and two additional years at the Royal Naval College at Dartmouth. At age 16, cadets who had changed their mind could leave the navy and those whose performance was unsatisfactory were dismissed. Those who remained served three years at sea as midshipmen, had three additional years of specialized training (some of it at sea), and were commissioned as lieutenants when they reached age 22.

IMPERIAL ENGLAND

The Empire

The British Empire arose more through commerce than through planned conquest. In 1830, England controlled the seas and accounted for about 45 percent of all world trade. Because it was the first country to industrialize, it had vast quantities of cheap manufactured goods to export. British ships, in return, brought back food and raw materials from countries around the world. Traders, merchants, bankers, investors, and immigrants settled wherever they discovered promising opportunities.

Until about 1870, the Empire grew slowly and haphazardly. When there was no established government in place (as in Australia or New Zealand), English explorers "claimed" territory for the Crown. In other places (as in India) traders initially made agreements with local rulers. New territories were added to protect the borders of existing colonies and ensure the safety of trade routes. Singapore, Hong Kong, and other ports were developed to serve British ships.

Before the Suez Canal opened in 1869, ships reached India and China by sailing around the southern tip of Africa. In 1806, the English paid the Dutch £6 million for their settlement at the Cape of Good Hope because it was an essential resupply point for ships. After the Suez Canal shortened the trip to Southeast Asia, England acquired new colonies in Burma, Borneo, and the South Pacific.

The 1876 Act of Parliament that made Victoria "Empress of India" crystallized the idea of empire. (The commercial East India Company and then the British government had ruled much of India for a century without calling themselves emperors.) In the 1880s, England joined what has been called the *scramble for Africa* in order to keep the continent (and its raw materials and trade routes) from being entirely controlled by France, Belgium, and Germany. Over the space of a few years, the African continent was carved up, territory grabbed, governments installed, and troops sent to protect the new colonies from their original inhabitants, who wanted their land back.

(It's important to recognize that borders in Africa were drawn by European conquerors who paid no attention to existing tribal territories. There were not, in the 1880s, central governments for countries named *Congo* or *Kenya* or *Nigeria*. The new states made little sense in terms of Africa's ethnic and cultural divisions—which is one reason that internal conflict continues in countries that became independent in the 1960s but kept the boundaries drawn on the map during the 1880s.)

The following colonies, protectorates, and occupied territories were under British rule at the Empire's high point in 1900: Aden, Antigua, Ascension, Australia, the Bahamas, Barbados, Basutoland, Bechuanaland, Bermuda, British Guiana, British Honduras, British North Borneo, British Solomon Islands, British Somaliland, Brunei, Burma, Canada, Cape of Good Hope, Cayman-Turks-Caicos Islands, Ceylon, Christmas Island, Cocos-Keeling Islands, Cook Islands, Cyprus, Dominica, the East African Protectorate, Egypt, Falkland Islands, Fiji, Gambia, Gibraltar, Gilbert and Ellice Islands, Gold Coast, Grenada, Hong Kong, India, Jamaica, Labuan, Lagos, Leeward Isles, Malay States, Maldive Islands, Malta, Mauritius, Montserrat, Natal, New Zealand, Newfoundland, Nigeria, Norfolk Island, Northern Rhodesia, Nyasaland, Papua, Pitcairn, St. Kitts and Nevis, St. Helena, St. Lucia, St. Vincent, Sarawak, Seychelles, Sierra Leone, Singapore, Southern Rhodesia, Straits Settlements (Singapore, Penang, Malacca), Sudan, Swaziland, Tonga, Trinidad and Tobago, Tristan da Cunha, Uganda, Virgin Islands, Windward Isles, Zanzibar.

In addition to ruling these territories, England exercised vast international influence. British investors, engineers, merchants, and businessmen built and ran electric companies, shipping lines, railways, telephone services, banks, and insurance companies around the world. The British consulate was the center of trade for much of South America as well as Russia, China, Persia, and Turkey. London's unquestioned role as the center of world commerce and investment supplied new wealth for mercantile leaders and a steady, prosperous life for the ever-increasing number of middle-class managers and superior clerks.

The Empire may not have had much of direct role in English life, but it supplied employment, adventure, and enterprise for ambitious people of all classes. The ease of emigration protected England from the social turmoil that many European countries experienced during the nineteenth century. A variety of organizations and charities helped artisans, families, working-class men and women, and even homeless children to get free or cheap passage to colonies such as Canada and Australia where jobs and land were plentiful.

The sense of empire (and pride in being an imperial nation) grew in the last decades of the century. Technology linked British possessions around the world. Steamships and the Suez Canal shortened the passage to India to 17 days. Australia could be reached in four weeks. More than half the world's merchant ships carried the British flag. By the century's end underwater cables and telegraphic land lines sent messages almost anywhere in the Empire in a matter of minutes. The mythology of popular imperialism used the colonies, the Union Jack, and pictures of heroic explorers and soldiers for patriotic and commercial purposes.

The term *colonies of white settlement* designated Australia, Canada, New Zealand, and sometimes South Africa—temperate territories with large numbers of English immigrants who had subdued the original population. Parliament realized that these colonies needed their own representative governments in order to prevent a repetition of what happened in the 13 American colonies in 1776. During the second half of the century, various forms of responsible self-government were established, although governors-general appointed by the queen retained their ceremonial roles.

In 1893, New Zealand became the world's first country to grant the vote on equal terms to all adults regardless of sex or race. In the rest of the Empire racial domination was the rule. There was no move towards permitting self-government in countries principally occupied by Africans, Chinese, Indians, or other people of color.

The Empire's administrators and businessmen developed a way of life devoted to remaining English even though their working years were spent abroad. Few of them came from the aristocracy. (The viceroy or governor might be a peer, but he usually spent most of his time at home and came out to the colony only for state occasions.) Middle-class men—often educated in lesser public schools—occupied positions they could not have achieved in England. At age 18 or 19, without any special training, they passed a foreign service examination or secured a commercial post through family interest and went abroad to the place where they would spend most of their life.

In most colonies a relatively small number of white men ran all the key institutions: the government, the army, the police, the banks, the shipping agencies, the important business firms. Their subordinates came from the native population, but there was no pretense of equality. In the earlier years of colonization, relationships had been more open. There were, for example, respectable marriages between English men and high-caste Indian women. By the latter half of the nineteenth century, however, social separation was the rule. The English lived in their own enclave, established a cricket club and an Anglican church, and eagerly entertained English travelers and military officers who passed through.

Careers in the Empire meant late marriage. A man went out to his posting and waited to be sure of his prospects. When he had a *home leave*—often after seven years or more—he went back to England and found a bride or married the woman who had been waiting for him. London department stores featured *India Outfits* and specialized trousseaus of clothing suited to the climate of other colonies. Chests of household goods and tinned foods packed for transport were also advertised. Private girls' schools offered short courses in domestic science and tropical hygiene that were tailored for intending colonists.

While emigrants to the colonies of white settlement quickly called themselves Canadians or Australians, residents elsewhere thought of England as home. They guarded against letting down their standards or "going native." Victorians were fully dressed by day and changed into something more formal for dinner even in remote tropical outposts. They sent their children back to England at a very young age—magazines advertised seaside boarding homes "suitable for colonial children until old enough for school." And they hoped that by middle age they would have accumulated enough money to buy a comfortable house and enjoy a pleasant retirement in England.

India: The Raj

England's most important, richest, and most distinctive overseas possession was India. The term *raj*, taken from the Hindu word for "rule," was first used in the form of *British raj* (British rule over India) and then transformed into *the Raj*—an all-encompassing word for the Indian subcontinent during the time it was under England's dominion.

The East India Company, a trading corporation owned by English investors, had been acquiring territory and influence since the early 1600s. By 1770 it was the effective governing agent in many parts of India. In May 1857, the Indian soldiers in three cavalry regiments killed their British officers and set off a rebellion against English rule, identified in history written by Englishmen as the *Indian Mutiny*. (Indian sources call it the *First War for Independence*.) In 1858, after the rebellion had been put down by troops brought in from other parts of the Empire, the East India Company was disbanded and the British government took over.

The post of Viceroy of India was a political appointment, generally given to an important aristocrat. About one-third of the territory was administered by some six hundred Indian rulers who governed their own states but swore allegiance to the Crown. The native rulers had Englishmen assigned to them as *residents* or *advisors*. Arrangements varied greatly, since each Indian ruler had signed a treaty defining his rights and powers.

Another 10 large provinces made up what was called *British India*: Bombay, Madras, Bengal, the Central Province, the United Province, Assam, Burma, Bihar, Punjab, and the North West Frontier. The government of British India was in the hands of the Indian Civil Service, which was responsible for defense, foreign affairs, finance, railways, the telegraph service, and the post office. Seven of the provinces also had local governments run by the Indian Civil Service to look after internal affairs.

All important posts in the Indian Civil Service were held by the British. In the lower and middle ranks were men from India who had received an English education in mission schools. (Technically, Indians were free to compete in the entrance exam for upper-level posts, but it was given in English in London and drew heavily on the subjects boys learned in public schools.)

A young Englishman appointed to the Indian Civil Service first served in one of the 250 local districts, where he might be responsible for police, courts, agriculture, or taxes. (Because taxes were

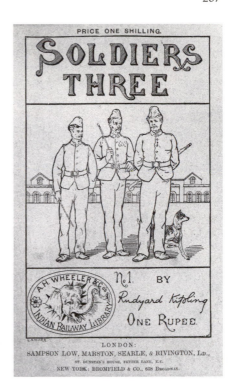

The cover of an inexpensive reprint of short stories about British soldiers in India written by Rudyard Kipling as a young journalist and originally published in the Sunday supplement of an English-language newspaper in the city of Allahabad, India. Notice that the book was sold for one shilling in England and, as part of the Indian Railway Library, for one rupee in India. The illustration was drawn by Rudyard Kipling's father, who was a professor in a Bombay art school. Courtesy of The Art Archive.

important in the imperial scheme of things, the district head was sometimes referred to as the *collector*.) His orders ultimately came from the India Office in London, but in an isolated location a district officer essentially operated on his own.

As he grew more senior, he could hope to be stationed near a regimental headquarters or in a larger city where there was a sizable English community. By the 1880s a distinctive Anglo-Indian life took shape: servants in plenty, polo, tea dances, garden parties, balls. The English in India were largely unmarried, but the wives of senior officials and higher-ranking army officers brought their sisters and cousins and nieces to share in the social life. In hot weather, women and children (and all men who could manage it) moved to hill stations at the foot of the Himalayas.

In the 1890s there were as many as 20,000 Britons in India, not counting the men in regular army regiments stationed there. About 1,300 were in the Indian Civil Service; 3,000 were officers in the Indian Army; and 10,000 or more were in business or represented London banking and commercial firms.

The Empire at Home

The Diamond Jubilee of 1897 was celebrated with a military procession drawn from all corners of the Empire: Canadian Mounties, New Zealand Maoris, the Royal Nigerian Constabulary, the Jamaica Artillery, native troops from the West Indies, British Guiana, Sierra Leone, Cyprus, Borneo, the Gold Coast, and India. The English royal family that rode through London's streets included grandchildren of Queen Victoria who occupied many of the thrones of Europe. For the Jubilee's final event, 165 ships of the Royal Navy passed in review at Spithead—a procession that stretched out for more than 30 miles.

By the end of the century, however, U.S. industry and German naval power threatened to challenge England's control of the seas and dominance of world markets. War against the Boers in South Africa revealed glaring weaknesses in the army's equipment and leadership. The response was a massive surge of patriotism. Symbols of the Empire and images of subject peoples were virtually inescapable: in songs and advertising, on postage stamps, in the popular press, in fiction for adults as well as for boys and girls.

When the war in South Africa was still going badly, the British garrison at Mafeking, in Bechuanaland, commanded by Colonel Robert Baden-Powell (who later founded the Boy Scouts) was surrounded and cut off from its sources of supply. After 217 days the siege of Mafeking was relieved on May 17, 1900, and streets all over England filled with cheering crowds. Bonfires and fireworks lit up the night. This celebration and jubilation did a good deal to paper over the rifts among the English people and to conceal the real changes that loomed on the horizon as the basis of economic and political power irrevocably changed.

One of the most popular writers of the 1890s was Rudyard Kipling, Bombay-born son of the Empire whose poems and stories about English soldiers and Indian life won him the Nobel Prize for literature in 1907. He made England aware of its place in the world; he assured his countrymen that English racial superiority brought the rule of law to grateful peoples everywhere. Yet Kipling did not write about colonels and commanders. His characters were engineers, common soldiers, and native children. He translated the power of Empire into a source of shared pride for ordinary English people, and when he wrote "Recessional" for the 1897 Diamond Jubilee it was not only a celebration of imperial glory but also a warning against putting too much trust in conquest and subjugation.

"RECESSIONAL," BY RUDYARD KIPLING

This poem was published in the London Times on the day of the Diamond Jubilee in 1897, which celebrated the 60th year of Queen Victoria's reign.

God of our fathers, known of old,
   Lord of our far-flung battle-line,
Beneath whose awful Hand we hold
   Dominion over palm and pine—
Lord God of Hosts, be with us yet,
Lest we forget—lest we forget!

The tumult and the shouting dies;
   The captains and the kings depart:
Still stands Thine ancient sacrifice,
   An humble and a contrite heart.
Lord God of Hosts, be with us yet,
Lest we forget—lest we forget!

Far-called, our navies melt away;
   On dune and headland sinks the fire:
Lo, all our pomp of yesterday
   Is one with Ninevah and Tyre!
Judge of the Nations, spare us yet,
Lest we forget—lest we forget!

If, drunk with sight of power, we loose
   Wild tongues that have not Thee in awe,
Such boastings as the Gentiles use
   Or lesser breeds without the Law—
Lord God of Hosts, be with us yet,
Lest we forget—lest we forget!

For heathen heart that puts her trust
   In reeking tube and iron shard,
All valiant dust that builds on dust,
   And guarding, calls not thee to guard,
For frantic boast and foolish word—
Thy mercy on Thy People, Lord!
Amen

An extraordinary transformation in daily as well as political life had taken place during Queen Victoria's reign. When she died on January 27, 1901, very few people still alive could remember the girl who had taken the throne almost 64 years earlier. The world into which she was born was irrevocably changed.

APPENDIX:
VICTORIAN RESEARCH
AND RESOURCES

Many books about various aspects of life in Victorian England have been published over the past century, from dense and thoroughly researched scholarly tomes to memoirs, picture-books, and chatty volumes intended for general readers. These secondary sources (that is, books describing or analyzing the period but written after it ended) are valuable as an overview to put information in context. Scholarly books often help in understanding and interpreting the facts, and also in appreciating novels written in the nineteenth century, which supply a compelling—if often partial—picture of Victorians' thoughts, concerns, experiences, and physical surroundings. For secondary sources the titles listed in "Further Reading" will provide a starting point and, usually, reference lists of additional materials. The most interesting new research on Victorian daily life, however, uses primary sources— that is, books and magazines and drawings and photographs produced between 1837 and 1901. Until very recently, very few primary sources from the Victorian era were available to people who could not travel to libraries in England. The 1861 edition of Isabella Beeton's *Book of Household Management,* for example, had been republished in paperback, but dozens of other books about cooking and servants and furnishing a home—some of which give quite a different picture of ordinary life—remained almost unknown.

All that is now changing very quickly. Although some new resources require access to a university library, other digitization projects bring authentic Victorian publications to anyone at a computer with a fast internet connection. The most significant for nineteenth-century England is Google Books, which is scanning out-of-copyright material from collections (including Oxford's Bodleian Library), making it possible to do research that would have required being in England as recently as 2006. This appendix is intended as a starting point to help you view what Victorians of all classes saw and read about fashion, manners, travel, health, work, wages, family budgets, and additional topics that have hardly yet been explored.

OVERVIEW AND METHODS

Finding Books Online

Searching for full-text primary sources can be frustrating and sometimes baffling. In Google, go first to http://books.google.com/ and then to the advanced book search; check "full view," put a search term in the title box (a full or exact title is not necessary), and restrict the dates. (Using the general search boxes at the top of the page will search the full text of all books, not just the title pages, and results may run into the thousands.) The resource sections that follow will suggest words or titles as starting points.

It may be necessary to click on the title page to find out where the book was published, since daily lives in the United States and in England could be very different. However, even books published in New York or Boston may have English origins: before international copyright became effective in the 1890s, U.S. publishers often simply reprinted British books. The back of the title page, the preface, or the table of contents may reveal a book's real origin. Google Books, for example, has a copy of *The Habits of Good Society: A Handbook for Ladies and Gentlemen* printed in New York in 1863 but first published in London in 1859. Note that you can not print pages directly from the screen; you must first download the entire book, after which you can glance through it off-line and print as much or as little as you choose.

Search results will improve with practice. Vocabulary differs: titles that include *cookery* instead of *cook book* or *receipts* instead of *recipes* are usually from England. *England guide* brings up not only guidebooks for tourists but also guides to marriage law, church doctrine, railway lines, and other topics. The "About this book" page sometimes has a blue underlined subject term; clicking on it may bring up additional books on the same topic. Putting the author's full name in the author search field may cause problems; a surname only is best if using a name. Be aware that the search function can make silly mistakes; its character recognition software is sometimes baffled by Victorian typography.

For illustrations and explanatory material, there are many useful and dependable Web sites—and also a great many with eccentric, partial, and erroneous information. Most sites recommended below are from universities, museums, organizations, and public bodies. Since Web addresses tend to change, both the current name and the URL are provided; with luck, the name should help if the address leads to "file not found." Finally, no subscription-only sites are listed; reference librarians in college and public libraries can help in finding additional online (as well as published) resources available through the library.

Other Full-text Sources

The oldest supplier of out-of-copyright books to download or read online is Project Gutenberg (http://www.gutenberg.org), although its books may not include their illustrations. Bartelby (http://www.bartleby.com) has older editions of many standard reference books. The University of Pennsylvania's Online Books Page (http://onlinebooks.library.upenn.edu) and the Internet Text Archive (http://www.archive.org/details/texts) both link to some material not listed elsewhere.

Full-text searchable newspaper archives can be essential for some projects. Although the London *Times* is accessible only through libraries that hold subscriptions, two other British newspapers are available at a modest fee. The Scotsman Archive (http://archive. scotsman.com) contains every issue of Edinburgh's *The Scotsman* from 1817 to 1950 (it was first a weekly and subsequently a daily). Searches can be saved; reading the full-text requires payment. The Guardian and Observer Digital Archive (http://archive.guardian. co.uk), which holds the weekday *Guardian* (1821–1990) and Sunday *Observer* (1791–1990, has a similar arrangement: free search, relatively inexpensive timed pass for reading and printing. The British Library sample newspaper site (http://www.uk.olivesoftware. com) holds full-page views of selected newspapers for a limited number of dates; its Collect Britain site at http://www.collectbritain. co.uk/collections/pip has the *Penny Illustrated Paper* from 1861

to 1913. Google's News Archive Search at http://news.google.
com/archivesearch searches the text of around 200 newspapers,
magazines and scholarly journals from 1750 to the present, most
of them from U.S. sources. The results page provides headlines
and either a free link to printable full text or information about
pay-per-view sources. In addition, the Nineteenth-Century Serials
Edition (http://www.ncse.ac.uk/index.html) contains ten years
(1880–1890) of the weekly book-trade magazine *Publishers' Circular*
and complete runs of five other titles: the *Monthly Repository of Theology and General Literature* (1806–1837); the Chartist *Northern Star*
(1838–1852); the mid-century political weekly *Leader* (1850–1860); the
monthly *English Woman's Journal* (1858–1864), voice of the women's
movement of its period; and *Tomahawk* (1867–1870), a weekly satirical
paper with elaborate full-page cartoons.

Widely Useful Victorian Web sites

The Victorian Web (http://www.victorianweb.org) is an academic
site with explanations, illustrations, and examples contributed by
scholars and teachers; a link in the upper-left corner of the home
page explains how to cite it as a source. The Nineteenth Century
City   (http://www.st-andrews.ac.uk/%7Ecity19c/viccity/home.
html); BBC History—Victorians (http://www.bbc.co.uk/history/
trail/victorian_britain); and Victorian London (http://www.victo
rianlondon.org), which is arranged in dictionary format with material taken directly from Victorian publications, should be checked
for all topics, whether or not specifically mentioned in the resource
section below. Bruce Rosen's Victorian History (http://www.vich
ist.blogspot.com) has short, well-illustrated essays on cabs, funerals, vegetarians, music halls, railways, and many similar topics.
The Victoria Research Web (http://victorianresearch.org), by and
for people who study the period, includes a link to the archives of
the VICTORIA discussion list, where questions have been asked
and answered since 1993.

At the United Kingdom National Archives (http://www.nation
alarchives.gov.uk), begin by exploring the menu under "Research,
Education, and Online Exhibitions." Among other useful materials,
its Learning Curve has documents, illustrations, worksheets, and
quizzes for students age 7–16. The Victorian Web Guide from the
Education Resource Service at http://www.ers.north-ayrshire.gov.
uk/primary/Victoriansweb.htm links to additional online resources,
some of them suitable for younger children. School History (http://

SchoolHistory.co.uk) has Victorian topics and resources at its sections for *primary* (age 4–11), *year 9* (age 13–14), and *AS/A2* (college prep). The English Heritage ViewFinder (http://view finder.english-heritage.org.uk) holds thousands of photographs of social, industrial, and architectural history; the photo essays are organized by theme ("domestic service," for example), and an advanced search can be controlled by date, topic, and additional restrictions.

London's Institute for Historical Research at http://www.british-history.ac.uk holds online versions of core historical works. Under "period" and then "the nineteenth century," the *Survey of London* provides street-level and sometimes even house-level descriptions, plans, and illustrations. Some volumes of the *Victoria County History*, the Lewis *Topographical Dictionaries* for England, Scotland, and Wales, and selected Ordnance Survey maps (which can be viewed by section) are also on the site, and materials are constantly being added. Another academic project, the major revision now known as the *Oxford Dictionary of National Biography*, is available only to subscribers, but its Oxford Biography Index (http://www.oup. com/oxforddnb/info/index) can be used to check the full name, title, and birth/death dates of prominent people from every field— nineteenth-century sources and even recent works often have errors. Historical Directories (http://www.historicaldirectories. org/hd/index.asp) contains the full text of many local directories listing residents and shops in a particular area at a certain date; most of them also have advertising pages that supply information about products and services in daily life.

RESOURCES

Beyond the general resources already mentioned, the sections below are broken into topics organized to follow the chapters of *Daily Life in Victorian England*. Within each section, full-text books are listed first, followed by Web sites.

The Foundations of Daily Life: Class and Money

On Google Books, *A Manual of Domestic Economy: Suited to Families Spending from £100 to £1000* by John Henry Walsh (1856) and an updated edition entitled *A Manual of Domestic Economy: Suited to Families Spending from £150 to £1500* (1874) include much general information on food, furniture, cooking, social duties, health, and servants as well as prices. *Wages and Earnings of the Working Classes* by Leone Levi (1867) is a detailed survey done for a Member of Parliament. Other titles (which will also suggest terms to use in searching for additional materials) include *The Progress of the Working Classes in the Last Half Century* by Robert Giffen (1884); and *Women's Work and Wages* by Edward Cadbury and others (1907).

Charles Booth carried out an extensive survey of conditions in London between 1886 and 1903. His papers in the Charles Booth Online Archive (http://booth.lse.ac.uk) include full digital images of 31 police notebooks, 4 notebooks about the Jewish community, 6 casebooks from the Stepney Poor-Law Union, and an online version of the 1898–99 map of London poverty. The map uses colors ranging from black (the poorest) through gold (the richest) to show residents' economic status; sections can be viewed side-by-side with a current map. Channel 4's Time Traveller's Guide to Victorian Britain (http://www.channel4.com/history/microsites/H/history/guide19/index.html) includes material on ways of life under "The Basics" and "Class and Customs."

Both "Economic Contexts" on the Victorian Web and "Finance" on Victorian London have specific examples of prices, wages, and family budgets. Additional links are under "United Kingdom and Europe" at Current Value of Old Money (http://www.projects.ex.ac.uk/RDavies/arian/current/howmuch.html).

The British Library's Evanion Collection of printed ephemera (http://www.collectbritain.co.uk/collections/evanion) includes trade catalogues, price lists and other advertising materials. The Sensation Press has assorted Victorian advertisements at http://www.sensationpress.com/victorianadvertising.htm. The Bureau de Change in the Sainsbury's Archives Virtual Museum (http://www.j-sainsbury.co.uk/museum/refram0.htm) has grocery store price lists for 1903 and a sample of arithmetic questions for children learning to do math in pounds, shillings, and pence.

Answers to the question "how much is that worth in today's money?" are complicated. Measuring Worth (http://www.measuringworth.com/ukcompare) has calculators that use five different indexes; Economic History Services (http://eh.net/hmit) also has several calculators and further explanations. An Excel worksheet for doing sums in the old currency down to the last farthing can be downloaded (about 900K) or opened directly and run from (http://victorianresearch.org/Pound_Calculator.xls); in either case, Excel must be available on your computer.

As for Victorian money itself, Pre-Decimal Sterling (http://gwydir.demon.co.uk/jo/units/money.htm) has pictures of the coins used before 1971. A related site provides tables of Imperial Weights and Measures (http://gwydir.demon.co.uk/jo/units/index.htm; please note that even when names, such as *pint* and *ton*, are the same, British measures are not identical to those in the United States). Photographs on the page Late Victorian Coinage (http://www.studium.com/2/viccoins.html) can be enlarged by clicking and have clear details but are not in relative scale; the Sainsbury Museum page at http://www.j-sainsbury.co.uk/museum/Coins.htm shows a full set in correct relative size but less clear images.

Working Life

Entering the three words *law master servant* in the Google Books title field will yield volumes covering workers in all fields; *The Factory and Workshop Acts* by George Jarvis Notcutt (1874) is also useful. Since laws relative to labor and working conditions were reformed often, it's especially important to pay attention to publication dates. The word *clerk* will produce books with practical advice for young men in virtually all areas of business and management (and also a good deal of fiction).

Books for domestic servants are also plentiful; typical titles for women are *Instructions in Household Matters; or, The Young Girl's Guide to Domestic Service* (1844); *The Servant's Behaviour Book* by Emily Augusta Patmore, (1859); and *The Young Servant's Own Book* (1883). On women's other employment, books written by and for social reformers include *The Condition of Working Women and the Factory Acts* by Jessie Boucherett and Helen Blackburn (1896). In the latter years of the century, practical guides for middle-class women began to appear. *How Women May Earn a Living* by Mercy Grogan (1883) has sections on teaching, medicine, nursing, bookkeeping, and a number of less-obvious possibilities. Both *What Our Daughters Can Do for Themselves* by J. E. Davidson (1894) and *Ladies at Work* by Mary Jeune (1893) were reprinted from women's magazines.

On the Web, see The Plight of Women's Work in the Early Industrial Revolution in England and Wales (http://www.womeninworldhistory.com/lesson7.html) and Spinning the Web (http://www.spinningtheweb.org.uk), developed by the Manchester City Council. Nettlesworth School Durham has information and illustrations for elementary-school children on "Industrial Revolution and Child Labour" at http://www.nettlesworth.durham.sch.uk/time/victorian/vindust.html; The National Archives Learning Curve covers similar issues at http://www.learningcurve.gov.uk/victorianbrit

ain/industrial/default.htm. Trade Union Ancestors (http://www.
unionancestors.co.uk) has resources on many nineteenth-century
trade unions, including the teachers' unions. Edwardian life at Hinch-
ingbrooke   (http://hinchhouse.org.uk/ninth/ech.html)   includes
information about the servants from the 1901 census, plus a table of
their wages and description of their schedules for a typical day.

Technology, Science, and the Urban World

Discoveries and Inventions of the Nineteenth Century by Robert Rout-
ledge was very popular and frequently updated. Google Books has
several editions from various dates, all with hundreds of illustrations. The transportation technology that transformed the Victorian world led to almost innumerable books; use *railway* in the title
box and carefully limit the dates. (*Railroad* is more common in the
United States.) Handbooks for travelers, with routes, timetables,
sights, and maps will be found by searching for *guide railway.*

For urban life, Victorian London has many full-text books, including the 1879 edition of *Dickens's Dictionary of London,* edited by the
novelist's eldest son, a small-print compendium of information
including omnibus routes, cab fares, names and prices of newspapers, postal information, and locations of churches, police courts,
schools, workhouses, lodging houses, hospitals, fire stations, banks,
clubs, theatres, and charities.

The Great Exhibition of the Industry of All Nations at the Crystal Palace in 1851 celebrated technology, industry, and the arts.
A Google Web search on either *Great Exhibition* or *Crystal Palace*
produces something like five million hits. Some of the best are:
the Victorian Web; Victorian Cities; Victoria Station (http://www.
victorianstation.com/palace.html); and the University of Kansas
library (http://spencer.lib.ku.edu/exhibits/greatexhibition). In
addition, *Great Exhibition* in the Google books title box leads to
the *Official Descriptive and Illustrated Catalogue* and a long list of
visitors' guides, many of which also have extensive advertising
sections.

Maps and plans can be found at the British Library's Streets of
London (http://collectbritain.co.uk/collections/crace). Baedeker's
Old Guide Books (http://contueor.com/baedeker/index.htm)
displays large-scale maps and street indexes from a 1905 London
guide. Canal and rail networks can be traced on some Victorian
maps towards the bottom of the page on British Isles Old Maps at
http://freepages.genealogy.rootsweb.com/~genmaps/genfiles/

COU_Pages/ENG_pages/aaEng.htm. Virtual exhibitions at the City of London Libraries and Guildhall Art Gallery (http://213.86 .34.242:8180/collage/app) include Henry Dixon's London (photographs from the 1860s–1880s) and London's Railways.

For industry and its technology, the Internet Modern History Sourcebook(http://www.fordham.edu/halsall/mod/modsbook2. html#index) has material on inventions, inventors, and workers' lives. The Steam Engine Library (http://www.history.rochester. edu/steam) has online books, many of them illustrated. The Time Traveller's Guide to Victorian Britain includes industrialization and science; see http://www.channel4.com/history/microsites/H/ history/guide19/index. The Victoria and Albert Museum pages on Industry and Transport are at http://www.vam.ac.uk/collections/ periods_styles/19thcentury/steam/index.html.

Several towns in the north of England maintain Web sites about industrialization, including Blackburn's Cotton Town (http://www. cottontown.org), Manchester's Spinning the Web (http://www. spinningtheweb.org.uk), and Liverpool's Historic Canning Area (http://canning.merseyworld.com).

York's National Railway Museum has online exhibits at http:// www.nrm.org.uk/collections/exhibition.asp; The Railways Archive (http://www.railwaysarchive.co.uk) holds full-text historical and archival sources. The Great Western Archive (http://www. greatwestern.org.uk) covers one of the major Victorian railway companies. The Heritage Railways Glossary (http://www.heri tagerailways.com/glossary/info.html) defines railway terms and supplies some technical information. A selection of contemporary reports from the *Illustrated London News* is at The Industrial Revolution and the Railway System (http://www.mtholyoke.edu/ courses/rschwart/ind_rev/indrev.html). National Archive Learning Curve materials on railways and their impact are at http:// www.learningcurve.gov.uk/victorianbritain/happy/default.htm.

Pictures of transport and other technologies can be located in the Science and Society Picture Library (http://www.scienceandsoci ety.co.uk). Many nineteenth-century pamphlets on transportation (including several railway timetables) held by the London School of Economics are available online. See the guide at http://www.lse. ac.uk/library/pamphlets/Transport/transport_pamphlets.htm; if the classmark (i.e., call number) is highlighted, click for access to the full text.

For ships and shipping, the National Maritime Museum at Greenwich has online displays at http://www.nmm.ac.uk/collections/

index.cfm. Through Mighty Seas (http://www.mightyseas.co.uk) has histories of more than 900 merchant sailing ships of the northwest England. Era of the Clipper Ships, although chiefly about American ships, has a page at http://www.eraoftheclipperships.com/british islestradewinds.html for the *Cutty Sark* and other British tea clippers, with links to additional British tall ship Web sites and museums. Great Ocean Liners Ship Histories at http://www.greatoceanliners. net/index2.html holds histories and illustrations of the transformed ocean transport from the second half of the century.

For Victorian science, The Complete Works of Charles Darwin Online at http://www.darwin-online.org.uk includes books, private papers, handwritten manuscripts, a bibliography, and supplementary materials. The full-text works include the first editions of *Voyage of the Beagle, Zoology,* and *Descent of Man;* all editions of *Origin of Species;* the Beagle diary and field notebooks, and Darwin's journal. There are also hundreds of illustrations. At http://darwin-online.org.uk/majorworks.html clicking on a title of a work brings it up, clicking on the finch icon leads to its illustrations, and clicking on the small image provides a much larger version. The University of Cambridge also holds the Darwin Correspondence Project (http://www.darwinproject.ac.uk) with the complete and searchable texts of around 5,000 letters written by and to Charles Darwin up to 1865, including all surviving letters from the years around the publication of *Origin of Species* in 1859.

The undergraduate Victorian Studies Online Teaching Anthology at http://etrc.lib.umn.edu/uvsota/index.htm, in the section "Science, Evolution, Eugenics," holds essays scanned directly from nineteenth-century periodicals. Like the comparable material in today's magazines, these essays often reveal varied and contradictory opinions.

Official Life: Government and the Law

Google book searches under the title words related to these topics almost always yield too many results; check for country, date, and contents before downloading. Frederic William Maitland's *Justice and Police* (1885) supplies a broad picture of the legal system. *Principles of the Criminal Law* by Seymour Frederick Harris and Charles Leete Attenborough (1899) describes the situation at the end of the period, after numerous reforms.

On the laws affecting private life, there are editions from 1858, 1886, and 1904 of *The Law of Wills, Executors, and Administrators* by

William Andrews Holdsworth, reflecting the major changes following the Divorce Act of 1857 and the series of married women's property acts from 1870 to 1882. For women's situation earlier in the century, Barbara Bodichon's 1854 *A Brief Summary in Plain Language of the Most Important Laws Concerning Women* is at http://www.indiana.edu/~letrs/vwwp/bodichon/brieflaw.html. Other useful volumes include *A Handy Book on the New Law of Divorce and Matrimonial Causes* by James Peter Byrne (1860) and *A Concise View of the Law of Husband and Wife* by Joseph Haworth Redman (1883). An 1881 edition of *Guide to the Unprotected in Every-Day Matters Related to Property and Income*, by "A Banker's Daughter" has information about house rental, marriage settlements, trustees, wills, and taxes, as well as other financial matters. *An Epitome of the Laws of Probate and Divorce* by James Carter Harrison (1883) also discusses marriage settlements. An inclusive treatment from the end of the century is *The Law of Domestic Relations: Including Husband and Wife, Parent and Child, Guardian and Ward, Infants, and Master and Servant* by William Pinder Eversley (1896).

The Workhouse at http://www.workhouses.org.uk is one of the most complete sites on any Victorian subject, with pictures, a history of the poor laws, a glossary, and a selection of literature and personal memoirs. Also see the British Library of Political and Economic Science Pamphlet Collection; many titles are available online at http://www.lse.ac.uk/library/pamphlets/SocialPolicy/social_policy_pamphlets.htm.

Old Bailey Online at http://www.oldbaileyonline.org has accounts of thousands of trials at London's central criminal courts from 1674 to 1913 as well as a large glossary of terms used in British criminal proceedings and authoritative background materials on policing, trials, verdicts, punishments, and the criminal justice system. The "schools" page includes images suitable for classroom use. The Harvard University Library Open Collections site http://digitalcollections.harvard.edu provides online access to "Studies in Scarlet," with some 450 trial narratives, and "Dying Speeches and Bloody Murders," an exhibit of the sensational accounts sold cheaply in the days before inexpensive newspapers. "Hanging Ballads" is a similar collection from the University of Glasgow library (http://special.lib.gla.ac.uk/teach/hang/text.html).

The official site of London's Metropolitan Police has a history page at http://www.met.police.uk/history; Scotland Yard History (http://www.historybytheyard.co.uk) has brief details of some cases online. London Police Divisions, a no-fee page from GenDocs

Genealogy Services at http://homepage.ntlworld.com/hitch/
gendocs/police.html has a short history of the London police, a
listing of the divisions and areas they covered in 1888, and some
additional resources.

The Jack the Ripper Casebook (http://www.casebook.org) is the
most complete archive of primary sources related to the 1888 "Ripper" murders. The Victorian section of Treasures from the National
Archives at http://www.nationalarchives.gov.uk/museum/dates.
asp?date_id=4 has an exhibit on Jack the Ripper and another with a
photograph of a child prisoner; at the bottom of that page are links
to other National Archives sites with material on crime and punishment suitable for school children.

The Australian site Convict Central (http://www.convictcentral.
com) provides information about British trials and sentencing as
well as convict settlements in Australia. Victorian Detective Fiction
(http://www.crimeculture.com/Contents/VictorianCrime.html)
has a short illustrated account of the Victorian origins of a very
popular genre.

The Material Substance of Private Life:
House, Food, and Clothes

Isabella Beeton's *Book of Household Management* (1861) is easily
found online. Other inclusive titles at Google Books range from John
Henry Walsh's well-organized *Manual of Domestic Economy: Suited
to Families Spending from £100 to £1000* (1856) and its 1874 update to
The Lady's Every-Day Book by Robert Kemp Philp (1875), jammed
with miscellaneous information: weaning an infant, archery, preventing moths, dry-cleaning carpets, stocking an aquarium, mixing a salad, and non-inflammable clothing all come up within five
pages.

On houses, the well-illustrated *Grammar of House Planning* by
Robert Scott Burn (1864) and *Our Homes, and How to Make Them
Healthy* by Shirley Forster Murphy and Robert Brudenell Carter
(1883) cover not only design and architecture but also domestic
technology. *English Country Houses* by William Wilkinson (1875)
has plans and sketches for 61 buildings including laborers' cottages; *The Englishman's House* by Charles James Richardson (1898)
also describes houses of many sorts; *The Gentleman's House* by
Robert Kerr (1865) is for the well-to-do. Books on furnishing and
decoration include *Hints on Household Taste* by Charles Locke East-
lake (1883) and the 1877 *Suggestions for House Decoration* by Rhoda

Garrett and Agnes Garrett, who ran a successful decorating business in London. There were also books on individual rooms: *The Drawing-room* by Lucy Orrinsmith (1878); *The Bedroom and the Boudoir* by Mary Anne Broome, Lady Barker (1878). *The Dining-room* by Martha Jane Loftie (1878) covers table setting as well as furniture, with many illustrations.

Several pages of full-text cookbooks (often in many editions from varied dates) can be found by using *cookery* in the Google Books title field. Some of the more important are *A New System of Domestic Cookery* by Maria Eliza Rundell; *Modern Cookery* by Eliza Acton (first published in 1845; most editions also include a helpful glossary of terms); and *A Shilling Cookery for the People* by Alexis Soyer. Textbooks for elementary-school girls, who learned cooking to prepare them for both domestic service and family life, include the well-illustrated *Food and Home Cookery* by Catherine M. Buckton (1879) and *Domestic Economy: a Class-book for Girls* by S. S. Wigley (1877). *The Scholar's Guide to Household Management and Cookery* by W. B. Tegetmeier (1876), in full-text on Victorian London, includes inexpensive recipes, pictures of cooking equipment, and diagrams of working-class cottages.

General information on clothing is found in books such as *The Hand-book of Dress-making* by Mary J. Howell (1845) and *How to Dress on £15 a Year* by Millicent Whiteside Cook (1874). A textbook for teachers, *Needlework and Cutting-out* by Kate Stanley (1883), includes instructions for underwear and baby clothes to be made by working-class schoolgirls.

On the Web, The Internet Library of Early Journals (http://www.bodley.ox.ac.uk/ilej) has scanned 10 years of *The Builder*, a weekly magazine of architectural and construction news with many plans and illustrations. A virtual tour of the Linley Sambourne House, home of a comfortable middle-class London family, is at http://www.rbkc.gov.uk/linleysambournehouse/tour/default.asp; the Sherlock Holmes Museum at http://www.sherlock-holmes.co.uk/home.htm provides the same for a late-Victorian flat. Photographs of Victorian Kitchen and Table Tools are at http://www.calacademy.org/research/anthropology/kitchen. Sainsbury's Virtual Museum (http://www.j-sainsbury.co.uk/museum/museum.htm) displays materials from a grocery chain with Victorian origins.

For the names and descriptions of many kinds of Victorian horse-drawn vehicle, see the Glossary of Carriages (http://www.arnkarnk.plus.com/glossary.htm) and a site with illustrations from many historical periods, the Florida Educational Clearinghouse

library of free clip art at http://etc.usf.edu/clipart/galleries/
Transportation/horse-drawn_transportation.htm.

Among the most useful sites for clothing are the Victorian Web's
page on costume (under "visual arts"); Bissonnette on Costume: A
Visual Dictionary of Fashion (http://dept.kent.edu/museum/cos
tume), with photographs annotated and explained by the museum's curator; and the Fashion Plate Collection (http://content.lib.
washington.edu/costumehistweb). Hundreds of additional fashion plates can be found with an advanced search in "Art & Literature" limited by the keywords *England* and *women* of the New
York Public Library Digital Gallery at http://digitalgallery.nypl.
org/nypldigital.

Victorian Era Fashion History (http://www.fashion-era.com/
the_victorian_era.htm) is an elaborate commercial site covering
many topics. Although the text sometimes has oversimplified information and factual errors, many illustrations are worth seeing. The
Secret History of the Corset and Crinoline (http://www.fathom.
com/course/21701726) was prepared by the costume department
of the Victoria and Albert Museum and should be entirely trustwor-
thy. London's Science Museum covers Dress, Fashion and Moder-
nity in Victorian Women's Magazines at (http://www.fathom.
com/course/21701733/index.html). Victorian and Edwardian
Photographs—Roger Vaughan Personal Collection (http://www.
rogerco.freeserve.co.uk) displays a large number of photographs
organized by date as well as a useful "Date an Old Photo" section,
which explains how to guess the date of a photograph by looking
closely at costume details.

Family and Social Rituals

Etiquette in the Google Books title field locates many examples,
but most borrow heavily from earlier titles. In addition, many of
the books were inexpensive editions, clearly meant for people without a lot of extra income, although the information is often inappropriate for someone of little means. It's advisable to look at several,
from different dates, and to judge everything with a dose of common sense. *Courtship and Marriage: And the Gentle Art of Home-mak-
ing* by Annie S. Swan (1894) and *Letters to a Bride including Letters to
a Débutante* by Lucie Heaton Armstrong (1896) were initially published in women's magazines. Books with model letters also reveal
information about social relationships; *letter writer* is the search
term to use to find books about writing letters. Victorian London has

the full text of *The Ladies' and Gentleman's Model Letter Writer* under *L* in the bibliography's alphabetical list. Other family and social topics on Victorian London are found under Childhood, Death and Dying, Publications, and Women. Mourning is treated on Remembering the Dead from the Australian Museum Online at http://www.deathon line.net/remembering/mourning/victorian.cfm.

Education

Education in the title field of Google Books, even when limited by full view and date, yields hundreds of titles; it's important to check for place of publication because of the significant differences between England and the United States. To locate schoolbooks used by Victorian children, try adding *school, school board, text,* or *class book* to a title search. *Sonnenschein's Cyclopædia of Education* by Alfred Ewen Fletcher (1889) contains vast amounts of information.

The Schools for the People by George Christopher Trout Bartley (1871) describes the education of non-elite children before 1870; *The Elementary Education Act, 1870* by Thomas Preston (1870) explains the law that established hundreds of new schools. For teachers and their training, see books such as *The Teacher's Manual of Method* by William Ross (1858) and *The Training of Teachers in England and Wales* by Peter Sandiford (1910). Some issues of *The Practical Teacher,* a magazine including sample lessons, can be found by searching for that title.

Practical Education by Maria Edgeworth and Richard Edgeworth, initially published in 1798, was used for most of the century by English parents who educated their children at home. Another popular book for mothers is *Hints for the Improvement of Early Education and Nursery Discipline* by Louisa Hoare (first published in 1824). Books to help the governess include *The Governess: A Repertory of Female Education* (1855) and *A Word to a Young Governess* by Katharine Naish (1860). Some question-and-answer books for teaching are *The Entomological Researcher* by Mary Bristow Wood (1845); *The Key-Stone of Grammar Laid* by T. C. (1843); and *The Child's Guide to Knowledge* by Fanny Ward (1862).

For the reformed girls' education after mid-century, see *Work and Play in Girls' Schools* by Dorothea Beale and others (1898). *The Ladies' College & School Examiner* by M. A. Johnston (1867) has sample examination and essay topics. *The Englishwoman's Year Book and Directory* lists secondary schools, vocational schools, and colleges for girls and women. *Tom Brown's School Days* by Thomas Hughes

(1857) is the classic story about English public school life. *Public Schools Calendar* (1866) and *Our Public Schools* by James Minchin (1901) provide an overview; *The Great Schools of England* by Howard Staunton (1865) has many illustrations. For other books on elite boarding schools—both factual and fictional—use *Eton, Rugby, Harrow, Winchester, Charterhouse,* or other schools' names in the title field.

For higher education, see *British and American Education: The Universities of the Two Countries Compared* by Mayo Williamson Hazeltine (1880). Searching with *Oxford University, Cambridge University,* or *London University* in the title field will yield regulations, calendars, alumni lists, lectures, and so forth. Since men (and later women) of any age over 16 could enter London University by passing an examination, the search term *London matriculation* will discover books of questions that reveal the necessary preparation. Women in the Literary Marketplace at http://rmc.library.cornell.edu/womenLit/default.htm displays material about Girton at its "Education" link.

Health and Medicine

Initially published in 1769, William Buchan's *Domestic Medicine* appeared in more than a hundred editions and remained on doctors' shelves throughout the nineteenth century; it is a good source for understanding what Victorians knew about symptoms and diseases. Others include *The Dispensing Chemist's and Medical Pupil's Assistant* by John French Burke (1844) and *The Student's Guide to the Practice of Midwifery* by David Lloyd Roberts (1876). Putting *guide* and *medical* or *medicine* in the title search turns up other potentially interesting books, some meant for professionals and others for the home. Additional advice for nonspecialists is in *Household Medicine, Surgery, Sick-room Management, and Diet for Invalids* (1854) and *The Mother's Manual of Children's Diseases* by Charles West (1885). *Advice to a Wife* by Pye Henry Chavasse, a marriage manual including sexual information, was initially published in 1842; *What a Young Husband Ought to Know* by Sylvanus Stall (1899) is a sex manual for husbands.

Three of Florence Nightingale's books are available via Google Books. More specialized medical subjects include *Health in India for British Women* by Edward John Tilt (1875) and *The Dictionary of Watering Places at Home and Abroad* (1883), which lists the amenities of health resorts.

Antiquus Morbus (http://www.antiquusmorbus.com) defines medical terms. The Wellcome Library (http://library.wellcome. ac.uk) is the primary history of medicine collection in the United Kingdom. Although books can not be accessed online, the "Wellcome Images" link from the main page permits an advanced search of historical images by topic.

The UCLA Department of Epidemiology site John Snow, Cholera, and Public Health (http://www.ph.ucla.edu/epi/snow.html) holds Snow's *On the Mode of Communication of Cholera* (1855) as well as other books, articles, maps, and photographs. The British Library Learning Resources page Filth and Fever at http://www. bl.uk/learning/histcitizen/21cc/publichealth/publichealthintro. html displays primary sources on public health. A Chronology of State Medicine, Public Health is at http://www.chronology.org.uk. Contagion: Historical Views of Diseases and Epidemics at http:// ocp.hul.harvard.edu/contagion includes the nineteenth-century cholera epidemics and material on tuberculosis.

National Archives materials on public health are at http://www. learningcurve.gov.uk/victorianbritain/healthy/default.htm. The Social Policy guide of the LSE Pamphlet Collection (http://www. lse.ac.uk/library/pamphlets/Default.htm) includes health, housing, and poor laws. If the classmark (call number) for a pamphlet is highlighted, click on it for access to the full text.

The Great Ormond Street Children's Hospital provides a short history of its Victorian origin at http://www.ich.ucl.ac.uk/about_ gosh/history/index.html. Small and Special (http://www.smal landspecial.org) holds a database of the hospital's patients; use the link to "library" for profiles that can be read online. The History of Rotherham's Hospital (http://www.micklebring.com/hospitals. htm) draws on local history resources to trace the development of a hospital in Yorkshire. London's Florence Nightingale Museum home page is at http://www.florence-nightingale.co.uk/index.php.

Leisure and Pleasure: Holidays, Sports, and Recreation

Sports and *pastimes* are useful search words for a variety of leisure activities; books on individual sports can be located with terms such as *racing, rowing, cricket, athletics, football, cycling,* and so forth. Many female and family hobbies are covered in *The Illustrated Girl's Own Treasury* (1861) and *A Manual of Amusements, Exercises, Studies and Pursuits* (1888). Other useful search terms include *home music, garden, work-table* or *work table,* and *needlework.*

Popular magazines are currently being digitized. Both Google and Project Gutenberg hold some issues of *The Argosy* (monthly), *Chambers's Edinburgh Journal* (a weekly), and *Punch* (the venerable illustrated humor weekly). Project Gutenberg has issues of *Girl's Own Paper* (weekly) and *Strand Magazine* (monthly). Manybooks. net (http://manybooks.net) holds a good deal of very popular Victorian reading material. George W. M. Reynolds's penny weekly serial *The Mysteries of London* is on Victorian London at http://www.victorianlondon.org/mysteries/mysteries-00-introduction. htm and a gallery of illustrations from its "sequel," *Mysteries of the Court of London* at ERBzine (http://www.erbzine.com/mag17/1797a.html). Victorian valentines and holiday cards from the Lilly Library at Indiana University are displayed at http://www.indiana.edu/~liblilly/exhibits-online.shtml. Victorian Turkish Baths (http://www.victorianturkishbath.org) has illustrations, advertisements, endorsements, and other curious material.

For other public entertainments, The British Library's Collect Britain (http://www.collectbritain.co.uk/collections) displays posters and sheet music in the Evanion Collection. The Gilbert and Sullivan Archive (http://math.boisestate.edu/GaS) has librettos, pictures, scores, and audio files. The Victorian Plays Project at Worcester University (http://www.worc.ac.uk/victorian) is an extraordinary resource with downloadable PDF files for almost 300 popular plays. The Raymond Mander & Joe Mitchenson Theatre Collection (http://mander-and-mitchenson.co.uk) displays hundreds of images. Other sources include the Theatre Museum (http://www.peopleplayuk.org.uk/guided_tours/drama_tour/19th_century/default.php) and the Adelphi Theatre Project, an indexed database of performances, names, and dates at http://www.emich.edu/public/english/adelphi_calendar/acpmain.htm.

The range of popular scientific interest is suggested by Lateral Science (http://www.lateralscience.co.uk), which includes experiments from the 1854 *Young Man's Book of Amusement*—along with cautions for modern readers. The Natural History Museum at Tring has work by nineteenth-century wildlife artists among its online exhibits at http://internt.nhm.ac.uk/jdsml/nature-online/nature-navigator-gallery.

Children's toys and games are found at the Museum of Childhood (http://www.vam.ac.uk/moc/index.html), the Victorian Toys Slide show (http://www.topmarks.co.uk/slideshows/victorians.htm), and "Writing Blanks, Board Games and other Educational Games" in the Oxford Digital Library archive (http://www2.odl.ox.ac.uk/

gsdl/cgi-bin/library). The original version of *Alice's Adventures Under Ground* with Lewis Carroll's own illustrations is in a British Library Turning the Pages exhibit at http://www.bl.uk/onlinegal lery/ttp/alice/accessible/introduction.html. Exhibits of children's books include Kate Greenaway (http://www.geocities.com/loveil lust/kg/kgreenaway.html), Picturing Childhood (http://www. library.ucla.edu/libraries/special/childhood/pictur.htm#an), and Children's Literature, Chiefly from the Nineteenth Century (http://www.sc.edu/library/spcoll/kidlit/kidlit/kidlit.html). The online full-text illustrated children's books at the Baldwin Project (http://www.mainlesson.com) include many from Victorian England.

For adult popular reading, the British Library has the *Penny Illustrated Paper* from 1861 to 1913 at http://www.collectbritain.co.uk/collections/pip and other popular forms in Aspects of the Victorian Book at http://www.bl.uk/collections/early/victorian/intro.html (click on the thumbnails for further examples of each genre). Cornell University Library includes additional titles in Women in the Literary Marketplace, 1800–1900 at http://rmc.library.cornell.edu/womenLit/default.htm. Literary annuals can be seen at Forget Me Not (http://www.orgs.muohio.edu/anthologies/FMN) and The Keepsake (http://www.rc.umd.edu/editions/lel/keepsake.htm).

Sensation Press, which publishes reprints of Victorian light fiction, has online displays at http://www.sensationpress.com. Web sites devoted to some of the most popular writers include the Wilkie Collins Pages (http://www.wilkiecollins.com); Mary Elizabeth Braddon Pages (http://www.sensationpress.com/braddonindex.htm); Ellen Wood (Mrs. Henry Wood) Web site (http://www.mrshenrywood.co.uk); Charlotte Mary Yonge Fellowship (http://www.cmyf.org.uk/) and PDF files of many Yonge novels at http://www2.hn.psu.edu/faculty/jmanis/cmyonge.htm; Kipling Society Homepage (http://www.kipling.org.uk); Sir Arthur Conan Doyle Literary Estate (http://www.sherlockholmesonline.org) and Sherlockian Net (www.sherlockian.net).

Faith and Works: Religion and Reform

Crockford's Clerical Directory, published for the Church of England at irregular intervals from 1858, lists clergymen and related information. *Charity, confirmation,* and names of denominations are useful search terms. *My Life and What Shall I Do with It?* by Lucy March Phillipps (1861) is one of many books for women about their duty to the poor; the magazine *Work and Leisure* has advice, information, and advertisements for charitable workers.

The Church of England *Book of Common Prayer* used during the Victorian period was established in 1662. (Revisions in 1928 eliminated some material and changed language, especially in the marriage ceremony.) Online Anglican Resources (http://justus.anglican.org/resources) includes a Book of Common Prayer page; choose "Church of England" for links to many editions published in the nineteenth century. Project Canterbury (http://anglicanhistory.org/index.html) has other primary sources. There is a section on Church History at the tourism site Britannia (http://britannia.com).

The W. T. Stead Resource Site (http://www.attackingthedevil. co.uk) has information and primary sources about William Thomas Stead, a reforming newspaper editor, spiritualist, and pacifist. Hidden Lives Revealed (http://www.hiddenlives.org.uk) includes pictures and case files of children cared for by The Waifs and Strays' Society. It would also worth searching the Web under the name of any other Victorian charitable society—hundreds of them are listed in *The Englishwoman's Year Book and Directory* mentioned below— since some still exist and others have archives that may be digitized.

Victorian Morality

Many conduct manuals and books of moral instruction are in full text online, including *Self-help* and other titles by Samuel Smiles; the Sarah Ellis bestsellers *Mothers of England, Wives of England,* and *Daughters of England;* Dinah Mulock Craik's *A Woman's Thoughts About Women;* John Ruskin's *Sesame and Lilies;* and *Hints on Self-Help* by Jessie Boucherett, founder of the Society for Promoting the Employment of Women. There are also conduct books for men such as *Advice to a Young Man Upon First Going to Oxford* by Edward Berens (1832); *The English Gentleman: His Principles: His Feelings: His Manners: His Pursuits* (1849); and *The Character of the Gentleman* by Francis Lieber (1864). The *Englishwoman's Yearbook and Directory* was an annual volume with detailed information about women's education, employment, medical training, social service, amusements, and legal responsibilities. The extent of this information suggests how much women's actual status (if not always their sentimentally idealized role) had changed by the end of the Victorian period.

Additional titles about women's rights and ideals are at the Victorian Women Writers Project (contents list at http://www.indiana.

edu/~letrs/vwwp/vwwp-list.html) and in the University of Minnesota Undergraduate Victorian Studies Online Teaching Anthology (http://etrc.lib.umn.edu/uvsota/index.htm), where "Condition of Women" has primary sources scanned from periodicals that represent a range of conflicting opinions. The National Archives Learning Curve "Were Men and Women Equal in Victorian England" is at http://www.learningcurve.gov.uk/victorianbritain/divided/default.htm. For anyone visiting London a self-guided Woman's History Walk of Bloomsbury is at http://www.lesleyahall.net/lwhnwalk.htm.

England and Empire

Missionary in the title field yields dozens of books although many are from U.S. organizations. David Livingstone's *Missionary Travels and Researches in South Africa* (1857) includes many illustrations. *Exploration* is also a useful term and a geographical addition may further narrow the results and produce, for example, *First Footsteps in East Africa* by Richard Francis Burton, John Hanning Speke, and William C. Barker (some versions listed stop after the first volume, but the copy dated 1856 with 648 pages has the complete text).

Primary sources for military topics include the 1871 manual *The Soldier's Pocket-Book for Field Service* by Garnet Wolseley (later Commander-in-Chief) and *The Queen's Regulations and Orders for the Army* (1899). *Army List* in the title field produces several pages of results, including *The East-India Register and Army List* for 1845 and the annual Hart's *Army List* for many different years. *Navy List* does the same for naval officers, regulations, and ships; using *British Navy* for additional works eliminates books about the United States. For campaigns, use a nineteenth-century designation; *Crimea* supplies many histories and memoirs, including the original accounts sent to the *Times* by William Howard Russell and collected as *The War* (1856), but *Mutiny* and *Boer* will be needed for campaigns now often known by less Anglocentric terms. For the Raj, *India* yields Victorian histories, handbooks, travel guides, and special topics of all sorts, some of them illustrated. Project Gutenberg has *Observations on the Mussulmauns of India* by B. Mir Hasan 'Ali (1832); its author was an English woman married to a high-ranking Muslim man.

The British Empire (http://www.britishempire.co.uk), a large site run by a teacher, has biographies, chronologies, maps, articles, and an exhibit of souvenir paintings acquired by employees of the East India Company. The National Archives Learning Curve

British Empire exhibition at http://www.learningcurve.gov.uk/
empire/default.htm offers broad questions drawn from illustrations and primary sources. Channel 4's overview of the Empire is
in the "Further Afield" section of the Time Traveller's Guide to Victorian Britain (http://www.channel4.com/history/microsites/H/
history/guide19/index.html). The PBS teaching site Queen Victoria's Empire (http://www.pbs.org/empires/victoria/text.html) is
suitable for middle and high school students. A 200th anniversary
exhibition on the abolition of the slave trade is among the British
Library learning resources (http://www.bl.uk/learning/histcitizen
/campaignforabolition/abolition.html).

Additional primary sources and excerpts are in the Undergraduate Victorian Studies teaching collection at http://etrc.lib.umn.
edu/uvsota/index.htm, and the Fordham Modern History Source-
book at http://www.fordham.edu/halsall/mod/modsbook34.
html#India%20Under%20the%20British.

The Center for Research Libraries Digital South Asia Library at
http://dsal.uchicago.edu includes (under "reference resources")
the *Imperial Gazetteer of India*, with maps, city plans, and descriptive geographical and cultural information. The British Library's
Collect Britain (http://collectbritain.co.uk/collections) exhibit
"Svadesh Videsh" displays thousands of illustrations from a collection begun by the East India Company in 1801. William Carey
University's page on Baptist missionary work (http://www.
wmcarey.edu/carey/maps/maps.htm) provides online access to
many nineteenth-century maps of India.

Military history tends to focus on organization and battles rather
than social history. A good starting point is Land Forces of Britain, the Empire and Commonwealth at http://www.regiments.
org. Soldiers of the Queen (http://www.soldiersofthequeen.com)
is an online museum of Victorian-era photographs and articles. The
Victoria Cross Registers can be searched at http://www.nationalar
chives.gov.uk/documentsonline/victoriacross.asp.

The National Maritime Museum in Greenwich (http://www.
nmm.ac.uk) Collections Online displays more than 10,000 pictures;
the history section of the Royal Navy's official Web site (http://
www.royal-navy.mod.uk/server/show/nav.1242) has pictures and
information about noteworthy men, ships, and battles. Ships of
the Old Navy at http://www.ageofnelson.org/MichaelPhillips/
index.html lists the Navy's ships from the mid-eighteenth century
to about 1840. *Navy and Army Illustrated* (http://www.cyber-heri
tage.co.uk/armynavy) holds photographs and illustrations from a

magazine published in the 1890s—the site's appearance and organization are awkward, but the pictures are interesting.

A selection of web resources for Victorian wars includes National Archives material (http://www.nationalarchives.gov.uk/battles); National Army Museum online exhibitions (http://www.national-army-museum.ac.uk); The Second Anglo-Afghan War, 1878–1880 (http://www.angloafghanwar.info); Anglo Boer War (http://www.angloboerwar.com) and Anglo-Boer War Centenary Exhibition (http://users.westconnect.com.au/~ianmac5/exhibit1.html#index); Rorke's Drift, 1879 (http://www.rorkesdriftvc.com); Anglo-Zulu War materials (http://www.kwazulu.co.uk/home.html and http://www.anglozuluwar.com).

The Crimean War Research Society (http://www.crimeanwar.org) has a good overview by a dependable military historian. Crimean Texts (http://crimeantexts.russianwar.co.uk) displays primary sources. The Library of Congress holds 263 images in Roger Fenton Crimean War Photographs; begin with the background at http://www.loc.gov/rr/print/coll/251_fen.html. In addition, an online archive of Roger Fenton's Letters from the Crimea is at http://rogerfenton.dmu.ac.uk.

London's Florence Nightingale Museum (http://www.florence-nightingale.co.uk/flo2.htm) displays brief but authoritative information. Angels & Orderlies (http://www.dorsetbay.plus.com/hist/crimea/nurselist.htm) contains an alphabetical list of the nurses who served with Nightingale in the Crimea; also see Mary Seacole (http://www.maryseacole.com/maryseacole/pages). Army Nursing in the Boer War (http://www.pcansr.net) provides information about developments during the second half of the century.

GLOSSARY

Anglicans—members of the Church of England.

Anglo-Catholicism—a movement emphasizing the connections between the Church of England and the Roman Catholic Church.

Apothecary—lowest-ranking medical practitioner, but not simply a pharmacist; an apothecary could prescribe medicines as well as prepare and sell them.

Apoplexy—usually what we now refer to as a stroke, but sometimes applied to other seizures.

Apprentice—an apprentice was legally bound to work for someone for a certain period of time in order to learn a trade or profession.

Area—in town houses (especially in London), an excavated courtyard providing light for the basement kitchen.

Aristocrat—a member of the ruling class; a man with an inherited title. *Aristocracy* may be used to include nontitled people who are closely related to aristocrats.

Articled—bound as apprentice. An articled clerk was apprenticed to a solicitor.

Artisan—a worker skilled in a particular craft, especially one who makes a product, such as a saddler or a shoemaker.

Assizes—court sessions in provincial towns, usually held twice a year, when judges came from London to try serious cases.

Bailiff—the sheriff's officer who arrests a debtor or seizes the debtor's goods; also a name for the steward or agent who manages a landowner's property.

Bank Holiday—day when banks and government offices are closed; legal holiday.

Bank notes—a form of paper money issued by individual banks.

Banns—announcement, given in church, of an intended marriage.

Baron—lowest rank of the peerage; addressed as *Lord X*.

Baronet—hereditary rank just below the peerage. A baronet is addressed with *Sir* before his name but is a commoner rather than an aristocrat.

Barrister—member of the elite branch of the legal profession who can argue cases in court.

Bathing—refers to swimming as well as to taking a bath for cleanliness; a swimming pool is generally called *the baths*.

Bed—mattress and/or featherbed, not the furniture on which it rests, which was called a *bedstead*.

Below stairs—the kitchens and other basement rooms that were servants' territory.

Board school—tax-supported elementary school; equivalent of neighborhood public school in the United States.

Board wages—the extra money provided to buy food when servants remained in a house while the family was elsewhere.

Boudoir—a woman's private sitting room, where she conducts her household and business affairs, not (usually) the room in which she sleeps and dresses.

Boxing Day—the day after Christmas.

Carriage—horse-drawn vehicle designed to carry people rather than goods. On railways, the British term *carriage* is equivalent to the U.S. *passenger car*.

Canon—in the Anglican Church, a clergyman who helps the Dean in the operation of a cathedral and its services.

Chapel—a place of worship for Dissenters such as Methodists or Baptists; also a private place of worship attached to a house or college. *Church* was generally used only for Church of England buildings.

Chemist—pharmacist.

Chips—fried potatoes, equivalent to *french fries* in the United States.

City of London—the oldest part of London. By Victorian times, *the City* was a synonym for *the financial district*.

Clerk—any white collar employee, from copyist to manager.

College—one of the teaching bodies within a university. Also used for some secondary schools (e.g., Eton College) and for other educational institutions.

Come out—a girl *came out* when she took her place in society as an adult and was seen as eligible for courtship and marriage.

Constable—police officer of the lowest rank, equivalent to *patrolman*.

Coronet—the lowest rank for commissioned officers in the cavalry until 1871, when it was replaced by *second lieutenant.*

Corn—any edible grain, but especially wheat; the terms *maize* or *Indian corn* were used for the grain known as *corn* in the United States.

Corset—close-fitting body garment.

Costermonger—street vendor.

Countess—wife of an earl.

County town—town that is the center of government for a county or shire.

Craftsman—skilled worker, whether in traditional hand production or in some industrial process.

Curate—Church of England clergyman who does not have full charge of his own parish; he assists the rector or is a paid substitute when the parish has no resident clergyman.

d.—abbreviation for penny.

Dean—the clergyman in charge of operating a cathedral; he heads a chapter of canons appointed to assist him.

Dispensary—outpatient clinic; medical office providing free or low-cost medical advice.

Dissenter (also *Nonconformist*)—Protestant Christian who belongs to some group other than the Church of England: Baptist, Congregationalist, Methodist, Quaker, Unitarian, etc.

Doctor's Commons—until 1857, the court that had jurisdiction over legal matters related to marriage, divorce, and probate.

Don—a generic term for those who teach at Oxford or Cambridge. (It is not a formal position like *professor* and is never used as a title.)

Draper's—shop that sells fabrics and goods such as tablecloths.

Drawing room—room for sitting and entertaining; would be called *parlour* in a more modest house.

Dustman—trash collector; *dust* means general household refuse as well as fireplace ashes.

East End (London)—the area east (downriver) of the Tower of London, associated with docks, warehouses, poverty, traditional Cockneys, and (in Victorian times) Jewish, Chinese, and Irish immigrants.

Ensign—the lowest rank for commissioned officers in the infantry until 1871, when *ensign* was replaced by *second lieutenant*.

Entail—a legal restriction determining who can inherit a landed estate. It also generally prevented the owner from selling any of the property.

Esquire—used after a man's name among the landed gentry, barristers, and others who had high status but no inherited title. *Esquire* was used by custom and could be claimed by almost anyone; there was no actual rule for its use.

Established church—a church officially recognized and supported by the government; in England, the Church of England.

Fellow—in Oxford or Cambridge colleges, a graduate appointed to a paid position in the college to do teaching and research. Fellows were not allowed to marry until 1877.

First floor—one flight of stairs up from the ground floor; in the United States it would be called the second floor.

Form—equivalent of *class*: students at about the same level who are taught together. The term *form* was generally used in public schools and large private schools, but not in elementary schools.

Frock coat—man's coat in daily wear among the middle classes through most of the Victorian period, it was about knee length and was the same length in front and back.

Funds—government bonds, which were a safe though conservative investment.

Game Laws—laws that regulated the killing of pheasants, partridges, hares, deer, and rabbits.

Gaol—pronounced *jail*, which is what it means.

Gentry—substantial people who have high social status but are not titled, including landowners (also called landed gentry) and members of the upper middle class.

Governess—woman teacher of middle-class or upper-class girls.

Grammar school—a fee-paying secondary day school for boys; in Victorian times most were descended from charitable or religious schools endowed in the Middle Ages.

Greengrocer—retailer of fresh vegetables and fruit.

Grocer—retailer of food (especially staples) and household supplies.

Groom—stablehand; worker who takes care of horses.

Guinea—used as a term for the sum of 21 shillings, although the coin—of gold, bearing the impression of an elephant—was no longer minted after 1813.

High tea—informal but substantial late-afternoon or early-evening meal.

Home rule—government of a country by its own citizens; generally used to describe movements towards self-government in Ireland and in some British colonies.

Household troops (also called *the guards*)—army regiments stationed in London to protect the monarch and government. Their duties were largely ceremonial.

Hunting—the word was used by Victorians only for the sport of foxhunting, also called *riding to the hounds*.

Infants—in the language of schooling, infants were under age seven.

In-law—applies to anyone related by law rather than blood; *brother-in-law*, for example, means not only "spouse's brother" and "sister's husband" but also "step-brother" and a young girl may have a *mother-in-law* who is her father's second wife or, in our terms, her stepmother.

Inns of Court—London institutions where men were trained to become barristers.

Instant—the current month. For example, a letter written on March 4th was often dated "4th inst." and the same form was used in the birth-marriage-death notices printed in the London *Times*.

Journeyman—a *journeyman* is someone who had completed his apprenticeship at a skilled trade and worked for hire.

Justice of the peace—landowner who served as a magistrate and did some other local government duties.

Laudanum—solution of opium in alcohol, used as painkiller and sleeping medicine.

Livery—uniform supplied by an employer for male servants.

Lover—suitor or admirer.

Market day—regular day (usually once a week) when stalls were set up in a town to sell food and merchandise.

Morning calls—brief social visits, generally (despite the name) between 3:00 and 5:00 P.M.

Morning dress—daytime wear with arms and shoulders fully covered.

MP—Member of Parliament, that is, an elected member of the House of Commons.

Mutes—hired mourners; undertakers' assistants.

Nanny, nursemaid—servants who take care of children.

Navvy—laborer who does heavy pick-and-shovel work in excavation, construction, and railway building.

Nonconformist (also *Dissenter*)—Protestant Christian who does not belong to Church of England.

Nursery—children's room. In large houses, there was a day nursery where children ate and played, and a night nursery where children slept, along with the nursemaid or nanny.

Nursing a child—meant breast-feeding; also holding (and, often, rocking or amusing a baby one is holding).

Omnibus—the word is now shortened to *bus*.

Pantomime—traditional Christmas entertainment, usually based on a fairy tale or folk tale and including slapstick comedy, musical numbers, and, often, audience participation.

Parish—the area served by a church, and also, in England, a unit of civil administration although the boundaries of the Church of England parish and the local government parish were not necessarily identical.

Peer—member of the peerage; that is, a duke, marquis, earl, viscount, or baron.

Perpetual curate—clergyman who had full charge of a parish that had no resident priest.

Perquisite (or perk)—an unofficial but traditional fringe benefit in a particular occupation, such as the cook's practice of selling excess fat from roasted meat.

Pin money—money for a woman's personal use, as provided in a marriage settlement or other legal agreement.

Plate—silverware (both tableware and flatware).

Poaching—killing fish or game without the landowner's permission.

Poor Law—the Poor Law governed public assistance for people who were impoverished or disabled. The term is used as an adjective for welfare institutions or officials, as in *poor law hospital* or *poor law overseer*.

Porter—doorkeeper in charge of the entrance to a college, hotel, or other large building.

Preparatory schools (prep schools)—private schools for boys of about age 7–12 that prepared them for entry to the elite secondary schools known as *public schools*. Prep schools were usually (but not always) boarding schools.

Primogeniture—the right of an eldest son to inherit the entire estate.

Private school—a privately owned school of any sort, often run by a single individual.

Pub (short for *public house*)—inn, tavern.

Public school—large fee paying secondary school, primarily for boarders and, in Victorian times, socially exclusive.

Quarter days—traditionally mark the quarters of the business year: Christmas (December 25), Lady Day (March 25), Midsummer Day (June 24), and Michaelmas (September 29).

Queen's Counsel—high-ranking barrister entitled to use the initials Q.C. after his name. Appointment to the rank was called *taking silk*.

Railway—the usual British term; in the United States we generally say *railroad*.

Raj—British sovereignty in India.

Ranker—an ordinary soldier (member of the rank-and-file); in the United States generally called an *enlisted man*.

Rates—taxes paid to local authorities on buildings or land.

Scullery—room next to kitchen for wet and dirty chores. A low-ranking servant who scrubbed, washed pots, and hauled water was called a *scullery-maid* or a *scullion*.

Settlement—a marriage settlement secured certain property for the wife and sometimes also for any children of the marriage.

Semidetached house—a house that shares one wall with the house next to it; in the United States often called a *twin* or *duplex*.

Shop assistant—retail sales clerk.

Sister—fully trained nurse, especially the head nurse in a hospital ward.

Social season—in London, the period from May through July when fashionable people lived in their town houses and enjoyed balls, dinners, and entertainments.

Solicitor—lower-ranking member of the legal profession, who handles wills, contracts, and other business but does not argue cases in court.

Squire—principal landowner of a village or district.

Standard—level of achievement, as established for elementary school pupils by the government's department of education. Sometimes used as equivalent of *class* or *grade*.

Subaltern—commissioned army officer below the rank of captain; that is, lieutenants and coronets or ensigns. The latter two were called second lieutenants after the army reforms of 1871.

Surgeon—dressed wounds, set bones, pulled teeth, treated skin diseases, and gave other medical advice. A surgeon had lower social status than a university-trained physician.

Surgery—the place where a general practitioner saw patients, whether or not he was a surgeon; equivalent to *doctor's office*.

Tradesman—shopkeeper.

Training college—teachers' college.

Underground—short for *underground railway*, in other words, the London subway system.

Union—a group of parishes combined for the purpose of building a single union workhouse; therefore *union* is often used as a synonym for *workhouse*. The organized association of workers called a union in the United States is generally a *trade union* or *trades union* in Britain.

Valet—gentleman's personal servant.

Waistcoat—man's garment now usually called a *vest* in the United States.

Ward—an orphaned minor or mentally incompetent person whose interests were looked after by the court or by a guardian.

Wedding breakfast—wedding reception.

Work—when a lady's work is referred to, the word generally means needlework, embroidery, knitting, crochet, etc.

Workhouse—residential institution for everyone who needed public assistance; the able-bodied were required to do work in exchange for their food and lodging.

FURTHER READING

Many of these books have been published in several forms, often including revised and/or paperback editions, in both England and the United States. I have therefore provided the date of first publication but not the city and publisher.

Altick, Richard D. *Victorian People and Ideas.* 1973. Especially suitable as background for students in Victorian literature; chapters on social structure, political and technological change, art, and the intellectual and religious climate.

Best, Geoffrey. *Mid-Victorian Britain 1851–75.* 1971. A readable social history (see also the two books by J.F.C. Harrison); especially good on the environment, work, leisure, and social order.

Broomfield, Andrea. *Food and Cooking in Victorian England: A History.* 2007. Explains changes in food production and preparation, nutrition, and the meals of people in all classes; includes a glossary and selected recipes.

Burnett, John. *Plenty and Want: A Social History of Diet in England from 1815 to the Present Day.* 1966. Detailed scholarship with many examples of wages, prices, and menus.

Cunnington, C. Willett, and Phillis Cunnington. *Handbook of English Costume in the Nineteenth Century.* 1959. A decade-by-decade summary of styles, construction, and distinguishing features of the clothing, hats, hairstyles, shoes, and accessories of prosperous men and women.

Davidoff, Leonore, and Catherine Hall. *Family Fortunes: Men and Women of the English Middle Class, 1780–1850*. 1987. Study based on business records, wills, diaries, and family papers describes the institutions, ideals, and ways of life shaped by an emerging middle class.

Farwell, Byron. *Armies of the Raj: From the Great Indian Mutiny to Independence: 1858–1947*. 1989. A lively and readable account of the Royal Army, the Indian Army, and other military forces in India.

Farwell, Byron. *Mr. Kipling's Army*. 1981. A social history rather than a history of the army's organization and campaigns, illuminated by anecdotes and examples.

Flanders, Judith. *Inside the Victorian Home: A Portrait of Domestic Life in Victorian England*. 2004. Published in England in 2003 as *The Victorian House: Domestic Life from Childbirth to Deathbed*. Describes the upper-middle-class town house, room by room, with attention to furniture, decoration, and domestic technology; includes plans, illustrations, and explanatory quotations from memoirs and fiction.

Frost, Ginger. *Victorian Childhoods*. 2009. Studies children's experiences; chapters on home life, schooling, work, play, organizations, and outsiders such as orphans, paupers, and child criminals.

Girouard, Mark. *The Victorian Country House*. 1971. Describes architecture, planning, and interior organization; uses letters and diaries to depict the routine for guests, hosts, and servants.

Graham, Kelley. *"Gone to the Shops": Shopping in Victorian England*. 2008. The changing experience of buying both necessities and luxuries, and the growth of shopping as a pleasure.

Harrison, J.F.C. *The Early Victorians 1832–51* (1971) and *Late Victorian Britain 1875–1901* (1990). Readable brief social histories, especially good on class, social structure, work, values, and change.

Harris, José. *Private Lives, Public Spirit: A Social History of Britain, 1870–1914*. 1993. Examines late nineteenth- and early twentieth-century changes in family, work, religious belief, and political structures.

Holcombe, Lee. *Victorian Ladies at Work: Middle-Class Working Women in England and Wales, 1850–1914*. 1973. A ground-breaking history of women teachers, nurses, shop assistants, clerical workers, and civil servants.

Hoppen, K. Theodore, *The Mid-Victorian Generation, 1846–1886*. 1998. Covers political and economic topics as well as social history.

Horn, Pamela. *Labouring Life in the Victorian Countryside* (1976), *The Victorian Country Child* (1974), *The Victorian Town Child* (1997), and other well-illustrated books on similar topics have appeared in various editions from several publishers.

Hughes, Kathryn. *The Victorian Governess*. 1993. Detailed study of the training, work, and social status of actual governesses rather than the governess-heroines of fiction.

James, Lawrence. *The Rise and Fall of the British Empire*. 1994. Readable and even-handed study covering 1600 to 1993.

Mingay, Gordon E. *Rural Life in Victorian England.* 1977. Also published in an illustrated edition in 1990, the book deals succinctly with landowners, farmers, farmworkers, professional people, tradesmen, and others.

Mingay, Gordon E., ed. *The Victorian Countryside.* 2 volumes. 1981. Essays by experts, with many illustrations, covering all aspects and all classes in countryside and country towns.

Mitchell, Sally, ed. *Victorian Britain: An Encyclopedia.* 1988. A reference book with brief articles on people, events, issues, and movements; each entry has a bibliography of sources.

Melnyk, Julie. *Victorian Religion: Faith and Life in Britain.* 2008. Authoritative and readable study covers religion's role in the family and community as well as its clergy, creeds, and controversies.

Morris, Jan [James]. *Pax Britannica: The Climax of an Empire.* 1968. An evocative description of the British Empire at its high point in 1897, explaining how it grew, how it worked, and what the English felt about the Empire and its subject people.

Nelson, Claudia. *Family Ties in Victorian England.* 2007. Draws on economics, birth and death rates, memoirs, and legal documents to describe the realities as well as the ideology of Victorian family life.

Perkin, Harold. *The Age of the Railway.* 1970. A readable social history focused on railways' role in changing Victorian life.

Perkin, Harold. *The Origins of Modern English Society 1780–1880.* 1969. Describes the transformation of English social structure from a landed individual hierarchy to the class-based society of the nineteenth century.

Propas, Sharon W. *Victorian Studies: A Research Guide.* 1992; 2nd edition (significantly updated), 2006. Intended for librarians and serious scholars, a guide to resources, bibliographies, and lists of sources organized by field.

Searle, G. R. *A New England? Peace and War 1886–1918.* 2004. A narrative history of political, social, and cultural life from Victoria's golden jubilee to the end of the first world war.

Simon, Brian, and Ian Bradley, eds. *The Victorian Public School.* 1975. Sensible essays about the elite private educational institutions.

Sykes, Christopher Simon. *Country House Camera.* Also published as *The Golden Age of the Country House.* 1980. A large-format book of snapshots and photographs taken between 1850 and 1939 and found in private family albums supplies an incomparable picture of life among the landowning classes.

Thompson, F.M.L. *English Landed Society in the Nineteenth Century.* 1963. Treats the gradual decline in power of the aristocracy and gentry.

Thompson, F.M.L. *The Rise of Respectable Society: A Social History of Victorian Britain, 1830–1900.* 1988. An overview with chapters on the economy, the family, marriage, childhood, homes, work, play, and authority.

Tobias, J. J. *Crime and Police in England 1700–1900.* 1979. Summarizes the shift
    from amateur to professional in policing, trials, and punishment.
Waller, P. J. *Town, City and Nation: England, 1850–1914.* 1983. Describes and
    analyzes urban growth, population, structure, government, and
    municipal services.
Winstanley, Michael J. *The Shopkeeper's World, 1830–1914.* 1983. Concen-
    trates on small shops, shopkeepers' political influence, and the
    actual working of businesses ranging from pawnbroker to high-
    class grocer.
Wohl, Anthony, *Endangered Lives: Public Health in Victorian Britain.* 1983.
    Detailed and readable account of sanitation, pollution, industrial
    disease, epidemics, and steps towards reform.
Young, G. M., ed. *Early Victorian England 1830–1865.* 2 volumes. 1934. The
    first broad description of Victorian cultural and social history, writ-
    ten when many people who remembered the nineteenth century
    were still alive.

INDEX

About the Author

SALLY MITCHELL is Professor Emerita of English and Women's Studies at Temple University. She has published extensively on Great Britain, the Victorian era, and women's issues, including *Victorian Britain: An Encyclopedia* (1988), which was named an ALA Outstanding Reference Work. Her most recent work, *Frances Power Cobbe: Victorian Feminist, Journalist, Reformer,* was published in 2004.